Organisational Behaviour

Organisational Behaviour

S. Fayyaz Ahmad
Nazir Ahmad Gilkar
Javid Ahmad Darzi

ATLANTIC
PUBLISHERS & DISTRIBUTORS (P) LTD

Published by

ATLANTIC

PUBLISHERS & DISTRIBUTORS (P) LTD

7/22, Ansari Road, Darya Ganj,
New Delhi-110002
Phones : +91-11-40775252, 23273880, 23275880, 23280451
Fax : +91-11-23285873
Web : www.atlanticbooks.com
E-mail : orders@atlanticbooks.com

Branch Office
5, Nallathambi Street, Wallajah Road,
Chennai-600002
Phones : +91-44-64611085, 32413319
E-mail : chennai@atlanticbooks.com

Printed in India at Glorious Printers, A-13, D.S.I.D.C.,
Jhilmil Industrial Area, Delhi-110095

Preface

We are fast becoming part of a new era of management. No longer does a manager sit in an ivory tower and afford to issue directives from a distance. The traditional authority structure is giving way to employee involvement, work teams, team spirit, participative decision-making, flexible work structures, etc. The management is becoming more and more aware of the fact that an organization has no life but for the people in it. Accordingly, it is becoming more and more people oriented as against task orientation of the yesteryears.

Organizational Behaviour is the study and application of knowledge about how people, individuals and groups act in organisations. It interprets people-organisation relationships in terms of the whole person, whole group, whole organization and the whole social system. This study, complex as it is, has acquired new dimensions, with the dynamic social changes and technological advancements of the past. Changing demographics, cultural diversity, and awareness of rights and privileges have prompted a new look at the entire organizational structure, examples, and systems.

The present book covers extensively, various facets—both micro and macro—in the field of Organizational Behaviour, and analyses the means of achieving human, organizational and social objectives through better relationships. Each idea has been reinforced with some specific real life example indicating where such idea has been successfully employed. Integrative case studies have been included in the chapters to facilitate easy understanding and applied use of the concepts. These case studies have been carefully selected to ensure that they are relevant to organizational environment both globally as well as within the country.

The book covers all the major concepts and principles of management, organization theory and organizational behaviour, taking care of both the traditional and transitional viewpoints. The concepts have been supplemented with relevant examples and practical situations. In the book, an attempt has been made to understand the impact of behavioural sciences on employees through individual determinants such as perception, personality, motivation, and learning. Other group interactions and organization system issues affecting human behaviour in organizations such as group dynamics, communication, leadership, power and politics, conflict resolution and organization structure and change management implications, have also been dealt with in this book.

The subject matter of the book is divided into fifteen chapters under five main sections as detailed in the table of contents. A variety of questions like descriptive, application oriented, multiple choice objective type have been included.

The book is intended for a wide audience. It will be useful not only to the students of Management, Human Resource Management and Organizational Behaviour, but also to the researchers in the field of Behavioural Science, and management practitioners who want to understand and enrich their understanding of human behaviour and thus manage their workforce more effectively. It will also fulfil the needs of students of Psychology, Sociology and those pursuing the courses like MBA, MFC, M.Com, BBM, BBA, and DBA.

We express our sincere thanks to all those individuals and organizations who have directly or indirectly contributed to the writing of this textbook. Our special thanks are due to Mr. Muzamil Mattoo of Vision Computers for meticulously computer designing the contents of this book. We also express our appreciation to M/s Atlantic Publishers & Distributors (P) Ltd for undertaking the professional printing and publication of this book.

S. Fayyaz Ahmad
Nazir Ahmad Gilkar
Javid Ahmed Darzi

Contents

PART V

PART I

Organisational Behaviour (OB)

1

Learning Objectives

- Concept and Characteristics of OB
- Relationship between Management and OB
- Emergence of OB
- Managerial Roles and Skills
- Disciplines Contributing to OB
- Need to Study OB
- Emerging Trends in OB

ORGANISATION–CONCEPT

The term 'organisation' can be used in a number of ways. We may speak of organisation as an activity that is the important function of management. In an organisation people are united for a common purpose.

Mooney and Reiley in this regard opine, "Organisation is the form of every human association for the attainment of a common purpose." Organisation, therefore, is simply people working together for a common goal.

Organisational Behaviour–Meaning

Organisational Behaviour is (i) the study, and (ii) application of knowledge about how people as, (a) individuals and (b) groups act within an organisation. It strives to identify ways in which people can act more effectively. Organisational Behaviour (OB) is a scientific discipline in which a large number of research studies and conceptual developments are constantly adding to its knowledge base. It is also an applied science, in that information about effective practices in one organisation are being extended to many others.

Organisation Behaviour provides a useful set of tools at many levels of analysis:

> It helps managers look at the behaviour of individuals within an organisation. It also aids their understanding of the complexities involved in inter-personal relations, when two people (two co-workers or a superior-subordinate pair) interact.

At the next level, Organisational Behaviour is valuable for examining the dynamics of relationship within small groups, both (i) formal, and (ii) informal, when two or more groups need to coordinate their efforts, such as engineering and sales, the managers become interested in the intergroup relations that emerge.

> They include two culturally different groups, or labour and management.

Finally, organisations can also be viewed and managed as whole systems that have inter-organisational relationships, e.g. managers and joint ventures.

Definitions

Many behavioural scientists and researchers have defined organisational behaviour. Let us consider some of them:

> *"OB is a field of study that investigates the impact that, (i) individuals, (ii) groups, and (iii) structure have on behaviour within organisations, for the purpose of applying such knowledge towards improving organisation's effectiveness."*
>
> (Stephen P. Robbins)

> *"OB can be defined as the: (i) understanding, (ii) prediction, and (iii) control of human behaviour in organisations."*
>
> (Fred Luthans)

"OB is the study of human behaviour in organisational setting, the interface between human behaviour and the organisational context and the organisation itself."

(W. Ricky, G. Griffin, Moorhead)

"OB is the study of the behaviour of individuals and groups in organisations and organisations themselves, as they (i) act, and (ii) interact to attain desired outcomes."

(Stephen P. Robbins)

MANAGEMENT AND ORGANISATIONAL BEHAVIOUR–RELATIONSHIP

OB represents the behavioural approach to management. The recognized approaches to management include: (i) process, (ii) quantitative, (iii) system, and (iv) contingency approaches. In other words OB does not intend to portray the whole of management. Organisational structure and management processes (decision-making and communication) play an integral and direct role in OB.

OB is concerned with people, (i) individually, and (ii) groups who act in organisations. Management is concerned with the optimum attainment of organisational objectives. However, since these goals are unattainable without human input, therefore, OB is a significant (i) segment, or (ii) subset of management.

The subject of OB is intended to support the knowledge necessary to a manager. The understanding of (i) individual, and (ii) group behaviour is important for what it can contribute towards the (i) education, and (ii) development of one's managerial talent. When managers perform managerial functions –planning, organising, directing and controlling, they need to know what impact of their actions has on people. Since managers get things done through and with people, an understanding of behaviour of people is critical for a manager. But, of course, managers also work with physical inputs (equipment and inventories) and financial inputs, a manager requires knowledge of subjects that go beyond human behaviour.

It can be, therefore, concluded that: (i) management, and (ii) OB are interrelated. They cannot be separated from each other. Management without OB cannot work successfully and OB has no (i) meaning, and (ii) use without management.

Organisational Behaviour–Characteristics

There are contributions from different parent disciplines to the knowledge of organisational behaviour (OB). As such, it is very difficult to categorise the various characteristics of OB. However, some generalisations can be brought out, viz.:

1. Interdisciplinary Approach

Behavioural science is basically an inter-disciplinary approach. An inter-disciplinary approach integrates the relevant knowledge drawn from different disciplines for some special purpose. Many of its core concepts are borrowed from other fields like: (i) Psychology, (ii) Sociology, (iii) Anthropology. Besides, it also takes relevant concepts from (i) Economics, (ii) Political Science, (iii) Law, and (iv) History, etc. These disciplines exist separately, but behavioural science integrates the relevant contents of these disciplines to make them applicable for organisational analysis.

2. Application Orientation

The basic objective of behavioural science is to make application of various researches to solve the organisational problems, particularly related to human behaviour. Unlike pure sciences which concentrate on fundamental researches, behavioural science concentrates on applied researches. Though many of the researches may be carried on in laboratory situations and controlled conditions, yet they are meant for general application in organisational analysis.

3. Humanistic Orientation

Behavioural science focuses the attention of people from humanistic point of view. It is based on the belief that (i) needs, and (ii) motivation of people are of high concern. There is an acceptance of the value of the individual as a (i) thinking, and (ii) feeling being and without these considerations, the organisation may not be fully operational as a social entity. Further, there is optimism about the innate potential of man to be (i) independent, (ii) creative, (iii) productive, and (iv) capable of contributing positively to the organisational objectives. The man will actualise these potentials, if given proper (i) conditions, and (ii) environment.

4. Environmental Focus or Systems Orientation

Behavioural science is a total system approach wherein the living system of an organisation is viewed as an enlargement of the man. The systems approach is an integrative approach which takes into account all the variables affecting organisational functioning. In fact, the systems thinking in organisational analysis has been developed by behavioural scientists. Behavioural science, while analysing organisational behaviour, does not take human beings in isolation but as the product of socio-psychological factors. Thus, his behaviour can be analysed keeping in view his (i) psychological framework, (ii) interpersonal orientation, (iii) group influence, and (iv) social and cultural factors. Man's nature is quite complex and behavioural science by applying systems approach tries to find solution of this complexity.

5. Oriented towards Organisational Objectives

Behavioural science being an applied science and emphasizing human aspects of the organisation, is oriented towards organisational objectives. Though an organisation may have several objectives and sometimes conflicting with individual objectives, it should not be understood that behavioural science only emphasizes the achievement of individual objectives at the cost of organisational objectives. In fact, behavioural science tries to integrate two types of objectives so that both are achieved simultaneously. For this purpose, it suggests various behavioural approaches.

6. Three Levels of Analysis

OB is the comprehensive study of behaviour of (i) individuals, (ii) groups in organisations, and (iii) organisations themselves, as they act and interact to achieve the desired objectives. Therefore, OB involves three levels of analysis. It is concerned with: (i) individual behaviour, (ii) group behaviour, and (iii) the behaviour of the organisation itself.

7. Goals of OB

OB is an academic discipline concerned with (i) understanding, (ii) predicting, (iii) describing, and (iv) controlling human behaviour in an organisational environment. It throws light on the whole complex of human factor in organisations by identifying cause and effect of that behaviour.

ORGANISATIONAL BEHAVIOUR–EMERGENCE

Although the field of organisational behaviour is only a few decades old, yet it has a very rich heritage. The purpose of this discussion, therefore, is to trace some of the important phases and provide a historical foundation for modern organisational behaviour.

The Classical Era

The classical era covered the period from about 1900 to the mid-1930s. It was during this period that the first general theories of management began to evolve. The classical writers on management and organisation were primarily interested in (i) structural, (ii) formal, and (iii) technical aspects of the enterprise. F.W. Taylor, Henri Fayol and Max Weber who are considered the pioneers in the field of classical theory were mainly preoccupied with these issues. Consequently the human side of the organisation received insignificant treatment from them. Employees were considered simply as hands to produce.

A few writers and managers, however, recognised the importance of individuals and social processes in organisations. Prominent among them are Robert Owen, Hugo Munsterberg and Mary Parker Follet. However, their ideas were a minority view, not widely known by practicing managers.

The Hawthorne Studies

A series of research studies was conducted between 1924 and 1932 that did much to change management's perception of the individual in the workplace. These studies were conducted at Western Electric Company near Chicago (USA). Several researchers were involved. Prominent among them were Elton Mayo (Harvard faculty member), Roethisberger (Sociologist and Wiliam Dickson (Company Representative). The Hawthorne studies created quite a stir among the managers and management researchers. The findings of these extensive experiments led the researchers to conclude that the human element in the work-place was considerably more important than previously thought.

Human Relations Movement

In response to the Hawthorne studies, a new school of thought 'Human Relations' emerged. The basic premises underlying the human relations movement were that people respond primarily to their social environment, that motivation depends more on social needs than economic needs and that satisfied employees work harder than unsatisfied employees. Besides Elton Mayo, two more pioneers of Human Relations were Abraham Maslow and Douglas McGregor. This movement generated tremendous interest among managers with regard to the human side of the organisation. Managers were encouraged to adopt more humanistic, soft, sympathetic and consultative approaches towards their subordinates. Specific techniques like employee counseling, participative leadership and group dynamics were developed for popularizing the philosophy of human relations. The first behavioural approach to management tried simply to treat people as human beings, satisfy their needs by listening to their complaints and involving them in certain decisions.

Emergence of Organisational Behaviour

The Hawthorne studies and the Human Relations Movement played major roles in developing the foundation of the field organisational behaviour. However, the human relations approach was too simplistic in its assumptions and was more prescriptive in nature. This provides the ample opportunity for organisational behaviour to emerge as a refined and sophisticated discipline.

The field of organisational behaviour really began to emerge in the late 1950s and early 1960s. The organisational behaviour moved from the simple assumptions and models of the Human Relationists to the concept and methodologies of scientific discipline. The subject of organisational behaviour is more descriptive in nature than Human Relations, which was prescription oriented.

Organisational behaviour remains an important field, because the work of organisations is done primarily by people and thus understanding their behaviour is extremely important in the organisational context. In view of its inherent importance and excitement, organisational behaviour has become one of the most popular subjects in the area of business studies. It is thus, a beginning of an academic discipline. There is a growing consensus among academicians about the nature and scope of organisational behaviour, which is a sign of its development as a discipline.

Organisational Behaviour–Concepts

The human behaviour in the organisation is involved at the three major levels: (i) individual, (ii) group, and (iii) organisation. Therefore, the concepts of primary interest to organisational behaviour can be grouped into categories that correspond to the three levels of organisational behaviour. Since change can affect any or all of the three levels simultaneously and is usually considered as a separate category of topics. A very brief description of the main concepts of organisational behaviour is listed below:

(a) Individual Concepts

Individual concepts relate to the behaviour of an individual, who is the basic component of an organisation. These concepts include: (i) perception, (ii) personality, (iii) learning, (iv) creativity, (v) needs, (vi) motivation, (vii) attitudes, (viii) behaviours, and (ix) stress.

(b) Group Concepts

These concepts involve the interaction between (i) two, or (ii) more people in an organisational setting and include topics like (i) group dynamics, (ii) intergroup conflict, (iii) leadership, and (iv) power and politics.

(c) Organisational Concepts

Organisational concepts pertain to the organisation itself and include: (i) job design, (ii) performance appraisal,

(iii) rewards, (iv) problem-solving, decision-making, (v) communication, (vi) organisational structure, and (vii) organisation design.

(d) Concepts of Change

Change refers to a planned effort to alter one or more parts of an organisation in a systematic and logical fashion. Topics covered are (i) organisational change, and (ii) organisational development.

MANAGERIAL ROLES

In addition to the four managerial functions of (i) planning, (ii) organising, (iii) directing, and (iv) controlling, there are ten managerial roles that are commonly defined. These roles were developed by Henry Mintzberg in the late 1960s after careful study of executives at work. He divided these roles into three categories, viz.:

Interpersonal Roles	Informational Roles	Decisional Roles
–Figurehead	–Monitor	–Entrepreneur
–Leadership	–Disseminator	–Problem solver
–Liaison	–Spokesperson	–Resource allocator
		–Negotiator

Interpersonal Roles

Managers spend a considerable amount of time in interacting with other people both within their own organisation and outside. These people include: (i) peers, (ii) subordinates, (iii) superiors, (iv) suppliers, and (v) government officials. All these interactions require an understanding of interpersonal behaviour. Studies show that interacting with people takes up nearly 80 per cent of managers' time. These interactions involve the following three major interpersonal roles:

(a) Figurehead Role

Managers act as symbolic figureheads performing (i) social, or (ii) legal obligations. These duties include: (i) greeting visitors, (ii) signing legal documents, (iii) taking important customers to lunch, or (iv) speaking at functions in institutions, etc. These duties are ceremonial in nature but are important for the smooth functioning of the organisation.

(b) Leadership Role

Since the manager is responsible for the activities of his subordinates, he must (i) lead and (ii) coordinate their activities in accomplishing goals. He must motivate them to perform better. He must be an exemplary leader so that his subordinates follow his directions with respect and dedication.

(c) Liaison Role

In addition to their constant contact with their own (i) subordinates, (ii) peers, and (iii) superiors, the managers maintain a network of outside contacts in order to assess the external environment of (i) competition, (ii) social change, or (iii) changes in governmental rules and regulations. This can be achieved by attending (i) meetings, (ii) professional conferences, (iii) trade exhibitions, and (iv) establishing informal personal contacts with outside agencies.

Informational Roles

By virtue of his interpersonal contacts, a manager emerges as a source of information for a variety of issues about the organisation. In this capacity a manager executes the following three roles:

(a) Monitor Role

The managers are constantly monitoring their environment both: (i) internal, and (ii) external. They collect and study information regarding their organisation and outside environment affecting their organisation. This can be done by reading reports and periodicals, through gossip, etc.

(b) Disseminator Role

The managers must transmit the information to their (i) subordinates, (ii) peers, etc. about the changes in (i) policies, (ii) procedures, etc. This can be done through (i) memos, (ii) phone calls, and (iii) group meetings.

(c) Spokesman Role

A manager is a spokesman of his unit. He represents his unit either (i) sending relevant information to people outside his unit, or (ii) making demands on behalf of his unit. This may be in the form of precedent making a speech to a lobby on behalf of an organisational cause, or an engineer suggesting a product modification to a supplier.

Decision Roles

On the basis of the information received, a manager makes decisions and solves organisational problems. In that respect, a manager plays four important roles:

(a) Entrepreneur Role

As entrepreneurs, managers are constantly involved in improving their units and facing the dynamic technological challenges. They are constantly looking for (i) product improvement and (ii) new productions. If necessary they arrange capital for new products. They take suggestions from the employees to improve the organisation. This can be done by holding strategy meetings with (i) project managers and (ii) R & D personnel.

(b) Conflict Handling Role

The managers are consistently involved as arbitrators in solving differences among the (i) subordinates or (ii) employees' conflicts with the management. These problems may involve: (i) labour disputes, (ii) customer complaints, (iii) employee grievances, (iv) machine breakdowns, (v) cash flow shortages, and (iv) inter-personal conflicts. Managers must anticipate such problems and take preventive/corrective actions.

(c) Resource Allocator

The third decisional role of a manager is of a resource allocator. The managers establish priorities among various projects and programmes. They assign jobs to personnel. They allocate their own time to different activities. They allocate funds for new equipments, advertising and pay hikes, etc.

(d) Negotiator Role

The managers represent their units in negotiating deals within and outside the organisation. HR Manager negotiates contacts with the unions. Sales manager negotiates prices with prime customers.

MANAGERIAL SKILLS

A skill is an (i) acquired and (ii) learned ability to translate knowledge into performance. All managers need to possess various types of skills, viz.:

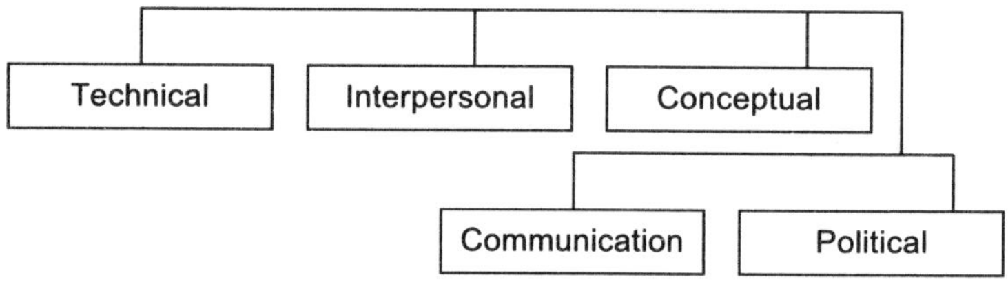

1. Technical Skills

Technical skills basically involve the use of (i) knowledge, (ii) methods, and (iii) techniques in performing a job effectively.

> Engineers, accountants and computer programmers have technical skills acquired through: (i) education, and (ii) training. This is a specialized (i) knowledge, and (ii) expertise which is used in day-to-day problems and activities.

This skill is highly necessary at the lower level of management and desirable at the middle management and even at the top level management.

2. Inter-personal Skills

Inter-personal skill is the ability to work with other people amicably. It involves: (i) patience and (ii) trust in inter-personal relationships. It is the ability to (i) lead and (ii) motivate others. This will create an environment in which the workers work together as a team with a sense of (i) belonging and (ii) dedication which is necessary for organisational success.

3. Conceptual Skills

Conceptual skill is the ability to view the organisation as a whole consisting of various parts integrated into a single unit. This skill, generally, depends upon an organised thinking process which deals with understanding various functions of an organisation. This skill is particularly required at the top level management because the executives have continuous contact with the outside world.

4. Communication Skills

Communication skills are, basic and important at all levels of management. A manager's best ideas will have little impact if they cannot be communicated effectively. Good communication is the foundation of sound management. Proper communication eliminates: (i) delays, (ii) misunderstandings, (iii) confusions, and (iv) conflicts and, thus, improves co-ordination and control.

5. Political Skills

Political skill is the ability to get your own way without being (i) selfish or (ii) self-oriented. It is the ability to get your share of power and use it without fear of losing it. It is the most complex skill. It is required to establish the right connections and impress the right people and then skilfully use these connections to your own advantage. Political skill is the most important at the middle level management because middle managers always want to reach the top level of management.

CONTRIBUTING DISCIPLINES

As we know organisational behaviour is an applied behavioural science. It is drawn from a number of applied behavioural disciplines, such as:

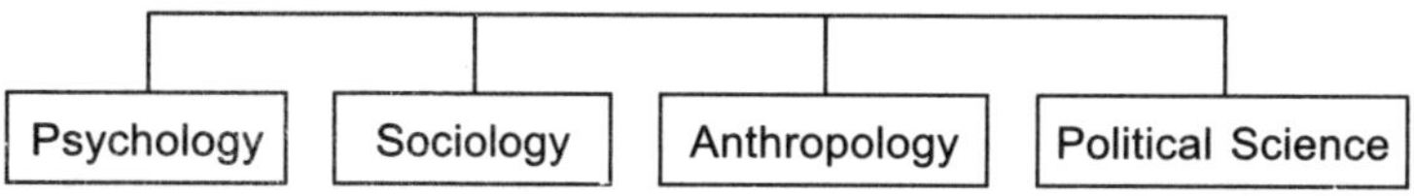

Psychology

Psychology is understood as the science of behaviour. It generally includes animals as well as human behaviour. Actually, psychology is concerned with individual behaviour. It has greatly contributed to the intra-individual dynamics of human behaviour. In other words, intra-personal aspects of organisational behaviour like motivation, personality, perception, attitude, opinions and learning owe their study to psychology.

Psychologists themselves are becoming increasingly important these days. The number of professional psychologists has also been growing. They hold important positions in many different fields.

> There are educational psychologists and counselors who work with school children.

> Industrial psychologists function mainly in industry, where they are involved in screening and training employees.

Sociology

Now we know that if psychology is the study of individual behaviour, sociology addresses itself to the study of group behaviour. It studies the behaviour of people in relation to their fellow human beings. Sociologists have enriched organisational behaviour through their contribution to the study of inter-personal dynamics, like: (i) leadership, (ii) group dynamics, (iii) communication, (iv) formal and informal organisations, etc.

Anthropology

Anthropology is the study of human race–its culture and society. As we know, culture has significant influence on human behaviour. It dictates what people learn and how they behave.

Every organisation has its own distinct culture. Some organisations, particularly close-ended, are secretive, publicity shy and less inclined to encourage participative management.

> Tatas take: (i) employee welfare and (ii) social responsibility as their main goals. The culture of the organisation will have an influence on an employee. His attire and discretion about things good and things bad, and his style of functioning are influenced by the culture of his organisation.

Political Science

Contributions of political scientists for better understanding of organisational behaviour are significant. Political scientists study the behaviour of (i) individuals and (ii) groups within a political environment. Specific topics of concern to political scientists are: (i) conflict resolution, (ii) group coalition, (iii) allocation of power, and (iv) how people manipulate power for individual self-interest.

ORGANISATIONAL BEHAVIOUR–NEED

A study of organisational behaviour is beneficial in several ways. The main reason for studying organisational behaviour is that most of us work in organisations, so we need to (i) understand, (ii) predict, and (iii) influence the behaviour of others in organisational settings. The below mentioned figure will help us to understand the dimensions:

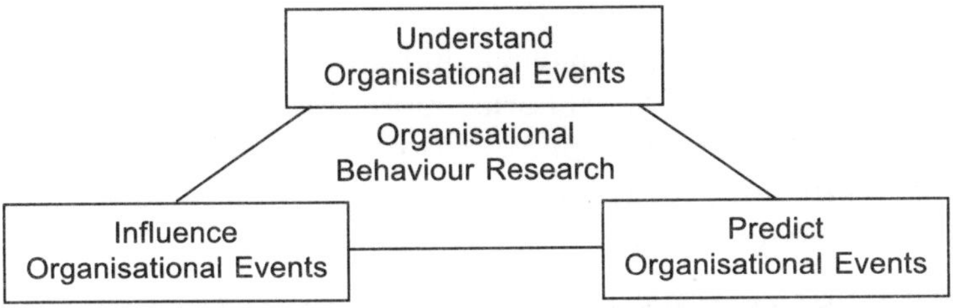

- Organisational behaviour helps an individual understand (i) himself and (ii) others, better. This will improve interpersonal relations considerably. Actually we want to understand why organisational events occur and to more accurately predict what to expect in the future. In other words, we need to map out organisational events so that we can participate more fully and comfortably in that area.
- A manager in a business establishment is concerned with getting things done through others. He will be successful in his job when he can motivate his subordinates to work for better results. OB will help the manager understand the basis of motivation and what to do to motivate his subordinates.

- The fields of OB will be useful to maintain cordial industrial relations.

> If an employee is slow in his work, or if his productivity is steadily declining, it is not always because of (i) denial of promotion or (ii) poor work environment.

> If the union of workers gives a strike call, the basic issue may not be (i) demands for more wages, (ii) higher bonus, etc. Often the indifferent attitude of the boss makes the workers lazy.

Actually human problems need to be tackled humanly. OB will be very useful in this context. It helps understand (i) the cause for the problem, (ii) predict measures for action, and (iii) control its consequences. It is also a human tool for human benefit.

- Another reason for studying OB is that we are interested in pursuing a career in management and want to learn how to predict behaviour and apply it in some meaningful way to make organisation more effective. Organisational Behaviour (i) theories and (ii) concepts will help us to influence organisational events and also efficient management of human resources.

ORGANISATION BEHAVIOUR–EMERGING TRENDS

We know that the pace of change is accelerating and most of the transformation is occurring in the workplace. Organisations are becoming leaner, employee expectations are changing, loyalties to organisations have become a thing of the past, competition is forcing organisations to think of improving productivity and globalization of business is exposing workers to new cultures and environments. In short, there are many (i) challenges and (ii) opportunities for OB in the coming years. Thus, the time has come to understand OB better than ever before. Let us take a brief look into a few critical issues confronting managers for which OB offers solutions, or at least some meaningful insights towards their solutions.

Globalization

The concept of global village results in exchange of cultures across the globe, location of manufacturing centers in various countries by treating the entire globe as a single village, producing the components in one country, assembling the product in the second country and marketing the product in the third country, financing from banks in the fourth country and getting insurance from companies in the fifth country and so on.

Most of the countries in the world globalized their economies by opening their economies to the rest of the world. Organisational operations have also moved beyond national boundaries.

> *Proctor* & *Gamble* manufactures shampoo in Vietnam, and imports to India for consumption purposes.

> - Telco is able to sell its small car *Indica* to many European countries.
> - Fiat is able to sell its Italy-designed Palio to India.

Then what does globalization mean for organisations behaviour? Plenty. Actually OB scholars have warned that organisational practices may not be applicable elsewhere because of different (i) cultures, (ii) religious, and (iii) ethnic belief systems. With increasing globalization, corporate leaders must heed these warnings and adjust OB practices accordingly.

Information Technology

Information technology is shaking up organisations and forcing organisational behaviour scholars to re-examine their concepts in the light of these revolutionary changes. As we know IT has given rise to virtual teams, and has made it possible for small businesses to compete in the global market place. Moreover, Information Technology challenges traditional businesses logic regarding (i) how employees interact, (ii) how organisations are configured, and (iii) how they relate to customers.

One of the critical efforts of IT on organisational behaviour concerns the way people perform their tasks and work with each other.

> Verifone, is the Howlett-Packard subsidiary that makes secure payment system. Verifone's software development group in India develops new code, then electronically sends it at the end of their day to Dallas for testing. This work is then forwarded to employees in Hawaii who integrate the code with existing software. By combining IT with global coordination, Verifone is faster than its competitors at bringing (i) products and (ii) services to market.

IT has also reshaped organisations and their interactions with other entities. We are now witnessing the emergence of the network organisation–an alliance of several organisations for the purpose of (i) creating a product or (ii) serving a client.

Workforce Diversity

Workforce diversity implies that organisations are turning heterogeneous entities visible in terms of differences in (i) gender, (ii) races, (iii) culture, (iv) ethnic groups, etc.

> In USA, the professional scene is mainly occupied by emigrants from other countries such as India, Italy and China.

> In India corporate scenario is changing. Women have left the four walls of the house and are actively participating in boardroom conferences.

It is quite common to find multicultural and diverse work groups in organisations. It may not be wrong to refer to organisations as a melting point for various (i) linguistic, (ii) regional, (iii) religious, and even (iv) national differences.

Usually, it is presumed that employees park their personal lives at the door. However, this presumption does not hold good today. Present day employees are keen to (i) retain and (ii) preserve their (i) cultural values and (ii) lifestyles. And it is now true of the organisations to adopt a more accommodative approach and learn to recognize and value the differences in their employees tastes and preferences.

The challenges before the manager is to learn and appreciate individual differences and treat everyone equally. Such an attitude will go a long way and help in the relations of good employees and thereby increased productivity.

> Many of the professionally managed organisations such as Infosys, Wipro, Satyam Infoway, Tata Sons, etc., have managers who have been trained to be sensitive to such issues and involved in (i) organizing, (ii) training, and (iii) revamping benefit programmes to employees to make them more comfortable in the organisational set-up.

It may not be wrong to comment that diversity if managed well cannot only lead to (i) creativity and (ii) innovativeness among employees but will also enrich decision-making through diverse perspectives. On the contrary, if diversity is managed badly it may result in (i) high employee turnover, (ii) inter-communication barriers, and (ii) inter-personal conflicts.

Empowering Employees

With the changes in workforce demographics, employee expectations and attitudes have also shifted. Traditional allurements such as (i) job security, (ii) attractive remuneration (iii) housing, and the like, do not (i) attract, (ii) retain, and (iii) motivate today's workforce.

Employees demand empowerment and expect quality of status with the management. Previous notions about managerial authority are giving way to employee influence and involvement along with mechanisms for upward communication.

> Citicorp Information Technology Limited (CITL) refers to its programmes as 'Associate Consultants'.

> Educational institutes like ICFAI prefer to address its teaching faculty as 'Faculty Associates', instead of the earlier trend as Lecturers.

With empowerment becoming the order of the day, employees are enjoying riding in the driver's seat, testing greater freedom and choice to participate in organisational affairs. Very often they (i) manage and (ii) perform high risk tasks along with a complete sense of ownership.

Empowerment has changed the conventional superior-subordinate relationship. Managers have learnt to give up control, allow employees to shoulder more responsibility and be involved in the actual decision-making process.

For the manager of tomorrow, there is a need to adopt flexible leadership styles, practice to manage by walking around and act as facilitators of work by using types of 'Power' not necessarily the power of their positions.

Business Ethics

Ethics refers to the study of moral principles or values that determine whether actions are right or wrong and outcomes are (i) good or (ii) bad. Actually we rely on our ethical values to determine "the right thing to do".

Managers and employees in today's organisations are always under pressure to register increased turnover, and strengthen bottomlines. They are, therefore, tempted to (i) cut corners, (ii) bend rules, and (iii) resort to questionable practices.

> Microsoft Corporation has come under scrutiny for allegedly undermining competition and forcing computer makers to bundle its products.

> Royal Dutch/Shell actively fights against corruption in the oil industry, yet the energy giant fired several employees after investigating 23 cases of bribery in one year.

Organisations resort to different ways to enforce ethical behaviours on their employees. They draw elaborate codes of conduct and expect all employees to adhere to the guidelines. They offer seminars, workshops and conduct training programmes to improve ethical behaviours. Organisations provide in-house advisors who can be contacted for assistance in dealing with an ethical issue. They are also creating protection mechanisms for employees who reveal internal unethical practices. It is, thus, the duty of today's manager to create an ethically healthy climate for his/her employees, where, they can do their work productivity and with clear conscience.

Statement showing number of frauds as reported by Public Sector Banks to Reserve Bank of India during the years 2002-03 and 2004 (till March)

Name of the Bank	2002	2003	2004
State Bank of India	416	477	68
(Overseas Branch)	04	10	00
State Bank of Bikaner & Jaipur	20	19	07
State Bank of Hyderabad	39	48	18
State Bank of Indore	18	18	01
State Bank of Patiala	11	08	17
State Bank of Mysore	09	15	02
State Bank of Saurashtra	09	08	04
State Bank of Travancore	08	15	03
Allahabad Bank	49	36	09
Andhra Bank	49	52	12
Bank of Baroda	85	146	68
(Overseas Branch)	01	09	03
Bank of India	77	97	38
(Overseas Branch)	02	02	01
Bank of Maharashtra	06	10	02
Canara Bank	192	164	48
(Overseas Branch)	0	0	0
Central Bank of India	45	108	22
Corporation Bank	44	101	11
Dena Bank	26	46	14
Indian Bank	75	75	16
Indian Overseas Bank	48	54	14
Oriental Bank of Commerce	28	24	08
Punjab National Bank	65	267	64
Punjab & Sind Bank	22	30	06
Syndicate Bank	118	103	34
Union Bank of India	64	59	15
United Bank of India	45	42	10
UCO Bank	42	91	14
Vijaya Bank	26	59	11

Source: Ministry of Finance, Govt. of India.

Statement showing details of cases registered by C.B.I. against the bank officials of Public Sector Banks in which raids have been conducted by C.B.I. during 1.1.2004 to 30.6.2004

Name of the Bank	No. of Cases Registered	No. of Officials Raided
State Bank of India	05	07
State Bank of Indore	01	02
State Bank of Travancore	02	02
Allahabad Bank	02	05
Andhra Bank	02	01
Bank of Baroda	01	02
Bank of India	01	01
Canara Bank	03	02
Central Bank of India	06	02
Corporation Bank	01	03
Dena Bank	02	02
Oriental Bank of Commerce	02	06
Punjab National Bank	05	06
Syndicate Bank	02	01
UCO Bank	04	03
United Bank of India	02	02
Vijaya Bank	01	02

Source: Ministry of Finance, Govt. of India.

Ethics is important for organisations for more than one reason:

- Ethics corresponds to basic human needs;
- Ethics creates credibility with the public;
- Ethical values bestow management with credibility before employees;
- Ethics helps improve decision-making process; and
- No law can protect society but ethics can.

Stimulating Innovation and Change

In today's competitive environment, organisations must foster innovation and manage change successfully. Success comes to those organisations that (i) maintain their flexibility, (ii) continually improve their quality, and (iii) outbeat their competitors with innovative products and services. Employees are key to (i) innovation and (ii) change. The challenge for managers is to stimulate employees creativity and tolerance for change. The field of OB provides ideas and techniques to help realize these goals.

CASE STUDY

How is this stuff going to help me?

Ms. X wants to be a manager. She enjoyed her accounting, finance and marketing courses. Each of these provided her with some clearcut answers. Now the professor in her organisational behaviour course is telling her that there are really very few clearcut answers when it comes to managing people. He has discussed some of the history of behavioural management and says that behavioural science concepts play a big role in the course. She is very perplexed. She came to the school to get an answer on how to be an effective manager but this course surely does not seem to be heading in that direction.

DISCUSSION POINTS

(1) How would you relieve Ms. X's anxiety? How is a course in organisational behaviour going to make her a better manager?

(2) Why did the professor start off with a brief introduction to the behavioural science framework.

(3) How does a course in organisational behaviour differ from courses in other fields such as accounting, finance or marketing?

KEY CONCEPTS

1. **Organisational Behaviour**
   - Organisation–Concept
   - Management and Organisational Behaviour–Relationship
   - Organisational Behaviour–Emergence
   - Managerial Roles
   - Managerial Skills
   - Contributing Disciplines

5. **Motivation**
   - Introduction
   - Motives–Types
   - Motivating
   - Motivation–Significance
   - Motivation–Nature
   - Motivation–Types
   - Motivation–Process
   - Motivation–Meaning
   - Motivation–Theories
   - Discussion Points
   - Questions

6. **Job Stress**
   - Stress–Meaning
   - Stress–Factors
   - Stress–Causes
   - Stress–Consequences
   - Job Stress–Coping Strategies
   - Stress and Job Performance
   - Discussion Points
   - Questions

7. **Group Dynamics**
   - Groups–Definition
   - Groups–Features
   - Groups–Importance
   - Groups Dynamics–Meaning
   - Groups–Formation
   - Groups–Types
   - Groups Development–Stages
   - Groups vs. Work Teams
   - Work Teams–Types
   - Influences on Team Effectiveness

- Political Behaviour–Reasons/Universality of Political Behaviour
- Political Behaviour–Techniques/Types of Organisational Politics
- Managing Political Behaviour
- Discussion Points
- Questions

14. Organisational Culture and Climate

- Organisational Culture–Defined
- Organisational Culture–Characteristics
- Cultural Typologies
- Cultural Concepts
- Cultural–Functions and Dysfunctions
- Maintaining Cultures through Steps of Socialisation
- How Employee Learn Culture
- How Organisational Culture Impacts Performance and Satisfaction
- Organisational Climate–Defined
- Organisational Climate–Affecting Factors
- Organisational Culture–Emerging Issues
- Organisational Effectiveness–Meaning
- Organisational Effectiveness–Nature
- Discussion Points
- Questions

15. Organisational Structure

- Organisational Structure–Introduction
- Organisational Structure–Steps
- Organisational Structure–Elements
- Organisational Structure–Dimensions
- Organisational Structure–Determinants
- Discussion Points
- Questions

QUESTIONS

- Define the term organisational behaviour. Explain the features and different approaches to the study of organisational behaviour.
- Analyse the contributions of various disciplines to organisational behaviour.
- Discuss the scope of organisational behaviour. How is it an interdisciplinary subject? Why should we study the subject of OB?
- Sketch the historical growth of the subject of organisational behaviour. What are the major factors that determine individual behaviour questionnaire?
- "Behaviour is generally predicable". Do you agree or disagree? Discuss.
- "People influence organisations and organisations influence people." Explain the statement.
- "The field of OB has the potential to become prescriptive as opposed to descriptive." Substantiate the statement.
- What challenges and opportunities will you come across within the third millennium as a manager which have relevance to OB?
- As a manager do you also believe that understanding human behaviour at work is the single most important requirement for managerial success. Elaborate your answer.
- Do you agree that the field of OB contributes to both the effective functioning of organisations and the well-being of individuals. Is there any inconsistency among the goals?
- Indicate the correct response against the following multiple choice questions:
  - (i) The field of organisational behaviour is characterized by:
    - (a) an interdisciplinary focus and a prescriptive nature.

(b) a single disciplinary focus and a perceptive nature.

(c) the ability to prescribe how to induce change in consistent and predictable ways.

(d) a single disciplinary focus and a descriptive nature.

(e) an interdisciplinary focus and a descriptive nature.

(ii) When information is transmitted to others, the manager is carrying out the role of:

(a) Monitor

(b) Spokesperson

(c) Disseminator

(d) Leader

(e) Liaison

Individual Perception

2

Learning Objectives

- Meaning of Perception
- Perception vs. Sensation
- Importance of Perception
- Perceptual Process, Selectivity and Organisation
- Social Perception/Person Perception
- Perceptual Errors
- Impression Management

PERCEPTION–MEANING

The important cognitive factor of human behaviour is 'perception'. It is one of the most important psychological factors affecting human behaviour. It is the chief mechanism by which people come to know about their surrounding milieu. Thus, perception is the way an individual experiences the situation. It is a unique interpretation of the situation, not necessarily an exact recording of the situation.

There can be no behaviour without perception and perception lies at the base of every individual behaviour. The best supervisor is one who (i) accurately and (ii) precisely estimates employees' perception and makes his moves.

Fred Luthans opines perception as "*the process of (i) selection, (ii) organisation, and (iii) interpretation of sensation to provide a meaningful experience for the individual.*"

There are two basic elements in this direction, viz.:

- Perception is a process of (i) selecting and (ii) screening of stimuli which prevents an individual from processing irrelevant information;
- Information is processed thereby implying that it has been (i) ordered and (ii) classified in some logical manner to assign meaning to the stimulus situation.

PERCEPTION VS. SENSATION

There has been a great deal of misunderstanding about the relationship between (i) perception and (ii) sensation, though there is a clear distinction between the two.

Sensation may be described as the response of a physical sensory organ. The physical senses are: (i) vision, (ii) hearing, (iii) touch, (iv) smell, and (v) taste. These senses are continuously bombard by stimuli both (i) external and (ii) internal to human beings and reactions in a particular sense organ because of these take place. Examples of sensation may be (i) reaction of eye to colour, (ii) ear to sound, etc. These examples show that sensation deals with every elementary behaviour that is largely determined by physiological functioning.

Perception, on the other hand, is much more (i) complex and (ii) broader than sensation. It is a cognitive and psychological process of (i) sensing, (ii) filtering, and (iii) modifying raw data.

Dempsey's statement further clarifies the difference between the two.

> "*By means of my eye, I see, but it is not my eye but* I who see, I tend to see an object in totality, a thing with certain qualities, with a figure and form set *against a background.*"

Thus, in seeing process, both (i) sensation and (ii) perception are involved. Activation of eye to see an object is sensation and the inference what is being seen is perception. As sensation plays an important role in private lives of people, perception plays a crucial role in organisational life.

Perception–Importance

Perception is a cognitive process. In terms of S-O-B-C model (i.e. S = stimulus, O = organism, B = behaviour and C = consequences) which involves the 'O' selecting, organising and interpreting the 'S'.

The key to understand perception is to recognize that it is a unique 'interpretation' of the situation, not an exact recording of it.

The cognitive map of an individual is not a photographic representation of the physical world. It is, rather, a partial, personal construction in which certain objects selected out by an individual are perceived in an individual manner.

Thus, every perceiver is, to some degree, a non-representational artist, painting a picture of the world that expresses his individual view of reality.

Perception is a very complex cognitive process which provides a unique picture of the world which is quiet different from reality. The difference between: (i) perceptual world and (ii) real world is vital to the understanding of organisational behaviour as exemplified hereunder:

> If a supervisor's concern is to see some change in the behaviour of other people, and if, in turn, people's present behaviour is determined largely by their perception of the environment, then it is critical to understand their perception.

It is obvious from the example that the supervisor has to understand circumstances under which their behaviour might change.

> The universal assumption made by managers is that subordinates always want promotions, when in fact, many subordinates really feel psychologically 'forced' to accept a promotion. Manager's seldom attempt to find out, and sometimes subordinates themselves do not know, whether the promotion should be offered or otherwise.

It seems that: (i) perceptual world of the manager is quite different from perceptual world of subordinates. And both may be very different from reality.

If this is the case, what can be done about it from management standpoint? The best answer seems to be:

- A better understanding of the concepts involved should be developed.
- Direct application and techniques should logically follow complete understanding.

PERCEPTUAL PROCESS

A perceptual process consists of several sub-processes. These sub-processes are the internal cognitive processes, classified into five parts:

Perceptual Process

Stimulus	Registration	Interpretation	Feedback	Reaction

1. Stimulus

The first important sub-process in the perception is the presence of stimulus or situation. Perception begins when a person is confronted with stimulus or situation. This confrontation may be with the (i) immediate sensual stimulation, or (ii) total physical and socio-cultural environment.

> An employee who is confronted with (i) his supervisor or (ii) the total formal organisational environment. Either (i) one or (ii) both may initiate the working of the employee's perceptual process. This represents the stimulus interacting with the perception.

The presence of stimulus, though necessary for perception, is not an actual sub-process of perception. However, perceptual process cannot start in the absence of stimulus.

2. Registration

Actual perception starts with the registration phenomenon, which occurs because of the presence of stimulus. During registration sub-process–the physiological (sensory or neural) organs are affected. The physiological ability to (i) hear and (ii) see will affect perception.

3. Interpretation

Interpretation is the most significant cognitive aspect of perception. It involves attaching meaning to the stimulus, the other physiological processes, particularly learning, affect the interpretation of a situation.

> In an organisation, employees' interpretation of a situation are largely dependent upon their (i) learning, (ii) motivation, and (iii) personality.

4. Feedback

Feedback is the fourth sub-process which is important for interpretation of the perceptual event data.

> Psychological feedback that may influence an employee's perception is the (i) supervisor's raised eyebrow or (ii) change in voice inflection.

5. Reaction

The final aspect of perception is the resultant behaviour. The response may be (i) overt, such as, actions, etc., or (ii) covert, such as, change in attitudes. The behaviour is necessary if perception is considered (i) behavioural event or (ii) psychological process. Here again, behaviour is the result of perceptual process and not its sub-processes.

PERCEPTUAL SELECTIVITY

Perception is a selective process. As people can sense only limited amount of information in the environment, they are characteristically selective. By selection, certain aspects of stimuli are: (i) screened out and others are (ii) admitted. Those which are admitted remain in the awareness of people and which are screened out fall below the threshold.

With all this stimulation having effect upon people, (i) how and (ii) why they select only a very few stimuli at a given time. There are a number of factors which affect this selectivity, viz.: (i) external and (ii) internal.

1. External Attention Factors

Various external attention factors affect perceptual selectivity. The external attention factors consists of outside environmental influences, such as:

Intensity | Size | Contrast | Repetition | Motion | Status

(a) Intensity

Intensity accentuates and functions to increase the chances of selection.

> If the messages are bright and loud, then they attract people.

> Underlying a sentence calls for a more attention, and people generally pay more attention to it.

The greater the intensity of a stimuli, the more likely it will be noticed. An intense stimuli has more power to push itself for selection filters than does a weaker stimuli.

> A shout is more attention getting than a normal speaking voice.

The essence of intensity principle is that: (i) a loud noise, (ii) strong odour, or (iii) bright light will be noticed very easily than a (i) soft sound, (ii) weak odour, or (iii) dim light. The principle that, "*the greater the intensity of external stimuli, the more likely it will be perceived*", is sometimes invalid.

> By speaking loudly, the supervisor is actually turning the subordinate off instead of gaining attention.

The intensity principle is only one small factor in the perceptual process, which is only a part of the (i) cognitive process and (ii) what goes into human behaviour. Thus, intensity principle has to be considered in the light of the situation, i.e. frame of reference.

(b) Size

Closely related to intensity is the principle of size. It says that the larger the object, the more likely it will be perceived.

Size establishes dominance and overrides other things, and thereby enhances perceptual selection.

> The maintenance engineer may pay more attention to a big machine than to a smaller one, even though the small machine costs the same as the big machine.

> In advertising, a full page spread is more attention-catching than few lines in some corner of the newspaper.

(c) Contrast

Stimuli that contrast with the surrounding environment are more likely to be selected for attention than the stimuli that blend in:

> Want Made **Go** When
> **Time**
> Cause **Effect** Then
> Other **Should** Even.

When we initially look at the box, the first thing we probably notice is the word "Effect" that is written in bold. We notice the bold word because it is contrasted with other words in the box. A contrasting effect can be caused by (i) colour, (ii) size, or any other factor that is unusual (any factor that distinguishes one stimulus from others at present).

> A man walking down the street with a pair of crutches is more attention-catching than a common man.

The contrast effect also explains why a male person stands out in a crowd of females. There is nothing unusual about a male person but, when surrounded by females he stands out.

(d) Repetition

The repetition principle states that a repeated external stimulus is more attention-getting than a single one. A stimulus that is repeated has better chances of catching us during the periods when our attention to a task is waning. Repetition increases our (i) sensitivity or (ii) alertness to the stimulus. Thus, the greater the frequency with which a sensory stimulus is presented, the greater will be the chances we select it for attention.

> Repetition is one of the most frequently used techniques in advertising and one of the most common ways of getting our attention.

(e) Motion

Under motion principle, people pay more attention, in their fields of vision, to moving rather than stationary objects.

> Workers will notice materials moving by them on the conveyor belt, but they may fail to give prcper attention to the maintenance needs of the stationary machine next to them.

> The assembly line workers may devote their attention to the line of slowly moving materials, they are working on and fail to notice the relatively nice working conditions, e.g. (i) pastel-coloured walls, (ii) air conditioning, etc.

(f) Status

Perception is also influenced by the status of the perceiver. High status people can exert influence on perception of an employee than low status people.

Example: When we are introduced to the (i) Divisional Manager and (ii) Foreman, we are likely to remember the name of Divisional Manager than the name of the foreman.

2. Internal Attention Factors

The concept is set of an important cognition in selectivity. It can be said as an internal form of attention-getting based on the individual's complex psychological make up. Among the internal factors the most important are:

- Needs and Desires
- Personality
- Experience

(a) Needs and Desires

The needs and motives of people play a vital role in perception. Frustrated individuals' perception is entirely different from that of a happy going person. Some researchers contend that when pictures of individuals in social setting are shown to them, they perceive in different ways. People at different levels of (i) needs and (ii) desires perceive the same thing differently.

> There is a strong likelihood of attending to job threatening comments, if you feel insecure about your job.

> Power-seekers are likely to notice power related stimuli.

> Socially oriented individuals pay attention to inter-personal stimuli.

Thus, (i) expectancy, (ii) motives, or (iii) interests also affect people perception. It goes without saying that people are likely to notice stimuli relevant to current active (i) motives, and (ii) compatible with major personality characteristics.

(b) Personality

Individual personality is another internal factor that has profound influence on perceived behaviour. It is often said that (i) optimistic people perceive things in favourable terms, (ii) pessimistic beings in negative terms. Researchers contend that between these two extremes there exists a category who can see things more (i) accurately and (ii) objectively. Individuals who have real perceptive abilities, can function effectively without being defensive about their imitation in their personality. Research on the effects of individual personality reveals many truths:

- Secure individuals tend to perceive others as warm not cold.
- Thoughtful individuals do not expose by expressing extreme judgement of others.
- Persons who accept themselves and have faith in their individuality perceive things favourably.
- Self-accepting individuals perceive themselves as (i) liked, (ii) wanted, and (iii) accepted by others.

(c) Experience

Experience and knowledge have a constant bearing on perception. Successful experiences (i) enhances and (ii) boost the perceptive abilities and lead to accuracy of perception of individual, whereas failure erodes self-confidence.

PERCEPTUAL ORGANISATION

Perceptual organisation focuses on what takes place in the perceptual process once the information from the stimuli is received. This aspect of perception is commonly known as perceptual organisation. An individual not often perceives (i) patches of colour, (ii) light, or (iii) sound. Instead, the person will perceive organised patterns of stimuli and identifiable whole objects.

> When a male college student is shown a football, he does not normally perceive (i) the colour, (ii) quality, or (iii) the odour of leather. Rather, he perceives a football which has a potential of giving the perceiver fun and excitement as either (i) participant, or (ii) spectator.

Hence, the person's perceptual process organizes the incoming information, into a meaningful whole.

The important forms of perceptual organisation:

- Figure-ground
- Perceptual Constancy
- Perceptual Context
- Perceptual Defence
- Perceptual Grouping

1. Figure-ground

Figure-ground is considered the most basic form of perceptual organisation. In the perceptual field certain factors are considered significant and give meaning to the person, and certain others which are either (i) unimportant or (ii) cannot be studied are left as insignificant. The meaningful and significant portion is called 'figure' and the insignificant or meaningless portion is labeled as 'ground'.

> The written words on this page are the 'figure' and the white space is the 'ground'.

The information we classify as figure is assigned more importance than that which we view as background.

The employees psychological storage and subsequent interpretation of information will be affected by whether he classified the information as (i) figure or (ii) ground. What becomes (i) figure or (ii) ground is largely influenced by our needs and expectations.

2. Perceptual Constancy

Constancy is sophisticated form of perceptual organisation. It gives a person a sense of stability in a changing world. Constancy permits an individual to interpret the stimuli in such a manner that these stimuli (i) more or (ii) less accurately reflect the constancies of the real world. The stability of (i) objects and (ii) people, the consistency of these dimensions of our everyday world.

If constancy principle is not at work, the world becomes disorganized for the individual. Without perceptual constancy, the (i) shapes, (ii) sizes or (iii) colours of the objects would change as the person moves about and this makes his job uncomfortable and sometimes impossible.

Perceptual constancy does not result from ignoring any particular cue, it results from responding to patterns of cues, these cues are mostly learned by individuals.

The essence of perceptual constancy is that the (i) shapes, (ii) sizes, (iii) colours, (iv) brightness, and (v) location of an object are fairly constant regardless of the information received by the senses.

- A cricket ball is red in colour.
- All cricket players wear white uniform.

3. Perceptual Context

The highest, most sophisticated form of perceptual organisation is context. It gives (i) meaning and (ii) value to simple (i) stimuli, (ii) objects, (iii) events in the environment. The principle of context can be simply understood by the well-known doodles as under:

(a) the rate race

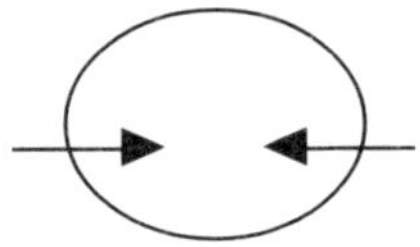

(b) two mice in a beer can

The visual stimuli without context becomes completely meaningless. But when the doodles are placed in a verbal context, they take on meaning and value to the person who perceives.

In an organisation, (i) a pat on the back, (ii) a suggestive gesture, and (iii) raised eyebrow, etc., will be meaningless without proper context. They will be made more meaningful if an employee receives a pat on the back for increase in performance and like that.

4. Perceptual Defence

People, often screen out perceptual stimuli that makes them (i) uncomfortable and (ii) dissatisfying. People have certain inherent tendencies to defend their reactions against new information, which would be conflicting with their existing impressions. Perceptual defence is performed by:

(a) denying (i) existence or (ii) importance of conflicting information;

(b) distorting the new information to match the old;

(c) accepting the existence of the new information that treat it as non-representative exception.

People, generally, build defences against stimuli that are either (i) personally or (ii) culturally unacceptable or threatening. From organisational point of view, perceptual defence plays an influential role in understanding superior-subordinate relationship.

5. Perceptual Grouping

Grouping principle of perceptual organisation is very elementary. It seems to be closely inherent. These groupings are based on certain uniformities. Usually several stimuli are grouped together into a recognizable pattern. When the simple grouping of stimuli are presented to people, they usually group them together into either.

The important forms of perceptual organisation:

- Closure
- Continuity
- Proximity
- Similarity

(a) Closure

When people are faced with incomplete information they have a tendency to fill in the gaps themselves. When presented with a set of incomplete stimuli, people fill in the missing parts and make it more meaningful. The tendency to organise perceptual stimuli so that they form a complete message is known as 'closure'.

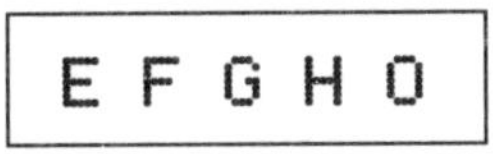

If we ask hundred people, it is quite obvious that all hundred people call them E, F, G, H, O. They would not call them a series of broken lines. What people do, they fill in the gaps and make a sense by perceiving them to be alphabets.

Managers, in organisations usually do not have complete message on the basis of which to judge the employees. Managers, in such cases, fill in the missing message and make decisions.

(b) Continuity

Continuity is closely related to closure. However, there is slight difference between the two. Closure supplies missing stimuli and the continuity principle says that, a person will tend to perceive continuous (i) lines, or (ii) patterns. This type of continuity may lead to (i) inflexible, or (ii) non-creative thinking. On the part of organisational participants only the continuous (i) patterns, or (ii) relationship will be perceived.

(c) Proximity

The principle of proximity or nearness states that: a group of stimuli that are close together will be perceived as a whole pattern of parts belonging together.

> Several workers who work on a particular machine may be perceived as a single whole. If the output is low, management may perceive all the workers as trouble making group, when in reality, some of the workers are (i) loyal and (ii) dedicated employees.

(d) Similarity

The principle of similarity states that: the greater the similarity of the stimuli, the greater is the tendency to perceive them as a common group. Similarity is conceptually related to proximity; but, in most cases, is stronger than proximity.

> In an organisation, all employees who wear white collars may be perceived as a common group; when, in reality, each employee is a unique individual.

Perception–Managerial Implications

A manager is concerned with the achievement of organisational objectives through specified behaviour of its members. Perception affects the outcome of behaviour. This is so because people act on the basis of what they see. Hence, in understanding behaviour, managers must recognize that facts people do not perceive as meaningful usually will not influence their behaviour, whereas the things they believe to be real, even though factually (i) incorrect or (ii) non-existent will influence it.

Thus, the understanding of human perception, particularly in the organisational setting, is important in (i) understanding and (ii) controlling the behaviour.

If management intends to improve the behaviour of individuals at work, which is largely the product of their perceptions of environmental factors, it should attempt to identify the situations under which their behaviour might be improved. The management can (i) control or (ii) influence the important environmental forces of perception. This is done in two ways:

(a) Managers decide what (i) structural and (ii) technological stimuli will be. Even though the individual filters the stimuli, the type of stimuli available to be filtered influences the resulting behaviour.

(b) Managers through the organisation, define the (i) ideas or (ii) beliefs of the group. They determine sanctions and thus establish the (i) word or (ii) punishment context of behavioural consequences.

Similar attempts can be made at group level also where various problems can arise because of mis-perception. Various conflicts among groups take place because of the mis-understanding of each group as (i) functioning and interests of others, some difficulties of administrative practices (ii) grow out of beliefs that different groups in the organisations are made up of different type of people. Once they see that people in other groups are different, they are predisposed to see the difference. If managers can produce an integrating situation which is (i) cooperative, rather than, (ii) competitive, the likelihood of seeing other people as similar is increased.

Managers can provide training facilities in behavioural science whereby people may learn to perceive correctly, however, it is difficult to point out the specific training to be provided for this purpose.

PERSON PERCEPTION

Of particular interest in organisational behaviour is the process of person or social-perception. Person perception is the process by which individuals attribute characteristics or traits to other people. It is closely related to the attribution process i.e. the ways in which people come to understand the causes of their (i) own and (ii) others behaviour.

The person perception process is the same as the general process of perception, i.e. the process follows the same sequence of (i) observation, (ii) selection, (iii) organisation, (iv) interpretation, and (v) response. However, the object being perceived in the environment is another person. Perceptions of (i) situations, (ii) events, and (iii) objects are important, but individual differences in perceptions of other people are crucial to understanding behaviour on work settings:

> We meet a new employee. In order to get acquainted and to make him feel at ease, we invite him to lunch. During lunch, he begins to tell us his life history and focuses on his accomplishments. Because he talks only about himself (he asks us no question about ourselves). We may form the impression that he is very self-centred.

Later, we may come to see other aspects of his personality, but our perceptions may always be strongly affected by his just impression, called the primary effect.

Actually, the factors influencing person perception are the same as those that influence perceptual selection. Both (i) external and (ii) internal factors affect person perception. However, we may usefully categorize factors that influence how a person perceives another as:

The Person Perceived

In person perceiving someone else, an individual processes a variety of cues about that person. Facial expressions, general appearances, skin colour, posture, age, gender, voice quality, personality traits, behaviour and the like. Some cues may contain important information about the person, but many do not.

> A person attempting to exert authority in a situation but also identified as very young may be viewed quite differently from an older person doing exactly the same thing.

People seem to have implicit personality theories about the relationships among (i) physical characteristics, (ii) personality traits, and (iii) specific behaviours.

> When we first contact with someone over the telephone, later upon meeting, did that person look and act as we expected?

The Perceiver

A person's own personality traits, values, attitudes, current mood, past experience, and so on, determine, in part, how that person perceives someone else.

> Someone with a strong need for ego satisfaction, may select out from a situation and emphasize signals that (i) either tend to satisfy, (ii) or deny, the desire for self-esteem.

> Listening to an employee describe the personality of a co-worker may tell you as much about the employees personality as it does about that of the person being described.

Accurately perceiving the personality of an individual raised in another culture is often difficult.

Example: Japanese Managers in the United States and the U.S. Managers in Japan may face dis-orienting experiences as they try to learn how to deal with business associates from the other cultures.

One reason is that the perceiver interprets perceptions of the other person's (i) traits and (ii) behaviour in the light of his/her own cultural (i) experiences, (ii) attitudes, and (iii) values. Often these factors are inadequate for making accurate judgement about (i) personality and (ii) behaviour of people from a different culture.

The Situation

The context in which we perceive events or objects is also important. There are elements in our surrounding environment which influence our perception.

> If the Managing Director of a company calls for a meeting with his General Managers and on that day a junior manager makes a small mistake, the General Manager is more likely to register and notice that, which otherwise or any other normal day would have been overlooked.

> If a person attired in a 'dhoti kurta' were to enter the office premises, he is likely to have more eyes compared to if he were to be attired in the same dress when walking around in the compound of his house.

This means that perception is influenced by various situational factors such as (i) time, (ii) location, (iii) light, (iv) heat, etc. These may simultaneously impact the perception process making it an extremely complex process.

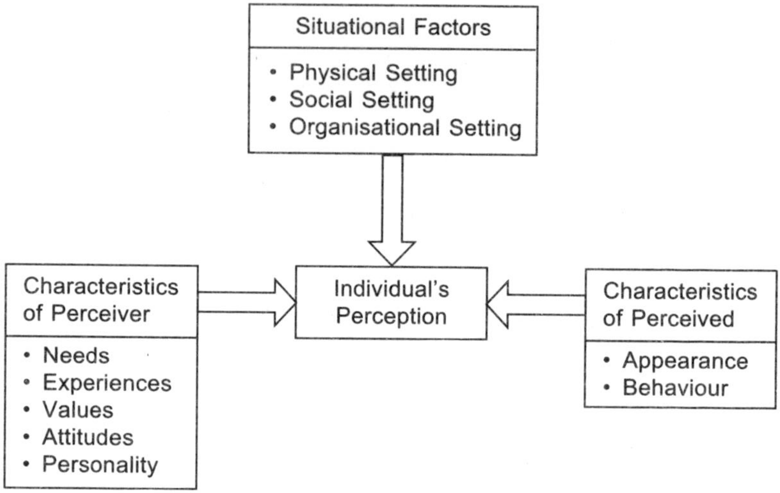

Multiple Influence on Perception

PERCEPTUAL ERRORS

The analysis of perceptual process indicates that perception is a complex process. It is influenced by a number of factors. Added to this, cognitive process plays a vital role in interpreting the information. Human beings are complex. Hence, they can not be objective regarding their judgements where environment is involved. A number of factors hinder our judgement about: (i) people, (ii) objects, and (iii) situations. We can perceive accurately, if these hindering factors are either (i) eliminated or (ii) controlled. It would be appreciated to know these factors in order to eliminate or control them. These hindering factors are also known as 'Perceptual Errors' or 'Barriers to Perceptual Accuracy'.

Perceptual Defence

Perceptual defence is the tendency for people to protect themselves against (i) ideas, (ii) objects, or (iii) situations that are threatening. The defence mechanism put up by the perceiver may assume any of the four forms:

- outright denial;
- modification of the data received;

- change in perception but refusal to change;
- change in perception itself.

The four defence mechanisms have been cultured from a study involving college students. The students were presented with a word 'intelligent' as a characteristic of a factory worker. This was conflicting to the notion about a worker held by the students. The defence put up by the students were:

- Some students denied that the factory workers could be intelligent.

  Denial Mechanism

- Some students said that the worker was intelligent but lacked initiative to rise above his group (associating intelligence with some other trait).

  Modification Mechanism

- A few students felt that the word intelligent conflicted with their understanding of a coworker. What they believed about the worker was that he was not too intelligent.

  Change in Perception but Refusal to Change Mechanism

- Many of the students felt that the worker was really intelligent. But this change in perception was very subtle.

  Change in Perception Mechanism

> He who crakes jokes he is witty.

Whatever the form of mechanism, perceptual defence is likely to play a useful role in understanding union-management and supervisor-subordinate relationship.

Stereotyping

Stereotyping is the tendency to assign attributes to someone solely on the basis of a category of people of which that person is a member.

> Mr. Jai, a newly appointed Accountant in the Department of Finance of Suraj Cables Ltd. entered the Department of Finance of the company. He saw a gentleman dressed in a suit carrying a briefcase entering the room of the Chief Finance Manager. Mr. Jai perceived that the gentleman is the Chief Finance Manager as we normally perceive managers are in full suit. But that gentleman was a cashier and carrying cash in the briefcase and he was on his way to the bank.

The perception of Mr. Jai was based on stereotype impression.

Actually, we have certain pre-established categories with certain characteristics and attributes based on the occupational/professional characteristics. We approach doctors, judges and teachers with most positive and obedience attributes, whereas, policeman with fear and submissive attributes. When a drug addict or an alcoholic approaches us, we perceive them most negatively.

The other stereotypes are:

Age Stereotype	Gender-role Stereotype

Age Stereotype

Age is one of the stereotypes which influences the organisational environment. We presume (i) physical qualities, (ii) psychological qualities, and (iii) intellectual qualities based on age. The stereotype of the young people include:

- Dynamic and dashing;
- Quick decision-making;
- More creative and innovative ideas;
- More physical capacities;
- Highly interested in new techniques and new methods; and
- Highly active.

The stereotypes of the older employees, as found by Rosen and Jardee, are as follows:

- More resistant to organisational change;
- Less creative and innovative;
- Less likely to take calculated risks;
- More conservative in nature;
- Lower in physical capacity;
- Less interested in learning new techniques;
- Less capable of learning new techniques;
- Gray hair.

Gender-role Stereotypes

We normally distinguish stereotype men and women into separate and distinct categories. The stereotype of men include:

- Tough leadership;
- Task centred leader rather than human relationist;
- High self-confidence;
- High competitiveness;
- Highly ambitious;
- Detailed analytical ability.

Stereotype of the women employees include:

- Highly emotional;
- Highly impulsive and submissive;
- Highly human relationists and inter-personal religionists;
- Low self-confidence;
- Less ambitious;
- More commitment and loyalty;
- Highly tolerant.

These stereotypes dominate/influence us to perceive the (i) objects, (ii) people, (iii) incidents in a pre-categorized or pre-determined structure. Hence, stereotyping hinders us from perceiving the objects as objectively as possible.

Halo Effect

Evaluation of another person solely on the basis of one attribute, either favourable or unfavourable is called the 'Halo Effect'.

Mr. Vijay of Industrial Finance Corporation attends the office on time every day while all other categories attend the office at least 15 minutes late. But Mr. Vijay is not efficient on job performance. But the manager of the branch ranked his performance on the best simply based on his punctuality in coming to the office.

This means the Halo Effect blinds the perceiver to take notice of the other attributes which also are to be considered if evaluation is to be obtained a complete, and accurate impression of the other person. Managers have to make efforts to guard against the halo effect especially during a preliminary interview with a prospective employee or rating on existing employee's job performance. One trait may be singled out and used for passing judgement on the performance of the individual:

The interviewer may perceive a beautiful candidate to be suitable to be a personal secretary, though actually she may be a poor typist and bad secretary.

Halo effect needs not always mean over-rating positive characteristics. An individual may be down rated based on the negative evaluation of his/her behaviour. This process is called Rusty Halo or Horns Effect.

Projection

Projection is the tendency for people to see their own traits in other people, i.e. they protect their (i) own feelings, (ii) personality characteristics, (iii) attitudes, or (iv) motives onto others.

Employees frightened by rumours of impending organisational changes may not only judge others to be more frightened than they are but may also assess various policy decisions as more threatening than warranted.

Projection may be especially strong for undesirable traits that perceiver possess but fail to recognize in themselves.

An individual who is himself not very energetic may see others as lazy or may explain their lack of achievement as resulting from their unwillingness to work hard.

> One who is dishonest may be suspicious of others and may perceive dishonest intentions in others where they don't exist.

Expectancy Effects

Expectancy effect in the perceptual process is the extent to which prior expectations bias perceptions of (i) events, (ii) objects, and (iii) people. Sometimes people simply perceive what they anticipate perceiving.

Expectancy effects may also bias perception even in less ambiguous situations.

> Our perception of a team to which we have been assigned recently may be positive if our supervisor told us that the team's work is important and that it will be staffed by talented people from several departments. However, our perception may be negative if he told us that the team exists solely for political reasons and contains some real 'deadwood' from other departments.

We might also perceive identical behaviour by other members of the team quite differently under each set of expectations.

As we know that experience and learning are important to the perceptual process, as a result, people often approach situations expecting certain things to happen or other people to have certain attributes. These expectations may strongly influence their perceptions of reality.

Another aspect of expectancy effect is the self-fulfilling prophecy. Expecting certain things to happen shapes the behaviour of the perceiver in such a way that the expected is more likely to happen.

> A team leader who has been led to believe that a new employee has a great potential might do two things:
>
> - to assess the employee's performance as being better than it really is (*an expectancy effect*).
> - to behave towards the new employee in such a way (e.g. providing encouragement or additional training) that the new employee's performance is, in fact, very good (*a self-fulfilling prophecy*).

IMPRESSIVE MANAGEMENT

The purpose of impression management or self-presentation is to regulate or monitor the perceptions of others from us. We mostly tend to try to present ourselves in a socially desirable or acceptable way in order to impress others. The employees tend to present themselves in an acceptable way to their superiors in order to be rated high in the performance appraisal or to be considered for continuation of employment or promotion or salary increase and the like.

The impression management strategies shown below include enhancing the positive behavioural outcomes and reducing the negative behaviour outcomes. In addition, the employees would like to give the impression that they are capable of more than what they are actually capable of. In addition, they use other strategies like (i) hiding the weaknesses, (ii) disassociation with the trouble makers, (iii) apologizing for their mistakes, (iv) associating with the positive impression makers.

Conformity

Agreeing with someone else's opinion in order to gain his/her approval.

> A manager tells his boss, "you are absolutely right on your reorganisation. Plan for the western regional office couldn't agree with you more".

Excuses

Explanations of a predicament-creating event aimed at minimizing the apparent severity of the predicament.

> Sales manager to boss, "we failed to get the ad in the paper on time, but no one responds to those ads anyway".

Apologies

Admitting responsibility for an undesirable event and simultaneously seeking to get a pardon for the action.

> Employee to boss, "I am sorry I made a mistake on the report. Please forgive me."

Acclamation

Explanation of favourable events to maximize the desirable implications for oneself.

> A salesperson informs a peer, "the sales in our division have nearly tripled since I was hired".

Flattery

Complimenting others, about their virtues in an effort to make oneself appear (i) perceptive and (ii) likeable.

> New sales trainee to peer, "*you handled that client's complaint so tactfully! I could never have handled that as well as you did*."

Favours

Doing something nice for one to gain that person's approval.

> Salesperson to prospective client, "I have got two tickets to the theater tonight that I can't use. Take them. Consider it a thank you for taking out the time to talk with me".

Association

Enhancing or protecting one's image by managing information about (i) people and (ii) things with which one is associated.

> A job applicant says to an interviewer, "what a coincidence. Your boss and I were roommates in college".

CASE STUDY

Space Shortage

Mr. Srinivasan is the Assistant Plant Manager of Triveni Aluminium Manufacturing Company. He is also the chairman of an ad hoc committee for space utilization having all departmental heads as members. The Plant Manager has entrusted the responsibility of ensuring optimum utilization of space in the company to Mr. Srinivasan. Presently, the company is plagued by two major problems: raising costs and shortage of space. To meet space shortage, an ambitious programme of plant expansion is envisaged. But before putting the stamp of approval on this programme, the Plant Manager wanted to know whether the existing space in the company has been put to judicious usage or not.

In the very first meeting of the committee, Mr. Srinivasan made his intentions clear. Irrational usage of space leads to uneconomical efforts and proves to be an expensive proposition in the long run. He also welcomed the members to air their opinions, regarding space utilization, freely. Immediately the office manager ventured to say: "I feel we are using every possible inch of the room that is available to us. We have people, piled on top of one another. It is only in the plant, I find many vacant spots." The production manager retaliated immediately thus: "It's unfortunate that my colleague has indulged in this dirty game of mutual recrimination and shifting of blame. Office people enjoy luxurious benefits and facilities. The supervisors in the plant don't find room to position filing cabinets even. In the recent past shortage of space has severely constrained our operations and my repeated complaints regarding this have not been taken care of by the 'top'. I know the success of the company is critically dependent on your performance. You people in the office do nothing except pushing papers around." You see, "those who live in glass houses should not throw stones on others".

At this stage, Mr. Srinivasan moderated the discussion thus: "It is obvious that we have different opinions and divergent views regarding our space problem. Before prolonging this discussion, I would like to sit through facts in a dispassionate manner. I will ask the Industrial Engineer to make an exhaustive study and provide necessary statistics on plant and office layouts. We shall be meeting again after a fortnight."

DISCUSSION POINTS

(1) What perceptual problems do you observe in this case?

(2) Do you think that Mr. Srinivasan's way of getting facts on plant and office layout will affect the views of office and production manager? What is the effect of such information on others in general?

QUESTIONS

- Define perception. Describe the steps in the perceptional process.
- Explain how:
  - (a) Perceptual Defence helps in understanding OB
  - (b) Perceptual constancy works in OB.
- Differentiate between:
  - (a) Perception and sensation
  - (b) Perception and attribution.
- Discuss the factors that influence the interpretation and information in the perception process.
- Why do people fail to perceive close to reality? As a manager you suggest suitable measures in this context.
- "The principle of figure-ground applies to our perception about objects." Explain with examples.
- Elaborate:
  - (a) Persons perception process, and
  - (b) Impressions management strategies. Discuss its managerial implications.
- Indicate the correct response against the following multiple choice questions:
  - Perception is:
    - (a) A single process consisting of the reception of information.
    - (b) A single process consisting of the inter-protestation of information.
    - (c) The processes used by the individual in receiving and interpreting information about his/her environment.
    - (d) A single process consisting of the transmission of information.
    - (e) The processes used by an individual to transmit information to others.

– ______ is one of the characteristics of the person that influences perception.

(a) projection

(b) size

(c) salience

(d) attribution

(e) stereotyping.

Individual Learning

3

Learning Objectives

- Definition of Learning
- Theories of Learning
- Reinforcement and Learning
- Schedules of Reinforcement
- Organisational Behaviour Modification–Concept
- Organisational Behaviour Modification–Steps
- Strength and Weakness of OB Modification

LEARNING–DEFINITION

A psychologist's definition is broader than the Layperson's view that, "*It's what we did when we went to school*". Actually each of us is continuously going "to school". Learning occurs all the time. A generally accepted definition of learning is:

> "*Any relatively permanent change in behaviour that occurs as a result of experience.*"

We can say that changes in behaviour indicate that learning has taken place and that learning is a change in behaviour.

This definition has several components that deserve clarification:

(i) Learning involves change, though not necessarily important in behaviour. This may be (i) good or (ii) bad from organisational point of view. People can also learn unfavourable behaviours.

Bad habits, stereotype, prejudice, work restrictions.

(ii) The change must be relatively permanent. Temporary changes may be only reflexive and fail to represent any learning.

(iii) This definition is concerned with behaviour. Learning takes place where there is change in actions. A change in an individual's (i) thoughts or (ii) attitudes, if accompanied by no change in behaviour, would not be learning.

(iv) Finally, some experience is necessary for learning. This may be acquired directly through observations or practice or it may result from an indirect experience, such as acquired through reading.

LEARNING–THEORIES

How do we learn? Three theories have been offered to explain the process by which we learn new behaviours. These are:

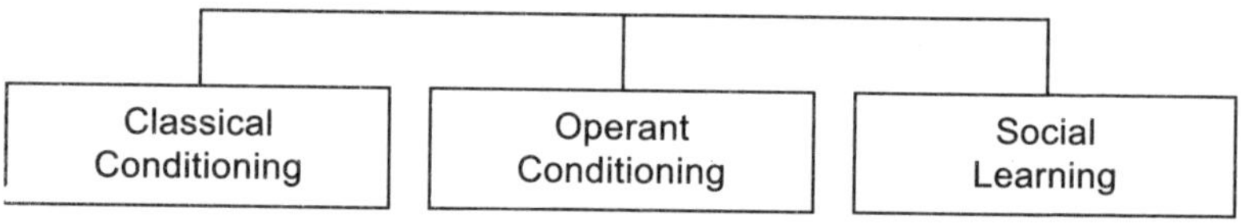

1. Classical Conditioning

Classical conditioning grew out of experiments to teach dogs to salivate in response to the ringing of a bell, conducted by a Russian Physiologist, Ivan Pavlov.

A simple surgical procedure allowed Pavlov to measure accurately the amount of saliva secreted by a dog. When Pavlov presented the dog a piece of meat, the dog exhibited a noticeable increase in salivation. Pavlov termed the 'food' an unconditioned stimulus (food automatically caused salivation) and the 'salivation'–an unconditioned response. When the dog saw the meat, it salivated.

On the other hand, when Pavlov withheld the presentation of meat and merely rang a bell (neutral stimulus), the dog did not salivate. Then Pavlov proceeded to link the meat and ringing of the bell. After repeatedly hearing the bell before getting the food, the dog began to salivate as soon as the bell rang, even if no food was offered. The dog had learned to respond, i.e., to salivate, to the ringing of the bell, Pavlov had conditioned the dog to respond to a learned stimulus.

Researchers called this the "*Law of Exercise*" which states that behaviour can be learned by repetitive association between (i) stimulus and (ii) response (S-R association).

Classical conditioning has a limited value in the study of organisational behaviour. It represents an insignificant part of total human learning. Classical conditioning is passive. Something happens and we react in a specific or particular way. It is elicited in response to a specific and identifiable event. It explains simple reflexive behaviours. But behaviour of people in organisations is emitted rather than elicited. It is voluntary rather than reflective. The learning of these complex behaviours can be better understood by looking at operant conditioning.

2. Operant Conditioning

Operant is defined as behaviour that produces effects. Operant conditioning, basically a product of Skinnering psychology, suggests that individuals emit responses that are rewarded and will not emit responses that are either (i) not rewarded or (ii) are punished. Operant conditioning is a (i) voluntary or (ii) learned behaviour in contrast to (i) reflexive or (ii) unlearned behaviour.

Operant conditioning acts on the environment to produce consequences. It is basically assumed that man's behaviour is determined by environment. An individual learns by producing alternations in their environment. Operant conditioning presupposes that human beings explore their environment and act upon it. In operant conditioning reinforcement is given when correct response is made.

Operant conditioning is a powerful tool for managing people in organisations. Most behaviours in organisations are: (i) learned, (ii) controlled, and (iii) altered by the consequences, i.e., operant behaviours. Management can use the operant conditioning process successfully to (i) control and (ii) influence the behaviour of employees by manipulating its reward system. If one expects to influence the behaviour, he must be able to manipulate the consequences.

In general, it can be concluded that the behavioural consequences that are rewarded increase the rate of response, while the oversize consequences decrease the rate of response.

3. Social Learning

Individuals can also learn by observing what happens to other people and just by being told about something, as well as by direct experience.

> Much of what we learn comes from watching (i) models, (ii) parents, (iii) teachers, (iv) motion pictures, and (v) television performers etc.

The view that we learn through both (i) observation and (ii) direct experience is known as social learning theory.

Social learning theory is an extension of operant conditioning, i.e. it assumes that behaviour is a function of consequences; it also acknowledges the existence of (i) observational learning, and (i) importance of perception of learning. People respond to how they perceive and define consequences, not to the objective consequences themselves.

From the social learning viewpoint, the influence of models is central. Four processes have been found to determine the influence that a model will have on an individual, viz.:

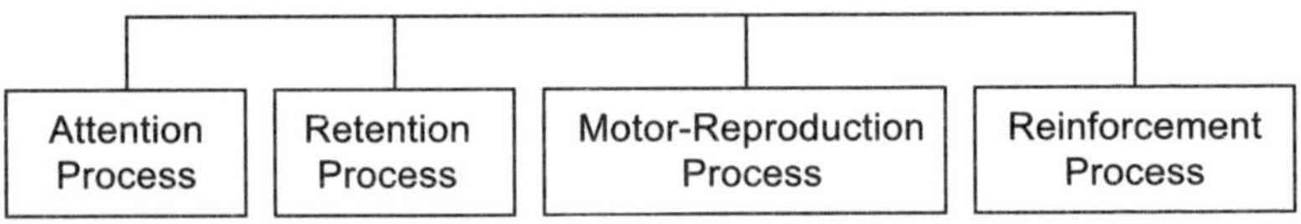

(a) Attention Process

People only learn from a model when they recognize and pay attention to its critical features. We tend to be most influenced by models that are (i) attractive, (ii) repeatedly available, (iii) important to us, or (iv) similar to us in our estimation.

(b) Retention Process

A model's influence will depend upon how well the individual remembers the models actions after the model is no longer readily available.

(c) Motor-Reproduction Process

When a person has seen a new behaviour by observing the model, the watching must be converted into doing. This process demonstrates that the individual can perform the modeled activities.

(d) Reinforcement Process

Individuals will be motivated to exhibit the modeled behaviour if positive (i) incentives or (ii) rewards are provided. Behaviours that are reinforced will be given (i) more attention, (ii) learned better, and (iii) performed repeatedly.

REINFORCEMENT–OPERANT CONDITIONING

Reinforcement is a fundamental condition of learning. Without reinforcement, no measurable modification of behaviour takes place. The term 'reinforcement' is closely related to the psychological process of motivation. However, motivation is a basic psychological process and, therefore, is (i) broader, and (ii) more complex than the learning principle of reinforcement. Motivation is an internal explanation of behaviour. And, reinforcement is an external explanation of behaviour. Thus, the (i) perspectives and (ii) explanation of behaviour due to (i) motivation and (ii) reinforcement are quite different.

Operational definition of reinforcement:

"*Anything that: (i) increases the strength of response and (ii) tends to induce repetitions of the behaviour that preceded the reinforcement.*"

> A reward can be a reinforcer when it increases the rate of response.

Four types of reinforcement strategies can be employed by managers to influence behaviour of employees, viz.:

Positive Reinforcement	Negative Reinforcement	Extension	Punishment

1. Positive Reinforcement

Positive reinforcement strengthens and increases the desirable behaviour by the presentation of attractive consequences (reward). In other words, a positive reinforcer is a reward that follows behaviour and is capable of increasing the frequency of that behaviour.

Effective reinforcers must meet two conditions:

(a) the reward should be contingent upon the rate of performance.

(b) the reward should match with the (i) need or (ii) desire of the performer.

Thus, when a response is followed with something pleasant, it is called positive reinforcement.

> Giving praise to an employee for the successful completion of a task is positive reinforcement.

There are two types of positive reinforcers, viz.:

(a) Primary Reinforcers

Primary reinforcers such as (i) food, (ii) water, and (iii) shelter are of biological importance. They are innately satisfying and have effects which are independent of experience.

(b) Secondary Reinforcers

Secondary reinforcers like (i) recognition, (ii) job advancement, and (iii) esteem results from previous association with a primary reinforcer.

2. Negative Reinforcement

The removal of punishment rather than the presentation of a reward is known as negative reinforcement. Negative reinforcers also serve to strengthen desired behaviour by:

(a) removing the environmental negative consequences and
(b) withholding the punishment for showing desirable behaviour.

People learn a negative reinforced behaviour through an 'avoidance' process. Avoidance learning techniques are used to strengthen desired behaviour.

> If your professor asks a question and you do not know the answer, looking on to your lecture notes makes impossible your being called on. This is a negative reinforcement. Because you have learned that looking busily on your notes prevents the professor from calling you.

3. Extension

Extension is an effective method of weakening the undesirable behaviour. It refers to non-reinforcement. It is based on the principle that:

"*If a response is not reinforced, it will gradually* disappear."

> If a teacher ignores a noisy student, the student may drop attention getting behaviour.

Extension is less painful than punishment because it does not involve direct application of aversive consequences.

> Students who perform well are praised, quite often, by the teachers. If they begin to slack off and turn out poor performers, teachers try to modify their behaviour by withholding praise.

Here, the teacher is not trying to punish the students by (i) imposing fine, (ii) rebuking openly in the class, or (iii) expelling them. The student is simply denied any feedback, if the students eventually show good performance, the teacher may again praise them, but if poor performance results again, extension will be re-employed.

4. Punishment

Punishment is a control device employed in organisations to (i) discourage and (ii) reduce annoying behaviours. It can take either of two forms. There can be (a) withdrawal or termination of desirable or rewarding consequences; or (b) an unpleasant consequence after a behaviour is performed.

Punishment reduces the response frequency. It weakens undesirable behaviour. The use of aversive control is the most controversial method of modifying behaviour because it produces undesirable by-products:

- Punishment reduces the frequency of undesired behaviour, but it does not promote desired behaviour.
- The frequency of undesirable behaviour is reduced only when the punishing agent is present. Punishment causes anxiety and suppresses the response which reappears when the punishing agent is absent.
- Punishment frustrates the punished and leads to antagonism towards the punishing agent. As a result, the effectiveness of the punishing agent diminishes over time.

SCHEDULES OF REINFORCEMENT

Reinforcement schedules indicate the timing of reinforcement. The effectiveness of the reinforcer depends upon its scheduling compared to its other features like: (i) magnitude, (ii) quality, and (iii) degree of association with the behavioural act. Essentially there are two types of reinforcement schedules:

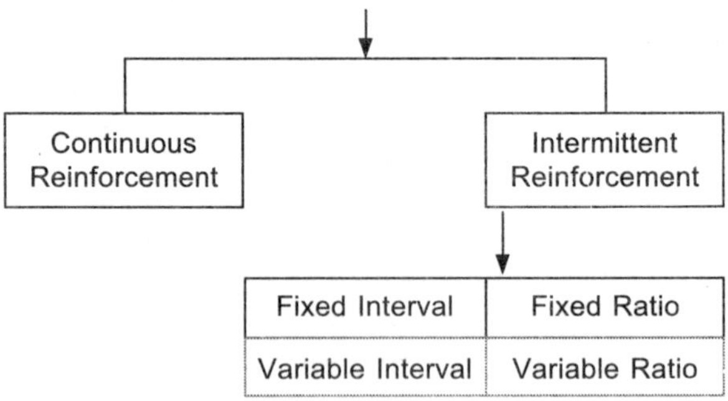

1. Continuous Reinforcement

Under this schedule, the individual receives a reward every time s/he performs a desired behaviour. With this schedule, behaviour increases very rapidly. But when the reinforcement is withdrawn, performance declines rapidly. Thus, it is very difficult to apply it in organisational context because it is not just possible to reinforce behaviour every time.

2. Intermittent Reinforcement

Under this schedule, the rewards (pay, praise, recognition, promotion, etc.), are administered on a random basis, because it is not possible to reinforce behaviours each time they occur. This schedule leads to slower learning but strong retention of a response than continuous reinforcement. This schedule has a wider application in organisational behaviour. Because, this factor is extremely relevant to the observed resistance to change in attitudes, values, norms, etc.

Intermittent schedules for administering rewards can be further classified into four types as listed below:

(a) Fixed Interval

This schedule demands that a fixed period of time should elapse before a reinforcement is administered. The critical variable is time and it is held constant. In many organisations monetary reinforcement comes at the end of a period of time. Most workers are paid hourly, weekly or monthly for the time spent on their jobs. This method offers the least motivation for hard work among workers because pay is tied to time interval rather than actual performance.

(b) Variable Interval

Under this schedule reinforcers are dispended unpredictably. The reward is given after a randomly distributed length of time. This is an ideal method for administering (i) praise, (ii) promotions, and (iii) supervisory visits. Variable interval schedules produce higher rates of response, and (i) more stable, and (ii) consistent performance.

> If the plant manager visits the production department at 11 a.m. approximately each day, performance tends to be high just prior to his visit and thereafter declines.

Under variable interval schedule the manager visits at randomly selected time intervals and no one knows surely when the manager will come. As a result performance tends to be higher and has less fluctuation than that under fixed interval schedule.

(c) Fixed Ratio

In this schedule, reinforcement is given after a certain number of responses. If the schedule is a fixed ratio, the exact number of responses is specified. Administering reward under this schedule tends to produce significant higher rate of response. Workers try to produce as many pieces as possible in order to pocket the monetary rewards.

> Fixed ratio schedule is the price rate system of wage payment.

(d) Variable Ratio

When the reward varies with the behaviour of the individual, he or she is said to be reinforced on a variable ratio schedule.

> Sales people on commission are individuals on such a reinforcement schedule.

On some occasions, they may make a sale after only two calls on potential customers. On other occasions, they may need to make twenty or more calls to secure a sale. Thus, the reward is variable in relation to the number of successful calls the salesperson makes.

LEARNING–MANAGERIAL IMPLICATIONS

The five specific applications of learning are:

1. Using Lotteries to Reduce Absenteeism

Management can design programmes to reduce absenteeism by using learning theory:

Example: In 1960, Harward Retail Store found that tardiness and absenteeism on the part of employees were too serious. The management used lottery programme with attractive prizes. What was unique about lottery were its eligibility requirements. Only employees with perfect attendance and no absenteeism were eligible to contest.

The program was successful. The attendance improved so much that even a storm had not prevented the employees from being present on work.

2. Well Pay vs. Sick Pay

Most of the organisations provide their salaried employees with paid sick leave as part of the employee's fringe benefits. But ironically, organisations with paid sick leave programs experience almost twice the absenteeism of organisations without such programmes. The reality is that sick leave reinforces the wrong behaviour–absence from work. Organisations should have programmes that encourage employees to be on the job and discoure unnecessary absence. When employees receive ten paid sick days a year, it is unusual of the employee who does not make sure that all his days are consumed, regardless of whether he is sick or not. This suggests that organisations should reward attendance, not absence. An attendance bonus programme which is practical in most organisations is designed to encourage good attendance.

3. Employee Discipline

Every manager will, at sometime, have to deal with an employee who drinks on the job, is insubordinate, steals company property, arrives consistently late for work or encourages similar behaviours. Managers will respond with disciplinary action such as oral reprimands, written warnings and temporary suspensions.

Disciplining employees for undesirable behaviours only tell them what not to do. It does not tell them what alternative behaviours are preferred. The result is that this form of punishment frequently leads to only short-term suppressions of the undesirable behaviour rather than its elimination. Continued use of punishment; rather than positive reinforcement, also tends to produce a conditional fear of the manager.

The popularity of discipline undoubtedly lies in its ability to produce fast results in the short run. Managers are reinforced for using discipline because it produces an immediate change in the employee's behaviour. But over the long run, when used without positive reinforcement of desirable behaviours, it is likely to lead employee frustration, fear of manager, reoccurrence of the problem behaviours and increase in absenteeism and turnover.

4. Developing Training Programmes

Learning is in itself developing effective training programmes. Social learning theory offers such a guide. It tells us that training should offer a model to grab the trainee's attention; provide motivational properties; help the trainee to file away that he has learned for later use; provide opportunities to practice new behaviours, offer positive rewards for accomplishment; and, if the training has taken place off the job, allow the trainee some opportunity to transfer what he has learned on the job.

5. Creating Mentoring Programmes

It is the unusual senior manager who, early in his career, did not have an older, more experienced mentor higher up in the organisation. This mentor provides advice and guidance on how to survive and get ahead in the organisation. Mentoring, of course, is not limited to the managerial ranks. Union apprenticeship programmes do the same thing by preparing individuals to move from unskilled status to that of a skilled journeyman.

A successful mentoring programme will be built on modeling concepts from social learning theory i.e., a mentor's impact comes from more than merely what he explicitly tells a protégé. Mentors are role models. Protégés learn to convey the attitudes and behaviours that the organisation wants by emulating the traits and actions of their mentors. They observe and then imitate.

ORGANISATIONAL BEHAVIOUR MODIFICATIONS–CONCEPT

Organisational behaviour modification is a sophisticated quantitative tool that is frequently employed to improve the organisational effectiveness. It contributes to the better understanding of human behaviour in organisations. It can be thought of as a powerful technique of human resource management.

OB modification is based on the idea that behaviour depends on its consequences; therefore, it is possible for managers to (i) control or (ii) effect a number of employee behaviours by manipulating their consequences.

OB modification relies heavily on the law of effect, which states that, "a person tends to repeat behaviour that is accompanied by favourable consequences (reinforcement) and tends not to repeat behaviour that is accompanied by unfavourable consequences".

> "*OB modification is a technique which may enable manpower management to (i) modify, or (ii) eliminate undesirable behaviour and replace it with behaviour that is more compatible with goal attainment.*"
>
> (Fred Luthans, Donald D. White)

> "*OB modification is the application of behaviouristic conditioning principles to practical problems.*"
>
> (Edwin A. Locke)

OB MODIFICATIONS–STEPS

As a specific approach to human resources management, OB modifications can be portrayed as a five-step problem solving model. The Figure hereunder shows this model. OB modification can be used in a step-by-step process to actually change performance related employee behaviours in today's organisations:

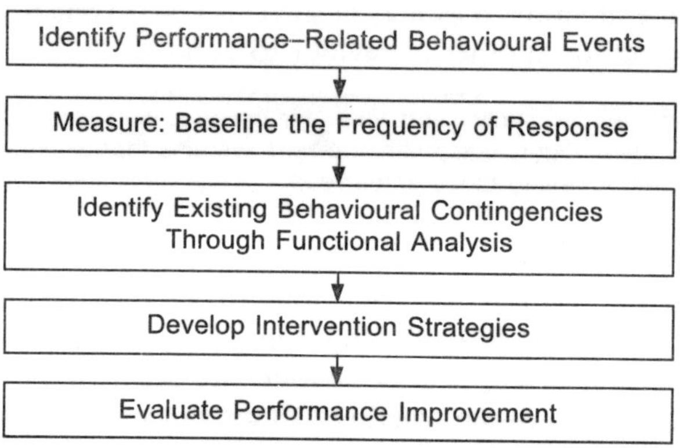

Steps in O.B. Modifications

1. Identification of Critical Behaviours

In this first step the critical behaviours that make a significant impact on performance are identified. In every organisation, regardless of type or level, numerous behaviours are occurring all the time. Some of these behaviours have a significant impact on performance and some do not. There are 5 to 10 per cent of behaviours that may account for upto 70 to 80 per cent of each employee's performance.

The process of identifying critical behaviours can be carried out in a couple of ways:

- One approach is to have the person closest to the job in question, the immediate (i) supervisor, or (ii) actual job holder, determine the critical behaviours. Its advantages are that the person who knows the job best can most accurately identify the critical behaviours and, because that person is participating, he may be more committed to carrying the OB modification process to its successful completion.
- Another approach to identifying critical behaviours would be to conduct a systematic behavioural audit. The audit would include internal staff specialists and/or outside consultants. The audit would systematically analyze each job, by using job analysis techniques.

If managers fail to identify the critical behaviour, they may unwittingly reinforce unintended behaviours. In such an unfortunate situation, they may mistakenly reward one behaviour while hoping for another behaviour to occur.

> Management normally wants their employees to work closely; yet it often uses highly competitive reward systems that discourage cooperation among these employees.

2. Measurement of the Behaviours

After the performance behaviours have been identified in step 1, they are measured. Without measurement of the rate at which the identified critical behaviours are occurring, there can be no way to determine whether OB modification has actually been effective in changing job related behaviours. Measurement involves collection and analysis of data before, during and after the behavioural change. The data before the beginning of the change process are called baseline data. Data collection removes ambiguity about the current level of the critical behaviour (e.g. absenteeism). It also helps managers to communicate the results of change process. Usually the data collected are pointed on simple graph. Baseline data identifies the precise extent of the problem and gauge the extent of behavioural change.

This step involves the determination of the rate at which critical behaviours are occurring. This information is necessary for evaluating the success of OB modification programme used. The observational data be gathered as inconspicuously as possible. For this purpose data straightforward observational techniques can be employed.

3. Functional Analysis of the Behaviour

This step involves a detailed examination of present behaviours being shown by employees to determine what consequences each produce, what conditions lead to their occurrence. The functional analysis brings out the problem solving nature of the OB modification.

This involves analyzing the contingencies that are reinforcing the critical behaviour and understanding. Workers taking unscheduled breaks and frequently wandering off the job may be a critical behaviour which needs to be changed. Upon the functional analysis it was found that clock serves as the cue for the critical behaviour.

> 8 a.m. to 10 a.m. working hours, 12 noon lunch, 1-3 p.m. break and 5 p.m. exit.

The functional analysis pinpoints one of the most significant practical problems of using OB modification approach to change critical performance behaviour. Only the contingent consequences have an impact on subsequent behaviour. The functional analysis often reveals that there are many competing contingencies for every organisational behaviour.

4. Development of an Intervention Strategy

The first three steps in an OB modification approach are preliminary to the action step, the intervention. The goal of the intervention is to strengthen and accelerate functional performance behaviours and/or weaken dysfunctional behaviours. There are several strategies that can be used but the main ones are discussed hereunder:

(a) A Positive Reinforcement Strategy

Positive reinforcement strengthens and increases the desirable behaviour by the presentation of attractive consequences (rewards). In other words, a positive reinforcer is a reward that follows behaviour and is capable of increasing the frequency of that behaviour.

A positive reinforcer uses as an OB modification intervention strategy, as long as it increases the performance behaviour. Most often money is thought of as the logical or sometimes the only positive reinforcer available to managers using this approach. However, money is potentially a very powerful reinforcer, but often turns out to be ineffective because it is not contingently administered as a consequence of the behaviour being managed.

Besides money, positive reinforcers that are also very powerful, readily available to all behavioural managers and costs nothing are the social reinforcers (attention, recognition and feedback) that have been effectively used as an OB modification strategy.

(b) A Punishment–Positive Reinforcement Strategy

There is a little debate that a positive reinforcement strategy is the most effective intervention for OB modification, yet realistically it is recognized that in some cases the use of punishment is to weaken and decelerate undesirable behaviours that need to be immediately decreased. However, many negative side effects accompany the use of punishment and it should be avoided if at all possible. Punished behaviour tends to be only temporarily suppressed.

> If a supervisor reprimands a subordinate for some dysfunctional behaviour, the dysfunctional behaviour will decrease in the presence of the supervisor but will surface again when the supervisor is absent.

In addition, a punished person becomes very anxious and uptight, reliance on punishment may have a disastrous impact on employee satisfaction and create unnecessary stress.

Punishment should never be used alone as an OB modification intervention. If punishment is absolutely necessary, it should always be used in combination with positive reinforcement.

5. Evaluation to Ensure Performance Improvement

OB modification attempts to meet the credibility and accountability problems head-on by including evaluation as an actual part of the process. In this last step, the need for four levels of evaluation is stressed, viz.:

(a) Reaction

The reaction level refers to whether the people using the approach and those having it used on them, like it. If OB modification is well received and there is a positive reaction to it, there is a better chance of its being used effectively. In addition, reaction evaluations are helpful because:

- positive reactions help ensure organisational support;
- they can provide information for planning future programmes;
- favourable reactions can enhance the other levels of evaluation; and
- they can provide useful comparative data between units and across time.

(b) Learning

The second level of evaluation is learning. This is especially important when OB modification is used for the first time. If its theoretical background and underlying assumptions are learned clearly, it will lead to its effective use.

(c) Behavioural Change

The third level is aimed at behavioural change. Are behaviours actually being changed? The charting of behaviours gives objective data for this level of evaluation.

(d) Performance Improvement

The fourth and final level performance improvement is the most important. The major purpose of OB modification is not just to receive a favourable reaction, but to learn the concept and change behaviours. These dimensions are important mainly because they contribute to the overriding purpose, which is to improve performance.

OB MODIFICATION–STRENGTHS AND WEAKNESSES

OB modification should not be treated as a panaceae for all organisational ills. OB modification requires significant administrative effort in managing reward contingencies. The criticisms will help managers in applying OB modification carefully and in designing effective reinforcement strategies that will encourage (i) creative, (ii) productive, and (iii) satisfied workforce. OB modification does not consist of a bag of tricks to be applied indiscriminately for the purpose of coercing unwilling people. Instead, it is a practical tool for (i) shaping, (ii) improving, and (iii) motivating behaviour of organisational participants. The strengths and weaknesses of behaviour modification are presented hereunder:

Strengths	Weaknesses
• It deals with observed behaviours. It can be put to testing and presents a set of tools by which people can learn new behaviours and skills.	• Use of behaviour modification on human beings is unethical, inhumane, and dictatorial.
• It presents managers a set of managerial tools with which they can effectively control and influence the behaviours.	• It ignores the importance of internal causes of behaviour.
• Principles of behaviour modification are simple and easy to understand. Managers can become effective users of behaviour modification.	• Behaviour modification is limited to job situations in which the target behaviour can be clearly defined.

CASE STUDY

Volunteers cannot be Punished

Ann Marie Jackson is the head of the volunteer agency in a large city. She is incharge of a volunteer staff of over twenty-five people weekly. She holds a meeting with this group in order to keep them informed and teach them the specifics of any new laws or change in State and Federal policies and procedures that might affect their work and she discusses priorities and assignments for the group. This meeting is also a time when members can share some of the problems and concerns for what they are personally doing and what the agency as a whole is doing. The meeting is scheduled to begin at 9 a.m. sharp every Monday. Lately, the volunteers have been filtering in every five minutes or so until almost 10 a.m. Ann Marie has felt she has to delay the start of the meeting until all the people arrive. The last few weeks the meetings have not started until 10 a.m.; in fact at 9 a.m. nobody has shown up. Ann Marie cannot understand what has happened. She feels it is important to start the meetings at 9 a.m. so that they can be over before the whole morning is gone. On the other hand, she feels that her hands are tied because, after all, the people are volunteers and she cannot punish them or make them get to the meetings on time.

DISCUSSION POINTS

(1) What advice would you give Ann Marie in times of reinforcement theory? Explain what is happening here and what Ann Marie needs to do to get the meetings started on time.

(2) What learning theories (operant, cognitive and social) could be applied to Ann Marie's efforts to teach their volunteers the impact of new laws and changes in State and Federal policies and procedures?

(3) How could someone like Ann Marie use modeling to train her staff to do a more effective job?

QUESTIONS

- Define learning? How does it help to solve organisational problems?
- Explain the principle of learning. Discuss various learning theories.
- Distinguish between:
  (a) Classical conditioning and social learning;
  (b) Operant conditioning and social learning.
- "Any observable change in behaviour is prima facie evidence that learning has taken place." Elaborate.
- As a manager you are confronted with the problem that your employees are not punctual in their duties. How will the different theories help you in this situation?
- As a manager how would you employ four basic reinforcement strategies in encouraging desirable behaviour and discouraging undesirable behaviour?
- Is any of the theories of learning in your opinion applicable to changing complex behaviours? Where the exhibited behaviour is a combination of many undesirable behaviours? Support your answer by justified reasoning and examples.
- Indicate the correct response against the following multiple choice questions:
  - Positive reinforcement, avoidance, extinction and punishment are ____ of reinforcement.
    (a) schedules;
    (b) kinds;
    (c) stimuli;
    (d) intervals;
    (e) none of the above.
  - To administer punishment effectively, it should
    (a) be applied after the undesired behaviour has been strongly reinforced.

(b) be applied immediately preceding the undesired behaviour.

(c) contain information on the consequence of a repeated occurrence of the same behaviour.

(d) suppress the undesired behaviour temporarily.

(e) focus on the person, rather than the behaviour.

PART II

Personality

4

Learning Objectives

- Meaning and Definition of Personality
- Factors/Determinants of Personality
- Theories of Personality
- Stages of Personality Development
- Personality Traits Relevant to OB

PERSONALITY–DEFINITIONAL ASPECT

The term '*personality*' is derived from the Latin word "*Per sona*" which means "to speak through". The Latin term denotes the masks which the actors used to wear in ancient Rome and Greece. Personality, thus, traditionally refers to how people influence others through their external appearance (actions). However, more external appearance, though important for personality characteristics, does not make the whole personality. But for academics personality includes:

- The external appearance and behaviour; or, social stimulus value.
- The inner awareness of self as a permanent organising force.
- The particular pattern or organisation of measurable traits both (i) inner and (ii) outer.

A thorough complete definition of personality, thus, becomes a jigsaw puzzle because human beings operate as a whole, not as a series of distinct parts. Though psychologists and social scientists unanimously agree to the importance of personality, still they are unable to come out with unanimous definition.

Personality has been defined by many people in different ways. Let us consider some of them:

> "*Personality is a set of distinctive: (i) traits and (ii) characteristics that can be used to (i) compare and (ii) contrast individuals.*"
>
> (Ricky W. Griffin, Gregory Moorhead)

> "*The sum total of ways in which an individual (i) reacts and (ii) interacts with others.*"
>
> (Stephen P. Robbins)

> "*How people affect others and how they (i) understand and (ii) view themselves, as well as their patterns of (i) inner and (ii) outer measurable traits and the person-situation interaction.*"
>
> (Fred Luthans)

> "*Personality refers to a relatively stable set of psychological characteristics that influence the way we interact with our environment.*"
>
> (Gary Johns)

> "*Personality refers to the relatively stable patterns of behaviour and consistent internal state that explain a person's behavioural tendencies.*"
>
> (R.T. Hagan)

> "*Personality is a stable set of characteristics and tendencies that determine those (i) commonalities and (ii) differences in the psychological behaviour (thoughts, feelings and actions) of people that have continuity in time and that may not be easily understood as the sole result of the (i) social and (ii) biological pressures of the moment.*"
>
> (Salvatore R. Maddi)

Kluckhohan and Murry have beautifully concluded that puzzling issue of 'personality' by stating that:

> "*To some extent, a person's personality, is like all other people, like some other people, like no other people.*"

PERSONALITY–DETERMINANTS

What determines personality? Of all the complexities and unanswered questions in the study of human behaviour, this question seems most difficult. The problem lies in the fact that the (i) cognitive and (ii) psychological processes, plus many other variables, all contribute to personality. However, for ease of study and analysis, the determinants of personality can be grouped in four categories, viz.:

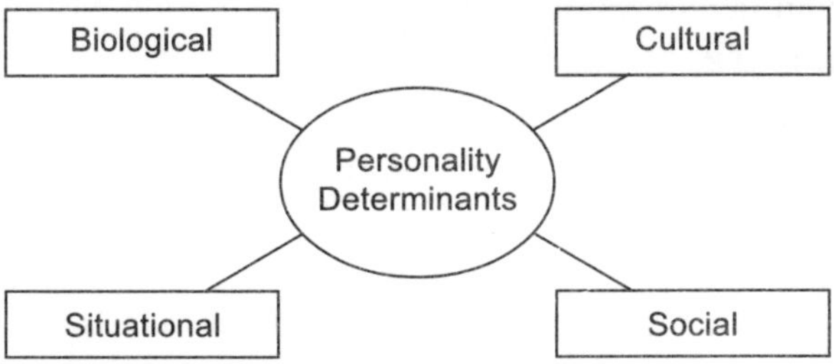

1. Biological Factors

Biological factors can be studied under three heads:

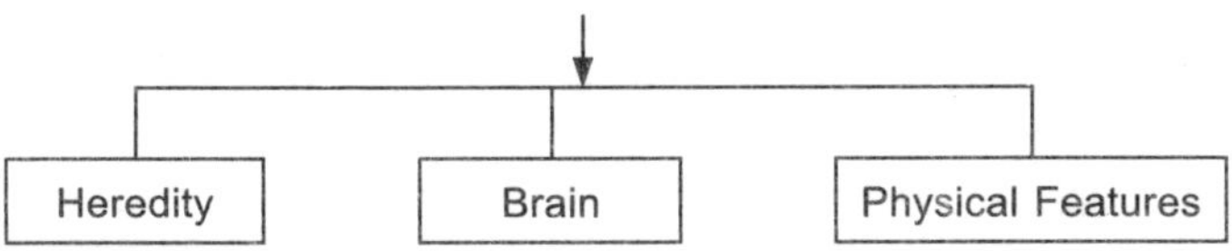

(a) Heredity

The relative effects of heredity comprise an old argument in personality theory. Certain characteristics, primarily physical in nature, are inherited from one's parent's transmitted by genes in the chromosomes contributed by each parent. Research on animals has shown that both: (i) physical and (ii) psychological characteristics can be transmitted through heredity. But research on human beings is inadequate to support this viewpoint. However, Psychologists and geneticists have accepted the fact that heredity plays an important role in one's personality. The importance of heredity varies from one personality trait to another.

(b) Brain

Another biological factor that influences personality is the role of brain of an individual. Though some promising inroads are made by the researchers, yet the psychologists are unable to prove empirically the contribution of human brain in influencing personality. Preliminary results from the Electrical Stimulation of the Brain (ESB) research gives indication that better understanding of human (i) personality and (ii) behaviour might come from the study of the brain.

(c) Physical Features

The third biological factors determining personality formation are (i) physical characteristics and (ii) rate of maturation. An individual's external appearance, which is biologically determined, is an important ingredient of personality. The fact that a person is: (i) tall or short; (ii) handsome or ugly, or (iii) black or white will influence others and this in turn will affect person's self-concept.

Paul H. Mussem observes that:

> "*A child's physical characteristics may be related to his approach to the social environment, to the expectancies of others and their reactions to him. These, in turn, may have impacts on personality development.*"

Similarly, a rapidly maturing boy or girl is exposed to different (i) physical and (ii) social situations and activities than those of slowly maturing child. Psychologists contend that the different rates of maturation will also influence the individuals personality.

2. Cultural Factors

Traditionally, culture is considered as the major determinant of an individual's personality. The culture largely determines: (i) what a person is and (ii) what a person will learn. The culture within a person brought up, is a very important determinant of behaviour of a person.

Culture requires both (i) conformity and (ii) acceptance from its members. There are several ways of ensuring that members comply with the dictates of the culture. The personality of an individual to a marked extent is determined by the culture in which he is brought up.

Accordingly, one psychologist opines:

"*Each culture expects, and trains, its members to behave in the ways that are acceptable to the group.*"

Inspite of the importance of the culture on personality, researchers were unable to establish linear relationship between these two concepts (i) personality; and (ii) culture.

3. Social (Family) Factors

Social factors are also important in shaping the personality of an individual. In order to understand the effect of a family on individual's personality, we have to understand the following processes:

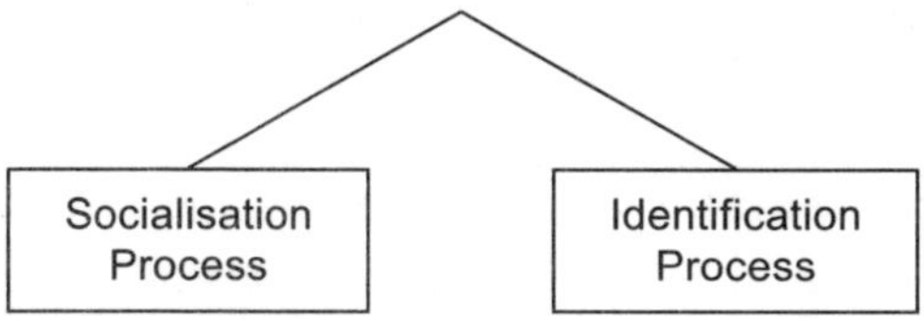

(a) Socialisation Process

The contribution of (i) family and (ii) social groups in combination with the culture is known as 'socialisation'. It is a process:

"*By which an individual infant acquires those behaviour patterns that are (i) customary and (ii) acceptable to the standards of his family and social group.*"

Socialisation process starts with initial contact between mother and her new infant. Later on, other members of the family influence this process.

(b) Identification Process

The identification process occurs when a person tries to identify himself with some person whom he feels ideal in the family. Generally, a child in the family tries to behave like his (i) father, or (ii) mother. He tries to emulate certain actions of his parents.

The identification process can be examined from three different perspectives:

- It can be viewed as the similarity of behaviour including (i) feelings and (ii) attitudes between child and model.
- It can be the child's (i) motives or (ii) desires to be like the model.
- It can be viewed as the process through which the child actually takes on the attributes of the model.

4. Situational Factors

Apart from the (i) biological, (ii) cultural, and (iii) social factors, situational factors also determine personality development. The effect of environment is quite strong. Knowledge, skill and language are obviously acquired and represent important modifications of behaviour. Learned modifications in behaviour are not passed on to children. They must be acquired by them through their (i) own experience and (ii) interaction with the environment.

In one research by Milgram, it was found that situations play a vital role in human personality. According to him, "*situations exert an important press on the individual. It exercises constraints and may provide a push. In certain circumstances it is not seen the kind of person a man is, as the kind of situations in which he is placed, that determines his actions.*"

Milgram certainly does not completely rule out the importance of the development aspects of personality. He rather demonstrated that the situation may potentially have a very big impact on the behavioural expression of personality.

PERSONALITY–THEORIES

Many personality theorists, not only from the field of psychology but even from other fields dealing with human behaviour also, have carried on researches to find an answer to the question, '*personality*'. However, these could not give the answer on which consensus could be reached; rather, these have resulted into a number of theories of personality because everyone has one's own definition of personality. Each theorist cannot really be grouped with another, even though he may have operated from similar positions. However, the most logical grouping of personality theories seems to be into:

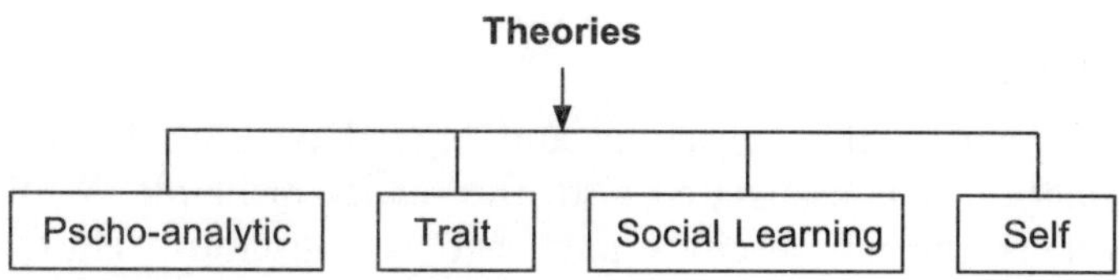

1. Psycho-analytic Theory

Psycho-analytic theory is based on the notion that man is motivated by unseen forces more than he is controlled by (i) conscious and (ii) rational thought. Although Sigmund Freud is closely related with this theory, others also made additional contributions.

According to Freud, human mind is composed of three elements: (i) the preconscious, (ii) the conscious, and (iii) the unconscious.

Freud developed an organisation of personality consisting of three structures within the human mind:

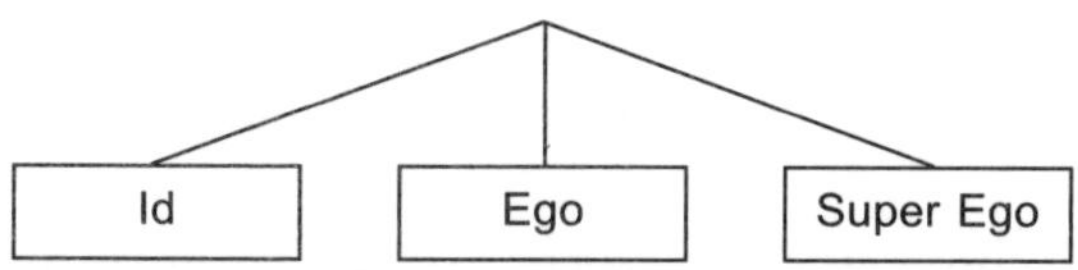

(a) The Id

It is the original and basic system of human personality. It consists of everything psychologically that is (i) inherited and (ii) present at the time of birth. Id that is (i) primitive, (ii) instinctual, and (iii) governed by the principles of greed and pleasure. Id represents a storehouse of all instincts, that unconsciously (i) direct and (ii) determine our behaviour. Id is largely (i) childish, (ii) irrational, (iii) never satisfied, (iv) demanding, and (v) destructive of others. But it is the foundation upon which all other parts of personality are erected.

Freud opines, "*Id is totally oriented increasing pleasure and avoiding pain, and it strives for immediate satisfaction of desires. It basically represents an individual's natural urges and feelings.*"

(b) The Ego

The ego is the conscious and logical part of the human personality. It is associated with the reality principle. While id represents the unconscious part, ego is conscious. Thus, ego keeps the id in check through the realities of the external environment through (i) intellect and (ii) reason. By the functioning of the (i) id and (ii) ego, many conflicting situations arise because id wants immediate pleasure, while ego dictates postponement to a more appropriate (i) time and (ii) place. In order to resolve the conflict, the ego gets support from the super ego.

(c) The Super Ego

The super ego represents (i) societal and (ii) personal norms. It serves as an ethical constraint on behaviour. It can be described as the conscience. The super ego provides norms to ego to determine what is right or wrong. However, a person is not aware of the working of the super ego, and conscience is developed by absorption of (i) cultural values and (ii) norms of society.

The psycho-analytic theory of Freud is based on a theoretical verification. The theory does not give a total picture of behaviour emerging from the personality. That is why, this theory is not relevant from behavioural science point of view. However, this theory gives an important insight into personality structure and the idea of unconscious motivation which can be used by behavioural scientists.

2. Trait Theory

Another useful way of looking at and understanding the structure of human personality is by considering the traits he possesses. Personality trait can be defined as, "*an enduring attribute of a person that appears constantly in a variety of situations.*"

The trait theory makes certain fundamental assumptions:

- Traits distinguish one personality from another.
- Individuals can be described in terms of construction of traits, e.g. affiliation, achievement, anxiety, aggression and dependence.
- Traits can be quantifiable and do not make measurement impossible.
- Traits are relatively stable. They exert fairly universal affects on behaviour regardless of the environmental situations.

The two most commonly known trait theories come from the classic work of (i) Gordon Allport and (ii) Raymond Cattell.

(a) Allport's Trait Theory

Allport bases his theory on the distinction between (i) common traits and (ii) personal dispositions. Common traits are used to compare people. He has identified six categories of values: (i) theoretical, (ii) social, (iii) economic, (iv) political, (v) aesthetic, and (vi) religious for comparative purpose. Besides the common traits, there are personal dispositions which are completely unique. These are (i) cardinal (most pervasive), (ii) central (unique and limited in number), or (iii) secondary (peripheral). This uniqueness emphasizes the psychology of the individual that Allport has developed. He gives more recognition to the (i) complexity and (ii) uniqueness of human personality.

(b) Cattell's Trait Theory

Cattell has taken different approach from that of Allport. Out of several different and sometimes overlapping words representing personality, Cattell has selected 171 words that can be used to describe personality. Using the factor analytic approach, he identified two categories of traits and called them (i) surface trait and (ii) source trait.

He determined 35 surface traits by finding cluster of traits that are correlated:

Wise–foolish
Affectionate–cold
Honest–dishonest

Such traits lie on the surface of personality. And are largely determined by the underlying source traits. He identified 12 source traits:

> Maturity *vs.* Immaturity
> Dominance *vs.* Submissiveness.

Overall, the trait theory has a great deal of intuitive appeal. It gives recognition to the continuity of personality. The trait theorists have also contributed (i) personality tests and (ii) factor analysis technique to the behavioural science.

The major drawback of this theory is that, it is descriptive rather than analytical. And is the long way from being comprehensive theory of personality.

3. Social Learning Theory

Social learning theory considers the 'situations' as an important determinant of behaviour. An individual's actions in a given situation depends on: (i) the specific characteristics of the situation and (ii) post reinforcement of behaviour in similar situations. When an individual encounters situations that are stable, then his behaviour will be more or less consistent.

The main focus of social learning approach is on the patterns of behaviour that an individual learns in coping with environment. Some behaviour patterns are learned or acquired through direct experience. Responses can also be (i) acquired or (ii) learned without direct reinforcement.

Social learning theories believe that reinforcement is not necessary for learning. But they accept that reinforcement facilitates learning by focusing attention. According to social learning school, much of human learning is (i) indirect and (ii) observational.

Reinforcement, though not necessary for learning, is very crucial for the performance of learned behaviour. The notable assumption of social learning theory in this connection is that people behave in ways likely to produce reinforcement. The reinforcement that controls the expression of learned behaviour may be:

(a) **Direct.** It refers to the social (i) approval or (ii) disapproval of aversive conditions, and other tangible rewards.

(b) **Vicarious.** It refers to observation of someone else receiving (i) rewards, or (ii) punishments for similar behaviour.

(c) **Self-administered.** It refers to evaluation of one's own performance with (i) self praise or (ii) reproach.

Social learning theory has been criticized on two solid grounds:

(i) It over-emphasizes the importance of situational factors in behaviour and neglects the individual differences.

(ii) The experimental methods used by social learning theorists are particularly sensitive to the impact of situational variables and are apt to emphasize change in behaviour.

But scientists cannot ignore the fact, the way the person perceives the situations is the most important factor in determining behaviour.

4. Self Theory

The psycho-analytic and trait theories represent traditional approaches to explaining the complex human personality. Of many other theories the one that has received the most recent emphasis is the self theory of personality. It attempts to integrate the various parts of the personality structure into a meaningful whole. Carl Roger is closely associated with this approach of self theory. Roger and his associates have developed this personality theory that places emphasis on the individual as an (i) initiating, (ii) creating, and (iii) influencing determinant of behaviour within the framework of environmental framework. According to Roger theory, there are three ingredients of personality, viz.:

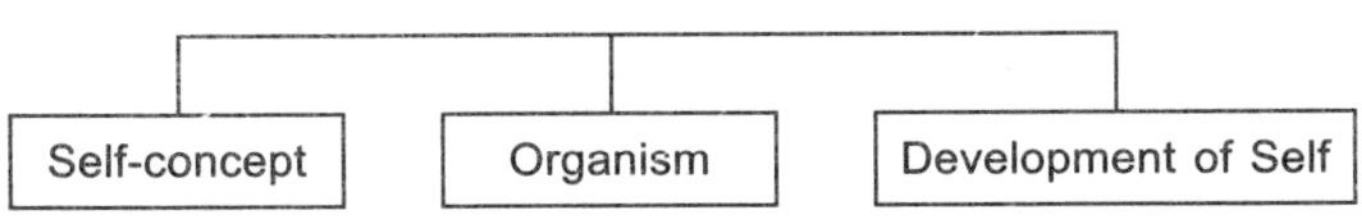

(a) Self-concept

The most important concept of Roger's theory is the self. The self consists of all the (i) perceptions, (ii) ideas, (iii) values, and (iv) characteristics that characterize 'I' or 'Me'. It includes 'what I am' and 'what I can do'.

Roger defines the self-concept as, "*an (i) organised, (ii) consistent, (iii) conceptual gestalt composed of perceptions of characteristics of the 'I' or 'Me'. And the perceptual relationships of 'I' or 'Me' to those perceptions'*. Here 'I' refers to the personal self. Personal self consists of a person's psychological processes such as (i) perception, (ii) motivation, and (iii) attitudes, that result in a composed whole.

The 'Me' refers to social self. It is the way a person (i) appears to others and (ii) thinks he or she appears to others.

The 'perceived self' influences both (i) the person's perception of the world and (ii) his behaviour. An individual with a strong, positive self-concept is likely to view the world quite differently from one whose self-concept is weak. An individual may be highly successful or respected, yet, may view himself as failure.

(b) Organism

The organism is essentially the locus of all experience. The totality of experience is the phenomenal field. This field is known to the person himself and is frequently referred as frame of reference.

Behaviour of an individual is largely determined by the phenomenal field not by the stimulating conditions of events in the external environment.

The individual evaluates every experience with his self-concept. These experiences may be (i) symbolized or (ii) unsymbolized. When they are symbolized they become part of individual's consciousness, when they are unsymbolized they remain outside the confines of the consciousness of an individual. The important thing here is that distorted symbolization gives rise to inappropriate behaviour.

(a) Development of Self-personality

Carl Roger feels that the fundamental force motivating the human organism, is self-actualization, i.e. a tendency towards: (i) fulfilment, (ii) maintenance, and (iii) enhancement of the organism. The tendency to self-actualization of both the (i) organism and (ii) self is subject to profound influence of the social environment, right from childhood. Actually, in the childhood itself, when the child's behaviour is evaluated continuously by their parents, he will be in a position to discriminate between thoughts and actions that are considered (i) worthy and (ii) unworthy. He will be able to exclude the unworthy experiences from his self-concept.

To conclude, the self theory is appreciated on the ground that it is organised around the concept of self. It is the one in which (i) personality and (ii) behaviour are largely determined by the individual.

Another positive point in favour of self theory is that the 'best vantage point for understanding is from the internal frame of reference of the individual himself. To Rogers individual is the centre of experience. To understand one's behaviour one should understand how that person views about himself.

In analyzing organisational behaviour, it would be beneficial for the manager to understand the self-concept because this unique concept influences the way he should apply various (i) reinforcement, (ii) motivation, and (iii) leadership techniques in the process of maintaining these required amount of output.

> Monetary rewards for (i) performance, (ii) authoritarian leadership style, and (iii) motivational strategies when applied to (i) an intelligent, (ii) independent, (iii) confident worker may be ineffective. These techniques may prove to be effective when applied to (i) unintelligent, (ii) insecure, and (iii) indecisive workers.

The self theory focuses on the person's world as he perceives it. It is the individual's perception and interpretation of the experiences that determine behaviour. But the trouble with the self-theory is that it vaguely defines the terms such as (i) self-actualization, (ii) self-concepts, etc., and such vague concepts will not be of much value in making precise predictions of behaviour of individuals if several other troubling criticisms are the accurate measurements of subjective experiences and the revealing of self.

PERSONALITY DEVELOPMENT–STAGES

The development of personality is traditionally an important area of understanding human behaviour. The developmental approach is actually a form of personality theory, but, in contrast to other personality theories, it is highly research-oriented. Modern developmental psychology does not get in the argument of: (i) heredity *versus* environment or (ii) maturity *versus* learning. The human beings consist of both (i) physiological and (ii) psychological interacting parts. Thus, (i) heredity, (ii) environment, (iii) maturity, and (iv) learning all contribute to the human personality.

The study of personality development can be divided into two separate but closely allied approaches, viz.:

- Adult Life Stages
- Immaturity to Maturity

One approach has attempted to identify specific (i) physiological and (ii) psychological stages that occur in the development of human personality. The other approach has tried to identify the important determinants of personality. The 'stage' approach is theoretical in nature, whereas the search for major determinants is more empirically based

(a) Adult Life Stages

The work of Daniel Levinson on adult stages has received considerable attention. At first, he believed that, "the life structure evolves through a relatively orderly sequence throughout the adult years". And, unlike other stage theories that were event oriented, e.g. (i) marriage, (ii) parenthood, or (iii) retirement, his theory was age based. He believed that there was little variability (a maximum of 2 or 3 years) in four identifiable stable periods:

1. Entering the adulthood (ages 22 to 28)
2. Settling down (ages 33 to 44)
3. Entering middle adulthood (ages 45 to 50)
4. Culmination of middle adulthood (ages 55 to 60)

He also identified four transitional periods:

1. Age thirty transition (ages 28 to 33)
2. Mid-life transition (ages 40 to 45)
3. Age fifty transition (ages 50 to 55)
4. Late adult transition (ages 60 to 65)

Like historically significant stage, theories of personality such as those by Freud and Erikson, Levinson's theory of adult life stages had a lot of (i) intuitive and (ii) popular appeal. The research is quite mixed.

(b) Immaturity to Maturity

Organisational behaviour theorist Chris Argyris has identified specific dimensions of the human personality as it develops. He proposes that the human personality, rather than going through precise stages, progresses gradually from (i) immaturity as an infant to, (ii) maturity as an adult. However, at any stage, people can have their degree of development.

Argyris carefully points out that the model does not imply that all persons (i) reach or (ii) strive for all dimensions on the mature end of the continuum. He further explains that:

- The seven dimensions represent only one aspect of the total personality. Much also depends upon the individual's, (i) perception, (ii) self-concept, (iii) adoption, and (iv) adjustment.
- The seven dimensions continuously change in degree from the infant to the adult end of the continuum.
- The model, being only a construct, cannot predict specific behaviour. However, it provides a method of (i) describing and (ii) measuring the growth of any individual in the culture.
- The seven dimensions are based upon latent characteristics of the personality, which may be quite different from the observable behaviour.

The Immaturity-Maturity Continuum

Immaturity Characteristics	Maturity Characteristics
Passivity	Activity
Dependence	Independence
Few ways of behaving	Diverse behaviour
Shallow interests	Deep interests
Short time perspective	Long-term perspective
Subordinate position	Super-ordinate position
Lack of self-awareness	Self-awareness and control

(a) Individuals have a tendency to develop from a stage of being passive as an infant to a state of increasing activity as an adult. A child is characteristically in the hands of his environment, his life is a series of events occurring without his choice. But an adult knows how to control (i) the environment and (ii) occurring of events.

(b) Human beings have a tendency to develop from a state of dependence on others as an infant to a state of relative independence as an adult.

(c) Individual, as a child, behaves in only a few ways but, as adult, he is capable of behaving in many ways. The adult is both (i) less predictable and (ii) more adaptable than the child.

(d) Individual has (i) casual and (ii) shallow interest as child, but develops (i) deeper and (ii) stronger interests as adult. Gradually he acquires a well defined set of interests, some of which offer him a great deal of satisfaction.

(e) Individual, as a child is almost exclusively concerned with the present, his time perspective is very short. As a mature, his time perspective increases to include the past and the future. His behaviour is influenced by past events also. He is also very much concerned with (i) what may or (ii) may not happen in future.

(f) Individual as a child is subordinate to everyone. As an adult he moves to (i) equal or (ii) superior position to others. Though he might be working as (i) superior or (ii) subordinate depending upon the situation, he does not think himself as being inherently to be a follower.

(g) Individual, as a child, does not have a habitual set of attitudes about himself. As an adult, he thinks about himself and is aware of the kind of person he is. He has ego and may go to some extent to protect it.

PERSONALITY TRAITS RELEVANT TO ORGANISATION BEHAVIOUR

The main reason that we are interested in individual personality in the study of organisational behaviour is the linkage between (i) personality and (ii) behaviour:

> "The CEO of Gillette India says, he retains the employees with (i) originality, (ii) confident, (iii) independent, and (iv) self-dramatizing even during reversionary periods as they perform better even in adverse situations. He also says, he fires the employees with (i) irresponsibility, (ii) self-doubting, (iii) communicative, (iv) rude, and (v) unassertive traits even in boom conditions as their behaviour does not match the organisational expectations."

His views indicate that personality has direct influence on (i) behaviour and (ii) performance of the people. Even the research findings indicate the same. Hence, we should study the influence of personality on organisational behaviour, as under:

Locus of Control

Locus of control refers to the extent to which individuals believe that they can control events affecting them. Locus of control may be (i) internal or (ii) external.

> The newly appointed CEO of Visakhapatnam Steel Plant of Steel Authority of India Limited (SAIL) believed that his traits could basically turn around the sick plant, while the CEO of Hindustan Cables Limited (HCL) believed that the financial assistance from the Government of India could turn around the sick company in 2001.

The former one is the internal locus of control whereas the latter refers to the external locus of control.

Locus of Control–Internal

Internal locus of control is the belief of an individual that his/her behaviour determines many of the events in his/her life. People with moderate strong internal locus of control are successful in their (i) jobs, (ii) career, and (iii) lives. They also (i) perform their job better, (ii) cope better in stressful situations, and (iii) are satisfied with the challenging jobs and performance based rewards.

Locus of Control–External

External locus of control is the belief of an individual that (i) chance, (ii) luck, (iii) fate, or (iv) other people determine what happens to him/her. People who believe in the external locus of control view that external environment or God or fate determine what should happen to them or will happen. People with moderately strong external locus of control may not be successful in their (i) jobs, (ii) career, and (iii) lives.

Self-Monitoring

Another personality trait that has recently received increased attention is called self-monitoring. It refers to an individual's ability to adjust his/her behaviour to external factors.

> The CEO of LG realized that the sales of the company were declining due to the cultural change. He immediately changed his leadership style and created empowered teams. This change in behaviour enabled the employees to develop a new refrigerator which could store the traditional Korean food. This product turned the company into a profit making company. Adjustment of the behaviour of the CEO is called self-monitoring.

Individuals high in self-monitoring can show considerable adaptability in adjusting their behaviour to external, situational factors. They are highly sensitive to external cues and can behave differently in different situations. High self-monitors are capable of presenting striking contradictions between their (i) public, (ii) personal, and (iii) private selves. Low self-monitors cannot deviate their behaviour. They tend to display their true (i) dispositions and (ii) attitude in every situation, hence there is high behavioural consistency, who they are and what they do.

The high self-monitors tend to pay closer attention to the behaviour of others and are more capable of conforming than low self-monitors. We might also hypothesize that high self-monitors will be more successful in managerial positions where individuals are required to play multiple and even contradicting roles. The high self-monitor is capable of putting on different 'faces' for different audiences.

Self-esteem

Self-esteem is the result of an individual's continuing evaluation of himself/herself. In other words, people (i) develop, (ii) hold, and (iii) sometimes modify opinions of their (i) own behaviours, (ii) abilities, (iii) appearance, and (iv) worth. These general assessments reflect responses to (i) people and situations, (ii) successes and failures, and (iii) opinions of others. Such evaluations are sufficiently (i) accurate and (ii) stable to be widely regarded as a basic personality trait or dimension.

Self-esteem affects behaviour in organisations and other social setting in several important ways. Self-esteem is related to initial vocational choice.

> Individuals with high self-esteem take risks in job selection, are attracted to high status occupation (e.g. medicine or law), and are more likely to choose unconventional or non-traditional jobs (e.g. forest ranger or jet pilot), than are individuals with low self-esteem.

> A study of college students looking for a job reported that those with high self-esteem:
> - received more favourable evaluations from recruiters.
> - were more satisfied with the job search.
> - received more job offers.
> - were more likely to accept jobs before graduation than were students with low self-esteem.

Self-esteem is also related to numerous (i) social and (ii) work behaviours.

> Employees with low self-esteem are more easily influenced by the opinion of other workers than are employees with high self-esteem.

> Employees with low self-esteem set lower goals for themselves than do employees with high self-esteem.

> Employees with low self-esteem are more susceptible than employees with high self-esteem to adverse job conditions such as (i) stress, (ii) conflict, (iii) ambiguity, (iv) poor supervision, (v) poor working conditions and the like.

In general sense, self-esteem is positively related to (i) achievement and (ii) a willingness to expend effort to accomplish tasks. Clearly, self-esteem is an important individual difference in terms of effective work behaviour.

Goal Orientation

Another individual difference of importance for behaviour in work settings is goal orientation or the preference for one type of goal versus another. Specifically, two orientations are considered important in terms of understanding some aspects of individual job performance.

- A learning goal orientation is a pre-disposition to develop competence by acquiring new skills and mastering new situations.
- A performance goal orientation is a pre-disposition to demonstrate and validate competency by seeking favourable judgement from others and avoiding negative judgements.

The implications of these goal orientations for work behaviour are dramatic. Employees with a strong performance goal orientation may avoid challenges at work and perform poorly when they encounter obstacles that are difficult to overcome. When faced with failure, such individuals are likely to become unhappy and dissatisfied and seek to withdraw from the situations in which they find themselves. But on the contrary, employees with a strong learning goal orientation strive to overcome failures and setbacks by increasing the efforts and seeking new solutions to the problems. They treat failures as a form of useful feedback, typically maintain their composure when challenged, and sustain or increase performance even they face obstacles that are difficult to overcome.

Introversion and Extroversion

The words introvert and extrovert are the most common descriptions of personality traits. These terms are normally associated with an individual's (i) sociability and (ii) interpersonal orientation. An introvert is (i) shy, (ii) quiet, and (iii) retiring, whereas an extrovert is (i) socially gregarious and (ii) outgoing.

Although some people exhibit the extremes of (i) introversions and (ii) extroversions, most are only moderately (i) introverts or extroverts, or/are even relatively balanced between the extremes. Introverts and extroverts appear in all (i) educational, (ii) gender, and (iii) occupational groups. As might be expected, extroverts are well represented in managerial occupations because the manager's role often involves working with others and influencing them to attain organisational goals. However, either (i) extreme extroversion or (ii) extreme introversion can interfere with an individual's effectiveness in an organisation.

One of the most striking implications of the introversion/extroversion personality dimension involves task performance in different environments. The evidence suggests that introverts perform better alone and in quiet environment, whereas extroverts perform better in an environment with greater sensory, stimulation, such as a noisy office with many people and a high level of activity.

Dogmatism

Dogmatism refers to the rigidity of a person's beliefs. The highly dogmatic individual perceives the world as a threatening place, often regards legitimate authority as absolute. And accepts or rejects other people on the basis of their agreement or disagreement with accepted authority. A high dogmatic (HD) individual is close minded and a low dogmatic (LD) person is open minded. As a result, HDs appear to depend more on authority figures in the organisation for (i) guidance and (ii) direction and are more easily influenced by them than are LDs.

> HDs typically need more group structure than do LDs to work effectively with others.

Hence, the performance of HDs assigned to (i) task forces and (ii) committees may vary somewhat, depending on how the group goes about its work. A high degree of dogmatism is related to a limited search for information in decision-making situations, which sometimes leads to poor managerial performance.

Authoritarianism

Authoritarianism is a concept developed by the psychologist Adorno during World War II to measure susceptibility to autocratic, fascistic, or anti-democratic appeals. Since that time, the concept has been extended to the authoritarian personality, a generic term used to describe an individual who has a strong belief in the legitimacy of established mechanisms of formal authority, views obedience to authority as necessary, exhibits a negative philosophy of people, adheres to conventional and traditional value system, is intellectually rigid, and opposes the use of subjective feelings. Authoritarians also tend to be rigid in the positions, place high moral value, on their beliefs, and are strongly oriented towards conformity to rules and regulations. They naturally prefer stable and structured work environments which are governed by clean rules and procedures. Similarly, authoritarians are likely to prefer autocratic or directive leadership and would exhibit high respect for individuals in positions of authority.

Personality–Type A and Type B

There is Type A Personality and Type B Personality.

Type A personality typifies a person who is always in a hurry, is extremely competitive and is often hostile and irritable. Opposite is Type B personality who is relaxed, incompetent and easy going.

> Mr. Ravi Rao of Hindustan Beverages Limited is exclusively competitive towards his rival company, takes his office work home, never enjoys leisure time, experiences a chronic sense of time urgency. His personality is termed as Type A personality. The personality with opposite traits is called Type B personality.

Profile of Type A personality includes:

- Always moving, walking rapidly, talking and eating rapidly.
- Feels impatient with the rate at which most events take place.
- Does two things at the same time.
- Can't cope up with leisure time.
- Obsessed with numbers.
- Measures success with quantity.
- Aggressive and competitive.
- Always under time pressure.

Profile of Type B personality includes:

- Not concerned about time, patient, mild mannered and never in a hurry.
- Does not brag.
- Plays for fun and relaxation rather than to exhibit their superiority at any cost.
- Relaxes without guilt.
- Has no pressing deadlines.

How do the two perform in organisations? Type A's are no doubt highly competitive and hardworking. But it is the Type B who climb up to the top of the organisation.

Type A's will make most successful salespeople and senior executives usually are Type B's. Why this paradox? The answer lies in the tendency of Type A's to trade off quality of effort for quantity. Executive positions usually go to those who are wise rather to those who are merely hasty, to those who are tactful rather than to those who are hostile, and to those who are creative rather than to those who are merely agile in competitive strife. (Stephen P. Robbins)

CASE STUDY

Cheerleader Versus Activist

Liz Schmit grew up in a Midwestern town of 25,000 people. She was the third generation of the Schmit family in this town.

Her grandparents, who had come from Germany, were retired, but they took care of her and her younger brother whenever her mother and dad had to go someplace–like a wedding or a funeral. Neither of Liz's parents had attended college, but once her father took an IQ test and scored almost in the genius category. Her parents always encouraged her to do well in school and saved their money so that she could go to State University. Liz also worked during the summer to save money for college. She did very well academically in high school and was a varsity cheerleader. She went to State University, joined a sorority, majored in English, graduated with honours and took a job with Landis and Smith Advertising Agency. Liz now 37 years old, has been with L & S for 15 years and has a good work record.

One of the Liz's coworker is Todd Long. Todd grew up in a suburb of Los Angeles. Both his parents had attended UCLA and he saw his grandparents, who were retired military people, only a few times. While Todd was growing up, his parents were a gone lot. His mother arranged for babysitter while she got her degree at UCLA. It was always assumed that when Todd graduated from high school he too would go to UCLA. Todd did not participate in many extra-curricular activities, but he graduated in the top 10 per cent of his high school class. At UCLA, he majored in Journalism and was very active in the student movement in the late 1960s. Upon graduation, he cut his hair and went to work for L & S. Todd, now 43, has been employed by L & S for 15 years and has a very good work record.

The job of copy editor is now open and Liz and Todd are the two top candidates. The Head of L & S, Stacy McAdams, made it clear that, "this job requires a good personality. The person will be in contact with all other the people in the office, and we need someone who can get along well with others and still be able to coordinate the work and meet our critical deadlines."

DISCUSSION POINTS

1. On the basis of the brief sketches of these two people, what do you think their personalities are like? Use the

determinants of personality and give an example of each determinant that can be found in the description of this situation?

2. Who do you think will get the job? You can discuss the male/female implications; however, solely on the basis of the personalities, that you outlined in question 1, who do you think would get the job? Who do you think should get the job?
3. What did the boss mean when she said that a "good personality" is required? Is there such a thing? Do you feel that personality has much of an input into this type of staffing decision? Should it have an input? Why?
4. Do you think the socialisation processes at L & S have completely overcome Liz's and Todd's biological, cultural and family influences? Why or why not?

QUESTIONS

- Define personality. How does the study of personality help in understanding OB?
- Analyse various personality development theories. Why do you interrelate the personality development, employee behaviour and job performance?
- Critically examine:
  (a) Freudian stages of personality development.
  (b) Erikson's stages of personality development.
- Comment on the humanistic approach to personality.
- Differentiate between:
  (a) Introvert and extrovert personality.
  (b) Authoritarian and bureaucratic personality.
- Write notes on:
  (a) Psycho-analytic theory of personality.
  (b) Trait theory of personality.
- "To some extent, a person's personality, is like all other people, like some other people, like no other people." Discuss.

- What do you know about hereditary factors that contribute towards formation of personality? How can you be sure that all such factors are hereditary in nature?
- Indicate the correct response against the following multiple choice questions:
  - Which of the following is associated with Sigmund Freud?
    (a) Behaviour is primarily caused by conscious motives.
    (b) Individuals pass through eight basic stages of development.
    (c) The progression between stages is marked by a crisis.
    (d) Behaviour is caused primarily by unconscious motives.
    (e) Individuals can be characterized in terms of a set of common traits.
  - __________ is associated with personality traits:
    (a) Raymond Cattell
    (b) Erik Erikson
    (c) Sigmond Freud
    (d) Jean Piaget
    (e) James Thompson

5

Motivation

Learning Objectives

- Meaning, Nature and Significance of Motivation
- Types of Motives
- Types of Motivation
- Content Theories of Motivation
- Process Theories of Motivation

INTRODUCTION

Motivation represents those forces acting within a person which causes them to behave in a specific and goal directed behaviour, because every human action is the result of a need or desire. One experiences a sort of mental discomfort as long as that need remains unsatisfied. The moment the action is initiated one makes an attempt to get over the discomfort. What causes an action? Is it the need or desire? What causes a need to be called the stimulus? Therefore, a manager's duty is to create the stimulus that causes a need which initiates action that leads to satisfaction. This should be a repetitive process for the action to continue. All this is called 'motivation' in management. Now we shall discuss:

- Motives
- Motivating
- Motivation.

Motives

The term motives is derived from the Latin word 'movere'. It means 'to move'. Motive is defined as an inner state that (i) energises, (ii) activates, and (iii) directs the behaviour of individuals towards certain goals. Motives are certain important needs of human beings. These needs have different degrees of strength.

The strong need or motive creates high tension or disequilibrium in a person and makes him restless until the need is fulfilled.

> The need for professional recognition makes the doctor restless until the co-doctors and patients recognize him as an efficient doctor. In order to reduce the tension, the doctor treats the critical cases.

Motives induce the individuals to channel their behaviour towards those actions which would reduce the disequilibrium. Thus, motives are drives which energize individuals to an action with a direction.

> The strong motive of earning large sums of money directs the students to take up the action of studying courses which have fast earnings.

MOTIVES–TYPES

Motives are classified into three categories:

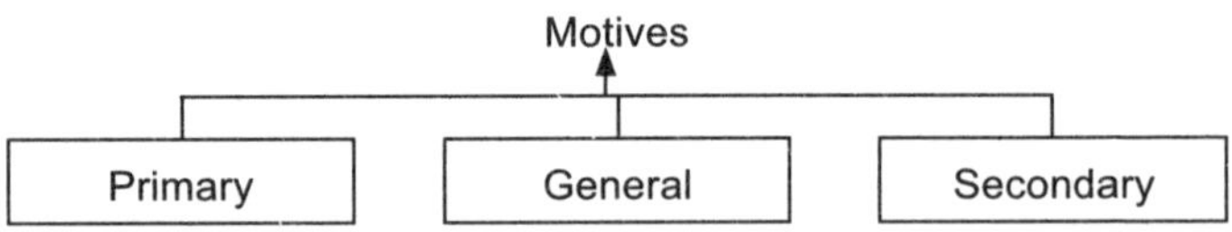

Primary Motive

Psychologists say that a motive in order to be a primary motive should be (i) unlearned and (ii) physiologically oriented. Such motives are also termed as physiological, biological, unlearned, or primary motives. The most common primary motives are (i) hunger, (ii) thirst, (iii) clothing, (iv) sleep, (v) sex, and (vi) maternal concern. Since human beings have a common physiological makeup, we all end up having the same primary needs.

General Motive

The motives which cannot be classified as (i) primary motives or (ii) secondary motives are categorized into general motives. These motives are unlearned but not psychologically based.

Primary motives tend to reduce the tension or stimulation whereas general motives encourage a person to increase the stimulation. Therefore, these needs are also called 'stimulus motives'. General motives play a more significant role in organisational behaviour than primary motives.

General motives include (i) curiosity, (ii) manipulation, (iii) activity motive, and (iv) affection motive. Human curiosity, manipulation and activity drives are quite intense.

> The teacher or examiner tries to confuse the students in order to create curiosity to learn deeper and exhibit the potentialities.

> Superiors allocate complex work to the subordinates in order to explore the employees curiosity, manipulation and activity drives. Similarly, employees should be allowed to exhibit their curiosity, manipulation and activity motives, in order to motivate them.

Affection motive is closely associated with the sex motive of primary motive and also affiliation motive of secondary motive. Hence, affection motive sometimes is classified as primary motive and sometimes as secondary motive. Affection motive plays a vital role in the organisations as most of the employees, in these days, are deprived of love and affection at home. Further, it plays a vital role in the general society also, due to the adages of 'love makes the world go round' and 'love conquers all'.

Secondary Motives

General motives play a significant role in organisational behaviour compared to primary motives. But secondary motives play further pivotal role in organisational behaviour. Primary motives do not play a significant role in developed countries.

However, it is not true in case of developing countries like ours. Secondary motives are closely related to learning concepts. Important secondary motives are (i) power, (ii) achievement, (iii) affiliation, (iv) security, and (v) status. The below mentioned table indicates few examples of key secondary needs.

Examples of Key Secondary Needs

Need for Achievement

Doing	better than competitors
Attaining or surpassing	a difficult goal
Solving	a complex problem
Carrying	out a challenging assignment successfully
Developing	a better way to do something

Need for Power

Influencing	people to change their attitudes or behaviour
Controlling	people and activities
Being	in position of authority over others
Gaining	control over information and resources
Defeating	an opponent or an enemy

Need for Affiliation

Having	a secure job
Being	protected against loss of income or economic disaster
Working	with people who are friendly or cooperative
Maintaining	harmonious relationship and avoiding conflicts
Participating	in pleasant social activities

Need for Security

Having	a secure job
Being	protected against loss or economic disaster
Safeguarding	against physical harm or hazardous conditions
Fighting	against illness and disability
Avoiding	taste or decisions with a risk of failure and blame

Need for Status

Having	the right ear and wearing the right clothes
Working	for the right company in the right job
Earning	a degree from the right university
Living	in the right neighbourhood and belonging to the country club
Enjoying	executive privileges

Power Motive

The power motive was advocated by Alfred Adler, a leading behavioural scientist, by developing the concepts of inferiority complex and compensation to explain it. The power motive can be termed as the need to manipulate others or the drive for superiority over others.

According to Adler, the feeling of inferiority is combined with an innate need for superiority and it is these two which will rule all behaviour. He communicates about how a person's lifestyle is characterised by striving to compensate for feeling of inferiority combined with the innate drive for power. In the organisation, this motive can lead to employees striving for organisational leadership and also the involvement of informal politics for this.

> This drive can be illustrated by quoting the example of the politicians who adopt various tactics to remain in power.

Achievement Motive

David V. McClelland, a Harvard psychologist has been studying on achievement motive. McClelland has written about all aspects of n-Ach (Achievement). Characteristics of a higher achiever have emerged out of his research. The achievement motive can be expressed as the desire of an individual to perform in terms of a particular standard of excellence or the desire to be successful in competitive conditions. The prominent characteristics of a high achiever are discussed hereunder:

Moderate Risk Taking

Taking moderate risks is probably the single most descriptive characteristic of the person possessing high achievement need. It seems that high achiever would take high risks. However, research gives a different answer from the commonsense. He/she will accept an assignment which carries moderate risk i.e., the assignment should satisfy two activities:

- It should not be so easy that there seems no challenge to be involved.
- Nor should the assignment be so difficult that he would find it very difficult to accomplish it.

Need for Immediate Feedback

Persons with high need for achievement prefer activities which provide (i) immediate and (ii) precise feedback information on how they are progressing towards a goal. Some hobbies and jobs offer such feedback and others do not.

High achievers generally prefer hobbies such as (i) wood work or (ii) mechanic which provide prompt, exact feedback and they shy from the coin-collecting type of hobby.

High achievers tend to get satisfied in jobs such as sales or management positions which are challenging and on which they are frequently evaluated by specific performance criteria.

Satisfaction with Accomplishment

High achievers do not want materialistic rewards. They want intrinsically satisfying rewards. A good illustration of this characteristics involves money. Though he likes to earn money a lot but not for usual reason of wanting money for its own sake or for the material benefits that it can buy. High achievers prefer a (i) complicated and (ii) challenging job even though it offers less salary compared to a simple job even if it offers higher salary.

Preoccupation with the Task

Once high achievers select a goal, they tend to be totally pre-occupied with the task until it is successfully completed. They cannot leave a job half-finished. They are not satisfied with themselves until they have but their maximum effort in completing the task. This type of dedicated commitment reflects his outward personality, which frequently has a negative effect on those who come in contact with him.

High achievers often strike others as being unfriendly and as 'loners'. They are very quiet and never talk about their accomplishments. They are realistic about their abilities and do not allow other people to get in the way of their goal accomplishment. Obviously, with this type of approach, high achievers do not always get along well with other people.

Affiliation Motive

Affiliation is a social need and members prefer to join groups in order to satisfy their need of belongingness/affiliation. Lower level employees have higher intense need to belong to a group. Affiliation motive plays a significant role in human resources management particularly in the area of commitment. Employees commitment level is enhanced by satisfying their social needs of belongingness.

Security Motive

The post-privatisation and globalisation era brought significant changes in the Indian business. The pre-liberalisation period (i.e. before 1991) provided job security to the employees particularly to those in public sector. Added to this, the fast technological advancement brought significant changes in the structure of employment.

Now, the Indian industry needs less number of people and as such, many industries started retrenching the employees through voluntary retirement scheme. Therefore, security of employment has become a complicated issue. Further, most of the employees have a fear of losing their jobs. Thus, the employees are deprived of the security need.

Status Motive

The capitalistic economic system along with the advanced technology created dynamic organisations. These dynamic organisations created challenging jobs. The candidates with the skills and knowledge suitable to the dynamic jobs are given quite attractive salary, lucrative perks like (i) free house, (ii) free car, (iii) telephone, (iv) club membership, (v) credit card, (vi) computer, (vii) internet connection and the like. Thus, the status and prestige motive of these dynamic employees is satisfied even though their need for job security is uncared for.

Thus, the status motive of the dynamic people is fulfilled in the free and high technology economies. Below mentioned table presents need hierarchy in different countries.

Need Hierarchy in Different Countries

Country	Need Priority
United States & Japan	Self-actualisation, esteem, safety, physiological and social.
France	Self-actualisation, esteem, physiological, safety and social.
Germany	Self-actualisation, physiological, esteem, social and safety.
India	Physiological, self-actualisation, esteem, social and safety.
Malawi	Physiological, self-actualisation, esteem, safety and social.
China (Esteem needs are not in evidence)	Self-actualisation, safety, psychological and social.

Source: Manab Thakur, et al., *International Management*, THH, 1997, p. 177.

MOTIVATING

Motivating implies that one person induces another person to engage in action or desired work behaviour by ensuring that a channel to direct the motive of the person becomes available and accessible to the person.

> Marketing Manager of XYZ Pharma Ltd. tells the sales force as: Those who achieve 200% targets will receive 200% of monthly salary as commission and will be promoted to Area Sales Manager. Thus the marketing manager induced the sales force to engage in extensive sales through the motives of commission and promotion.

Managers play a significant role in motivating the subordinates. They identify employees (i) talents, (ii) skills (iii) creativity, and (iv) innovative ideas. Thus, energize them to put these into action. Through this action, the managers help to convert the innovative and creative ideas of their subordinates into worthwhile action. Managers play a significant role in motivating their subordinates by chanellizing the employees' potentialities and work behaviour towards the organisational goals.

The managers also convert a weak desire into a strong desire and motive. This, in turn helps an employee to make use of his potentialities for his benefit and also for the organisation.

Below given table represents relationship among (i) motive, (ii) motivating, and (iii) motivation.

Motive, Motivating and Motivation–Relationship

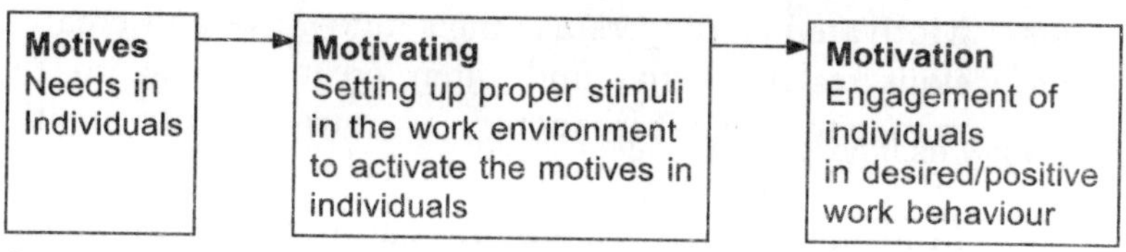

Source: Modified version from Uma Sekharan, p. 58.

MOTIVATION–SIGNIFICANCE

The word 'motivation' is used frequently and prominently by the people of different occupations and professions.

> A student says, "Mathematics teacher motivated me a lot positively during my school days and hence I am very much interested in Mathematics."

> A salesman says, "The new marketing manager does not motivate the sales force and hence the sales of our company are dwindling these days."

Scientists, researchers, politicians, managers and the like refer to the term 'motivation' quite often.

> We came across the word, 'motivation' in the Ramayana when Lord Anjaneya was encouraged/motivated by Jambavanta to fly over the sea by identifying the potentialities of Lord Anjaneya. This is a positive effort of motivation.

This simple example tells us what motivation would do. In other words, motivation makes the impossible things possible. Thus, motivation plays an important role in converting the human potentialities into performance. The increased attention towards motivation is justified by several reasons.

- Motivation identifies employee potentialities. Motivation makes the employee to know his potentialities.
- Motivation converts the potentialities into performance.
- Motivation converts motivated employees into committed and loyal employees.
- Motivated employees explore the alternative methods of performing a task and they select a better method than the existing method.
- Motivated employees use their innovative and creative skills, talents, etc., and often creative ideas to the management. This factor, in turn results in the upgradation of technology and technical know-how.
- Motivated employee has positive attitude towards quality and has concern towards quality improvement. This increased concern towards quality results in high quality in production/operation.

- Motivated workers exert all their energies towards the job. This, in turn, results in increase in employee efficiency and thereby productivity.
- The committed employees do the work in a better way and also reduce the wastage, which, in turn, contributes to higher productivity.
- Motivation maintains discipline, sound superior – subordinate relations and sound relations among colleagues. This, in turn, leads to congenial industrial relations.
- Motivation makes the people to understand each other completely, leads to group work and team spirit. These in turn, lead to unreserved cooperation and collaboration among members of a department and organisation.

MOTIVATION–NATURE

Motivation is mainly concerned with the directing of employees towards organisational objectives. The nature of motivation is discussed hereunder:

Motivation is a Continuous Process

As we have studied in economics, human wants are unlimited. It is said that, 'Even God cannot satisfy all human wants.' With the satisfaction of one want, another want preferably of the higher order is created. Thus, new wants emerge when the present wants are satisfied. All the wants cannot be satisfied at the same time. Wants are to be satisfied one after another continuously. Hence, motivation is also a continuous and an unending process.

Motivation is a Psychological Concept

Motivation is concerned with the psychological aspects of human being. The level of satisfaction, contentment, etc., by using the same reward/incentive vary from person to person. This is due to variation in (i) aspirations, (ii) attitudes, (iii) feelings, and (iv) perceptions of the individuals. Thus, motivation is reaction of the organs of the human body to the inducements/incentives offered.

The Entire Individual is Motivated

As we know, motivation is a psychological concept interacting with the total organs of an individual. Further, each individual is an integrated and comprehensive system. The entire system of an individual reacts to the motivation. Thus, the entire individual is motivated.

Frustrated Individual Fails to be Motivated

Some individuals are frustrated despite of the rewards due to the wide gap between their aspirations and rewards. Some of the frustrated persons become mentally ill and these persons cannot be motivated.

Goals Lead to Motivation

Goals form a part of motivational process. Goal achievement results in the satisfaction of want. Goal fulfilment leads to reduction of drives and fulfils deficiencies. Thus goal achievement ends the motivational process.

The Self-concept as a Unifying Force

Self-concept is the life position of a person that he formulates about himself during his childhood. He thinks himself in the same way during his lifetime until and unless a major change takes place in the rest of the lifetime. Therefore, those who formulated a positive view about themselves during the childhood, will be motivated by themselves in the rest of the lifetime. And the *vice versa* is true in case of negative self-concept.

MOTIVATION–TYPES

There are two ways by which people can be motivated:

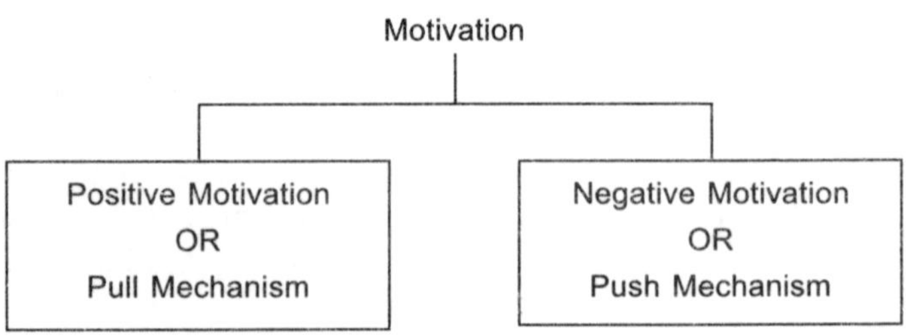

Positive Motivation or Pull Mechanism

People are said to be motivated positively when they are shown a reward and the way to achieve it. Such reward may be (i) financial or (ii) non-financial. Monetary motivation may include (i) different incentives, (ii) wage plans, (iii) productive bonus schemes, etc. Non-monetary motivation may include (i) praise for the work, (ii) participation in management, (iii) social recognition, etc. Monetary incentives provide the workers a better standard of life while non-monetary incentives satisfy the ego of a man. Positive motivation seeks to create an optimistic atmosphere in the enterprise. Positive motivation involves (i) identifying employee potentialities, and (ii) make him realize the possible result by achieving his potentialities.

Negative Motivation or Push Mechanism

One can get the desired work done by installing fear in the minds of people. In this method of motivation, fear of consequences of doing something or not doing something keeps the workers in the desired direction. This method has got several limitations. Fear creates frustration, a hostile state of mind and an unfavourable attitude towards the job which hinders efficiency and productivity. So the use of it should be kept to its minimum.

MOTIVATION–PROCESS

Motivation is a basic psychological process. Few people would deny that it is the most important factor in the micro approach to organisational behaviour. Many people equate the variables as (i) causes of behaviour and (ii) motivation. The causes of behaviour are broad and complex. These cannot be explained by motivation alone. However, motivation should never be underrated. Motivation is very important process in understanding behaviour along with the following variables: (i) perception, (ii) personality, (iii) attitudes, and (iv) learning. But it should not be thought of as the only explanation of behaviour. It acts and interacts with (i) other mediating processes, and (ii) the environment. Like the other mediating processes motivation cannot be seen. All that can be seen is behaviour.

The key to understanding the process of motivation lies in the meaning and relationship between the following:

Needs → Drives → Incentives

1. Needs

Needs are created whenever there are the imbalances, like (i) physiological or (ii) psychological.

> A need arises when cells in the body are deprived of food and water.

Although psychological needs may be based on a deficiency, sometimes they are not.

2. Drives

With a few exceptions drives or motives are set up to reduce needs. A physiological drive can be simply defined as a deficiency with direction. Physiological and psychological drives are action-oriented. These provide thrust towards reaching an incentive. They are at the heart of motivational process.

> The need for food and water are translated into the hunger and thirst drive.

3. Incentives

At the end of the motivation cycle is the incentive. It is defined as anything that will reduce (i) a need and (ii) a drive. Thus, attaining an incentive will tend to restore (i) physiological or (ii) psychological balance and will reduce drive.

> Eating food, drinking water will tend to restore the balance and reduce the corresponding drives.

MOTIVATION–MEANING

Today, all people (practitioners and scholars) have their own definitions of motivation. Usually, one or more of the following words are included in the definition: "desires", "wants", "wishes", "aims", "goals", "needs", "drives", "motives" and "incentives".

The term "motivation" has been derived from the Latin word 'movere', which means "to move". This meaning is evident in the following comprehensive definition:

> "*It is an inner process which (i) stimulates and (ii) energizes an individual to work with willingness for the achievement of certain goals.*"

On the analysis of this definition, we can derive the following characteristics of motivation:

1. Motivation is an Internal Feeling

Motivation is a psychological phenomenon which generates within an individual. Needs are feelings in the mind of a person that he lacks a certain thing. Such feelings affect the behaviour of the person.

2. Person in Totality, not in Part, is Motivated

Each individual in the organisation is a (i) self-contained and (ii) inseparable unit, and all his needs are interrelated. These affect the behaviour in different ways. Moreover, feeling of needs is a continuous process, as such, these create continuity in human behaviour.

3. Motivation Enables to Satisfy Same Needs

Motivation is the willingness to exert high level of effort towards organisational goals, conditioned by the effort and the ability to satisfy some individual needs.

4. Motivation = Anticipated Values × Perceived Probability

Motivation is the product of anticipated values from an action and the perceived probability that the values would be attained by the action. The anticipated value is called 'Valance' and the perceived probability is called 'Expectancy'. Thus,

Motivation = Valance × Expectancy

5. Motivation Involves the Arousal, Direction and Maintenance of Behaviour Towards a Goal

Basic Components of Motivation

Arousal	Direction	Maintenance	Goal

Compliment work — persist

Desire to make a good impression		Goal impression made
Desire to	.... Compliment work — persist	Goal
make a good	.... Work Extra Hard — Persist	impression
impression	.... Do Special Favours — Persist	made

MOTIVATION–THEORIES

From the very beginning, when human organisations were established, various people have been engaged in finding out the answer to the question relating to 'what motivates people'. Their approaches have differed resulting into a number of theories pertaining to motivation. Though all these theories try to focus attention on the basic issue, yet they differ considerably. These theories may be grouped into two categories viz.

Theories of Motivation

Content	Process
- Maslow's Hierarcy of Needs	- Equity Theory–J. Stacy Adam
- Alderfer's ERG Theory	- Expectancy Theory–Victor Vroom
- McClellands Theory of Needs	- The Porter and Lawler Model
- Hazberg's Two Factor Theory	- Goal Setting Theory

1. Maslow's Hierarchy of Needs

Perhaps the most widely known theory of individual needs and motivation comes from Abraham Maslow, who was a clinical psychologist in the U.S.A. He stated that people have five basic levels of needs which they tend to satisfy in the hierarchical fashion. He believed that once a given level of need is satisfied, it no longer serves to motivate. The next higher level need activates in order to motivate the individual.

He identifies five levels in his need hierarchy. They are:

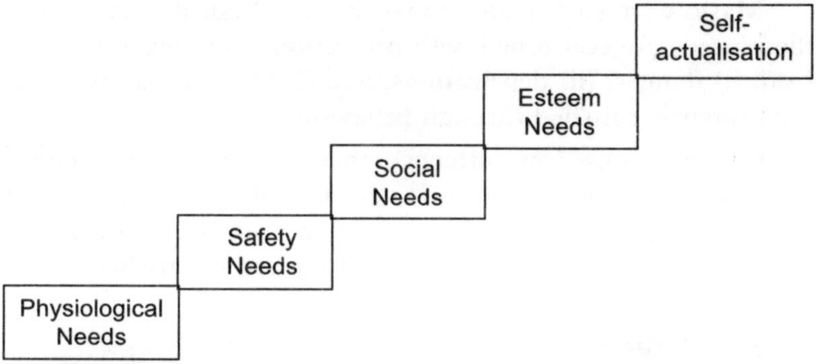

(a) Physiological Needs

Physiological needs are the biological needs required to preserve human life. These needs include (i) food, (ii) clothing, and (iii) shelter. According to the theory, once these basic needs are satisfied, they no longer motivate.

> A starving person will strive to obtain a carrot that is within reach. However, after eating his fill of carrots, the person will not strive to obtain another. He will be motivated only by the next higher level of needs.

These needs must be met at least partly before higher level needs emerge. They exert a tremendous influence on behaviour. As pointed out by Maslow, "man lives by bread alone". When there is no bread, physiological needs dominate when all needs are unsatisfied.

(b) Safety Needs

Once physiological needs become relatively well gratified, the safety needs begin to manifest themselves and dominate human behaviour. These include:

(i) Protection from physiological danger (fire, accident);

(ii) Economic security (fringe benefits, health, insurance programmes);

(iii) Desire for an orderly, predictable environment; and

(iv) Desire to know the limits of acceptable behaviour.

Maslow stressed (i) emotional and (ii) physical safety. Thus, these needs are concerned with protection from hazards of life from (i) danger, (ii) deprivations, and (iii) threat. Safety needs are primarily satisfied through behaviour.

Organisations can influence these security needs either (i) positively–through pension schemes, insurance plans, or (ii) negatively by arousing fears of being fired or laid off safety needs too are motivational only if they are unsatisfied. They have finite limits.

(c) Social Needs

After the lower order needs have been satisfied, the social or lower needs become important motivators of behaviour. Man is a gregarious being and he wants to (i) belong, (ii) associate, (iii) gain acceptance from associates, (iv) give, and (v) receive friendship and affection. Social needs tend to be stronger for some people than for others in certain situations.

In organisations, workers form informal group environment. Such environment is developed where the work is (i) routine and (ii) tedious. This situation is made worse when workers are closely supervised and controlled, but have no clear channel of communication with management. In this type of environment workers depend on informal groups for support of unfulfilled social needs such as affiliation.

(d) Esteem Needs

The esteem represents the higher level needs of humans. These needs are two-fold in nature (i) self-esteem and (ii) esteem from others.

- Self-esteem needs include (i) self-confidence, (ii) self-respect, (iii) achievement, and (iv) autonomy.
- Esteem from others are related to one's reputation needs (i) status, (ii) recognition, and (iii) appreciation.

Esteem needs have certain features in common:

1. They do not become motivators until lower level needs are reasonably satisfied.
2. These needs are insatiable, unlike lower order needs, these needs are rarely satisfied.
3. Satisfaction of esteem needs produces feeling of (i) self-confidence (ii) worth, (iii) strength, and (iv) capability of being useful and necessary in the world.
4. The satisfaction of esteem needs is not always through (i) mature or (ii) adaptive behaviour. It is sometimes generated by irresponsible actions.

(e) Self-actualisation Needs

Self-actualisation is the need to maximize one's potential, whatever it may be. This is related with the development of intrinsic capabilities which lead people to seek situations that can utilize their potential. This includes competence which has control over environmental factors both (i) physical and (ii) social.

> A man with high intensity of achievement needs will be restless unless he can find fulfilment in doing what he is filled to do.

As Maslow has put it, "self-actualisation is the desire to become what one is capable of becoming".

Maslow suggests that:

- The various levels are interdependent and overlapping.
- The lower level needs become substantially satisfied, and the higher level needs become dominant.
- The substantially satisfied needs no longer motivate.

2. Alderfer's ERG Theory

Clayton Alderfer reformulated Maslow's Needs Hierarchy Theory. He modified and reduced Maslow's five levels of needs to three levels and labeled them as needs for:

Herzberg's Two Factors	Maslow's Hierarchy of Needs	Alderfer's ERG Needs
Motivators	Self-actualisation	Growth
	Esteem	
Hygiene Factors	Social	Relatedness
	Safety	Existence
	Physiological	

(a) Existence Needs

The existence group is concerned with providing basic material existence requirements. They include the items that Maslow considered as (i) physiological and (ii) safety needs.

(b) Relatedness Needs

The relatedness needs stress the importance of (i) interpersonal, (ii) social relationships i.e., the needs of people for (i) affection, (ii) love, and (iii) friendship in their social environment and would thus include Maslow's social needs.

(c) Growth Needs

Finally, Alderfer isolates growth needs–an intrinsic desire for personal development. These include:

- The individual's desire to be (i) self-confident, (ii) productive, and (iii) creative.
- The desire to engage in tasks that require full utilisation of abilities and that develop additional capabilities or skills.

Alderfer's and Maslow's Theory–Difference. The difference between Maslow and Alderfer is that:

- Alderfer posited a "satisfaction–progression" and "frustration regression" process in his theory i.e. Alderfer agreed with Maslow that once one level of needs is satisfied, people will progress to the next level to satisfy the higher level needs.

> If relatedness needs are satisfied, people will move on to the growth needs to have them satisfied.

- Unlike Maslow, Alderfer also postulated that, if for some reason, people become frustrated in trying to satisfy their needs at one level, their next lower level needs will re-emerge and they will regress to the lower level to satisfy them.

> If relatedness needs are not satisfied and an individual experiences frustration in satisfying these needs, his existence needs will re-emerge and he will regress to this level and try to satisfy those needs.

- Alderfer's theory is a less restrictive model of the motivation process. It represents a simplification of Maslow's hierarchy of needs theory, not only by reducing the number of needs categories but by removing the restrictions about the activation of needs in any hierarchical order.
- Alderfer suggests that more than one need may be operative at the same time, whereas Maslow, felt a person primarily addresses one set of needs at a time.
- Alderfer also suggests that satisfaction of higher order needs leads to greater intensity of those needs.

3. McClellands Theory of Needs

Besides, many theories about motivation, there is another theory that uses needs as the central focus. David McClellands and his associates proposed that the organisation offers an opportunity to satisfy at least three needs:

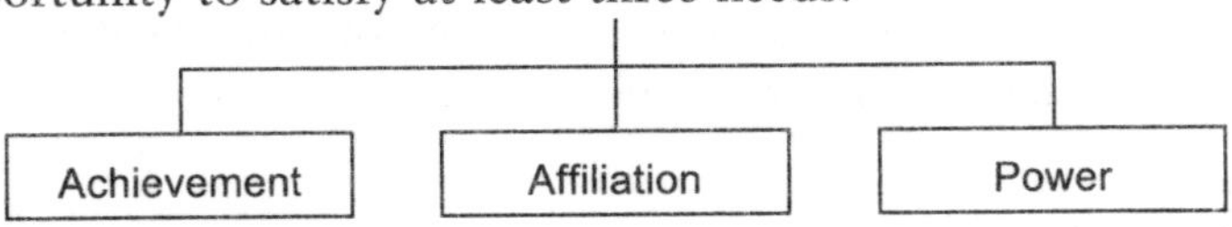

According to this theory, called "Achievement Motivation Theory", a major factor in willingness to perform is the intensity of the individual's needs for achievement.

(a) Need for Power (n Pow)

The power motive is discussed first because it has been formally recognized and studied for a relatively long time. This is the need to (i) dominate, (ii) influence, or (iii) control the activities of others.

The leading advocate of the power motive was the behavioural scientist, Alfred Adler. He explains the power needs as (i) the need to manipulate others or (ii) the drive for superiority over others.

Adler developed the concept of (i) inferiority complex and (ii) compensation. He felt that every small child experiences a sense of inferiority, when this feeling of inferiority is combined with innate need for superiority, the two rule behaviour–the person's lifestyle is characterised by striving to compensate for feeling of inferiority, which are combined with the innate drive for power.

McClelland and his associates have found that people with a high power need have a great concern for exercising (i) influence and (ii) control. Such individuals are generally seeking positions of leadership. They involve in conversation, as they are (i) forceful, (ii) outspoken, (iii) hard headed, and (iv) demanding.

(b) The Need for Affiliation (n Aff)

Since people are social animals, most individuals like to be with others in situations where they feel they belong to and are accepted. Sometimes affiliation is equated with social motives. However, the affiliation motive is not so broad. Affiliation plays a very complex but vital role in human behaviour. The study of affiliation is complicated by the fact that some behavioural scientists believe that it is an unlearned motive. However, the fact is partly true.

McClelland has suggested that persons who have high need for affiliation view the organisation as a chance to form new and satisfying relationships. They are motivated by jobs that demand frequent interaction with coworkers. Such people are not likely to succeed well at tasks that force them to work in isolation.

(c) The Need for Achievement (n Ach)

Over the years, behavioural scientists have observed that some people have an intense desire to achieve. McClellands research has led him to believe that the need for achievement is a distinct human motive that can be distinguished from other needs. It can also be (i) isolated and (ii) assessed in any group.

McClelland has identified four basic characteristics of high achievers. They are:

1. *Moderate Risk Taking*

Taking moderate risks is probably the single most descriptive characteristic of the person possessing high achievement need. It seems that a high achiever would take high risks. However, research gives a different answer from the commonsense. He/she will accept an assignment which carries moderate risk, i.e. the assignment should satisfy two activities:

- It should not be so easy that there seems no challenge.
- It should not be so difficult that he would face hardships to accomplish it.

2. *Need for Immediate Feedback*

Persons with high need for achievement prefer activities which provide (i) immediate and (ii) precise feedback information on how they are progressing towards a goal. Some hobbies and jobs offer such feedback and others do not.

High achievers generally prefer hobbies such as (i) wood working or (ii) mechanics, which provide prompt, exact feedback and they shy from the coin collecting type of hobby.

High achievers tend to get satisfied in jobs such as sales or management positions which are challenging and in which they are frequently evaluated by specific performance criteria.

3. *Satisfaction with Accomplishment*

High achievers accomplish a task intrinsically satisfying in and of itself. They do not necessarily want the accompanying material rewards. A good illustration of this characteristic involves money. Though he likes to earn money a lot but not for usual reason of wanting money for its own sake or for the material benefits that it can buy. Given the choice between a simple task for accomplishment with a good payoff, and a difficult task with a lesser payoff, other things being equal, high achievers generally choose the latter.

4. *Pre-occupation with the Task*

Once high achievers select a goal, they tend to be totally pre-occupied with the task until it is successfully completed. They cannot leave a job half-finished. They are not satisfied with themselves until they have put their maximum effort in completing the task. This type of dedicated commitment often reflects his outward personality, which frequently has a negative effect on those who come in contact with him.

High achievers often strike others as being unfriendly and as 'loners'. They are very quiet and never talk about their accomplishments. They are realistic about their abilities and do not allow other people to get in the way of their goal accomplishment. Obviously, with this type of approach, high achievers do not always get along well with other people.

5. *Herzberg's Two Factor Theory of Motivation*

For Several years managers had been wondering as to why their fancy personnel policies and fringe benefits were not increasing employee motivation on the job. To answer this, Herzberg provided an interesting extension of Maslow's need hierarchy and developed a specific content theory of work motivation.

Herzberg conducted a widely reported motivational study on about 200 accountants and engineers employed by firms in Pittsburgh, U.S.A. He used the critical incident method of obtaining data for analysis. The professionals were given the following direction by an interviewer, "Think of a time when you felt (i) exceptionally good or (ii) exceptionally bad about your job, either (i) your present job or (ii) any other job you have had.

This approach had been repeated many times with a variety of job holders in various countries. Responses obtained from this critical incident method were interesting and fairly consistent.

- Good feelings were generally associated with (i) job experiences and (ii) job content.
- Bad feelings were generally associated with the surrounding aspect of the job, i.e. the job context.

Herzberg concluded that:

- Job satisfiers are related to job context; and
- Job dissatisfiers are related to job context.

He labeled satisfiers 'motivators' and called dissatisfiers 'hygiene factors'. They came to be known as 'Herzberg's two factor theory of motivation'.

Herzberg's Two Factor Theory

Hygiene Factors	Motivators
Company Policy and Administration	Achievement
Supervisor	
Relations with Supervisor	Supervision
Relations with Coworkers	Recognition
Relations with Subordinates	Work itself
Working Conditions	Advancement
Salary	Responsibility

1. Hygiene Factors

Herzberg's theory is closely related to Maslow's Need Hierarchy. The hygiene factors represent the need to avoid pain in the environment. They are not an intrinsic part of a job, but are related to the conditions under which a job is performed. They are roughly equivalent to Maslow's lower level needs. These hygiene factors prevent dissatisfaction, but do not lead to satisfaction. These factors produce no growth in worker's output but they prevent loss in performance caused by work restrictions. Herzberg believed that hygiene creates a zero level of motivation and if maintained at proper level, prevents the occurring of negative type of motivation.

2. Motivators

Motivators are associated with positive feeling of employees about the job. They are related to the job content (work itself). They make people satisfied with their job. An increase in these factors will satisfy the employees; however, any decrease will not affect their level of satisfaction. If managers wish to increase (i) motivation and (ii) performance about the average level, they must enrich the (i) work and (ii) person's freedom on the job. Motivators are necessary to keep (i) job satisfaction and (ii) job performance high.

Maslow and Herzberg Models–Differences

Although there are marked similarities in the two models. However, many differences exist.

Issue	Maslow's Model	Herzberg's Model
Order of Needs	Sequential arrangements of needs.	No such hierarchical arrangement.
Emphasis	Descriptive	Prescriptive
Essence of Theory	Unsatisfied needs energize behaviour; this behaviour causes performance.	Gratified needs cause performance.
Motivator	Any need can be a motivator if it is relatively unsatisfied.	Only higher order needs serve as motivators.
Applicability	Takes a general view of the motivational problems of all workers.	Takes a micro-view, and deals with work-oriented motivational problems of professional workers.

Herzberg's Departure from Traditional View

Traditionally, job satisfaction and dissatisfaction were viewed as opposite ends of a single continuum. When certain things are present on a job (good pay, opportunity for growth, healthy working environment), the employee will be satisfied. When they are absent, he is dis-satisfied. The absence of dis-satisfaction is satisfactory.

Herzberg's findings indicate that dissatisfaction is not simply the opposite of satisfaction or motivation. One can feel no dissatisfaction and yet not be satisfied. Satisfaction and dis-satisfaction appear to be somewhat independent. They are not viewed as symmetrical items on the single scale, rather, they are viewed as attributes of different scales. The factors that cause (i) dissatisfaction are different from those that result in (ii) satisfaction. Satisfaction is affected by motivators and dissatisfaction, by hygiene factors.

Traditional View

Dissatisfaction ——— Satisfaction

Satisfaction and dissatisfaction are opposite ends of a single continuum.

Herzberg's View

Hygiene's

Dissatisfaction ←——→ No satisfaction

Motivators

No satisfaction ←——→ Satisfaction

Satisfaction and dissatisfaction are independent dimensions, satisfaction is affected by motivators and dissatisfaction by hygienes.

4. Equity Theory–J. Stacy Adam

Adam's theory of equity is one of the popular social exchange theories. It is perhaps the most exactly developed statement of how individuals evaluate social exchange relationships. It is probably the clearest of the process theories. The theory points out that:

- People are motivated to maintain fair relationships with others.
- People will try to rectify unfair relationships by making them fair.

This theory is based on two assumptions about human behaviour:

(a) Individuals make contributions (inputs) for which they expect certain outcomes (rewards). Inputs include (i) past training and experience, (ii) qualifications, (iii) organisational position, and (iv) how hard he works. Outcomes include (i) pay, (ii) status, (iii) promotion, (iv) fringe benefits.

(b) Individuals decide whether or not a particular exchange is satisfactory, by comparing their outcomes/inputs to those of others in the form of ratio. Equity exists when an individual concludes that his outcome/input ratio is equal to that of other people.

Categories of Inequality

Overpayment Inequity. The person gets more out of the job relative to what he puts compared to another:

$$\frac{\text{Person's outcomes}}{\text{Person's inputs}} > \frac{\text{Others' outcomes}}{\text{Others' inputs}}$$

Under-payment Inequity. In this situation the person and the others do the same job but other gets more. The person experiences internal tension:

$$\frac{\text{Person's outcomes}}{\text{Person's inputs}} < \frac{\text{Others' outcomes}}{\text{Others' inputs}}$$

Equity occurs when,

$$\frac{\text{Persons' outcomes}}{\text{Persons' inputs}} = \frac{\text{Others' outcomes}}{\text{Others' inputs}}$$

How to Escape Inequity

> 'X' and 'Y' are two typists who perform the same type of work in two different divisions of a company. 'X' is paid Rs. 1000 a month and 'Y' is paid only Rs. 800 a month. One day they met and found out this unfortunate payment plan.

According to equity theory both 'X' and 'Y' will feel upset by this inequity. 'X' will feel guilty for being paid more and 'Y' will resent the under-payment and will be frustrated.

Now the question arises: how to bring about equity in their relationship? Adam has studied the impact on equity either by (i) over-payment, or (ii) under-payment. His findings suggest:

1. The worker 'X' can do more or better work than Y and Y can do less or poorer work to equalize their ratios.

This is termed as 'behavioural inequity resolution strategy'.

2. Another method to lower one's inputs is to remain absent from work. 'X' and 'Y' can attempt to adjust their outcomes to resolve inequity.

   'X' may refuse pay hike and 'Y' can demand for a rise.

   If 'X' lowers his outcome and 'Y' raises his, they equalize their ratios and this may help to establish a fair relationship. Alternatively, they may decide to quit and get out of the relationship completely. Quiting a job, obtaining a transfer, absenteeism are common forms of leaving the field.

3. It is also possible to establish equity psychologically (psychological inequity resolution strategy) 'Y' can convince himself that 'X' actually works harder than 'Y'. Quiet often inequitable paid workers convince themselves that they are not working hard, thereby establishing equity between (i) themselves, and (ii) equitable paid workers. Thus, to restore equity, the person may alter the (i) inputs, or (ii) outcomes, cognitively distort the (i) inputs, or (ii) outcomes, leave the field, act on the other, or change the other.

5. Expectancy Theory–Victor Vroom

Victor Vroom in 1964, made an important contribution to our understanding of motivation. Contrary to most of the critics, Vroom proposed his expectancy theory as an alternative to the content theories, which he felt were inadequate explanations of the complex motivation process. In academic circles, his theory has become a popular explanation for work motivation and has generated considerable research.

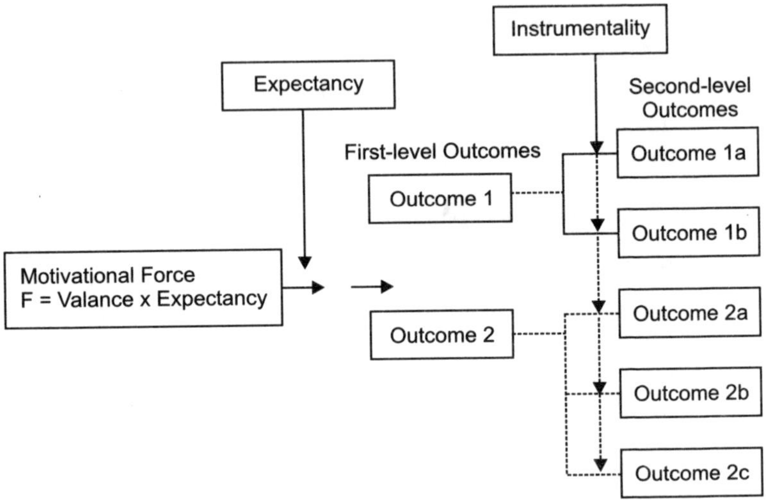

The Vroom Expectancy, or VJE, Theory of Work Motivation

Key Variables in the Model

The expectancy theory is based upon a rational-economic view of people. It views people as having their (i) own needs, and (ii) expectations which they desire from their work (obviously rewards). They use these to decide which company to join and how hard to work on the job. The theory assumes that people are decision-makers who choose among alternatives by selecting the one that appears most desirable at the time. Thus, motivation depends on the situation facing people and how it satisfies their desires. Both individual and situational differences are given due consideration.

The expectancy theory is built around three concepts, viz.:

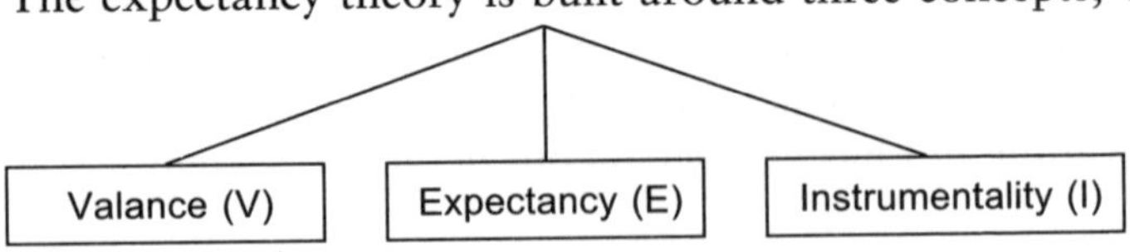

1. Valance. People have preferences (valances) for various outcomes or incentives that are potentially available to them. By valance, Vroom means the strength of an individual's preference for a particular outcome. Other terms equivalent to valance used in various theories of motivation are: (i) value, (ii) incentive, (iii) attitude, and (iv) expected utility.

In order for the valance to be positive, the person must prefer attaining the outcome to not attain it:

- The valance of zero occurs when the individual is indifferent towards the outcome.
- The valance is negative when the individual prefers not attaining the outcome.

An individual deserves promotion and feels that superior performance is a strong factor in achieving that goal. His first-level outcome are then (i) superior, (ii) average, or (iii) poor performance. His second-level outcome is promotion, the first-level outcome of high performance thus acquires a positive valance by virtue of his expected relationship to the preferred second-level outcome of promotion.

According to this example, a person would be motivated towards superior performance because of preference to be promoted. The superior performance (first-level outcomes), is being seen as instrumental in getting promotion (second-level outcome).

2. Expectancy. Another factor determining the motivation is expectancy, that is, the probability (ranging from 0 to 1), that a particular action or effort will lead to a particular first-level outcome. Expectancy differs from instrumentality. It relates efforts to first-level outcome, where instrumentality relates first and second-level outcome to each other. In summary, the strength of the motivation to perform a certain act will depend on the sum of the products of the values for the outcome times the expectancies.

3. Instrumentality. It refers to the relationship between (i) performance, and (ii) reward. It provides answer to such questions "will I be rewarded if I perform the job well". Instrumentality refers to the degree where a first-level outcome will lead to a desired second-level outcome. Perceived instrumentality is a subjective feeling. If people perceive that their performance is adequately rewarded, the perceived instrumentality will be positive. If they perceive that performance does not make any difference to their rewards, the instrumentality will be low.

In the example given above, instrumentality refers to the person's perception of the relationship between high performance (first-level outcome), and promotion (second-level outcome).

Implications of the Vroom Model for O.B.

Vroom's theory is different from the content theories because it depicts a process of cognitive variables that reflects individual differences in work motivation. It does not attempt to describe (i) what the content is, or (ii) what the individual differences are. Everyone has a unique combination of (i) valances, (ii) instrumentalities, and (iii) expectancies. Thus Vroom's theory indicates only the conceptual determinants of motivation and how they are related. It does not provide specific suggestions on what motivates organisational members as the other content theories do.

Although the Vroom model does not directly contribute to the techniques of motivating personnel in an organisation. It is of value in understanding organisational behaviour.

> It can clarify the relationship between (i) individual, and (ii) organisational goals.

Importance of the Vroom Model

The major reason why Vroom's model has emerged as an important modern theory of work motivation and has generated so much research is that it does not take a simplistic approach. The content theories over simplify human motivation. Yet the content theories remain extremely popular with practicing managers because the concepts are (i) easy to understand, and (ii) apply to their own situations.

The expectancy theory recognizes the complexities of work motivation. It is difficult to (i) understand, and (ii) apply. Thus, from a theoretical standpoint, the VEI model seems to help managers to appreciate the complexities of motivation, but it does not give them much practical help in solving their motivational problems. This is not criticism of the expectancy theory because the expectancy model attempts only to mirror the complex motivational process, it does not attempt to describe (i) how motivational decisions are actually made, or (ii) how to solve actual motivational problems facing a manager.

6. The Porter and Lawler Model

Early human relationists believed that employee satisfaction directly affected productivity. Employee satisfaction was perceived to be an antecedent conditions for productivity. Based on a belief that a happy worker is a productive worker. All the content theories completely assume that satisfaction leads to improve performance, dis-satisfaction detracts from performance. However, studies at a later stage (Vroom, 1964), had not found a strong relationship between (i) satisfaction, and (ii) performance. Most studies actually found a very low positive relationship between the two.

Porter and Lawler (1968), promoted the thesis that performance causes satisfaction. They tried to examine the complex relationship between (i) motivation, (ii) satisfaction, and (iii) performance. They pointed out that efforts do not directly lead to performance.

Performance in organisations, according to Porter and Lawler, appears to be a function of three important factors:

1. An employee must 'want' to perform; the desire of an employee to do the assigned job, one must be motivated.
2. Motivation alone will not ensure task performance. A person must have the necessary (i) abilities, and (ii) traits.
3. A person must have an accurate knowledge of the requirements of the job if he is expected to devote his energies fully on the assigned tasks, i.e., one must have fairly clear role perception.

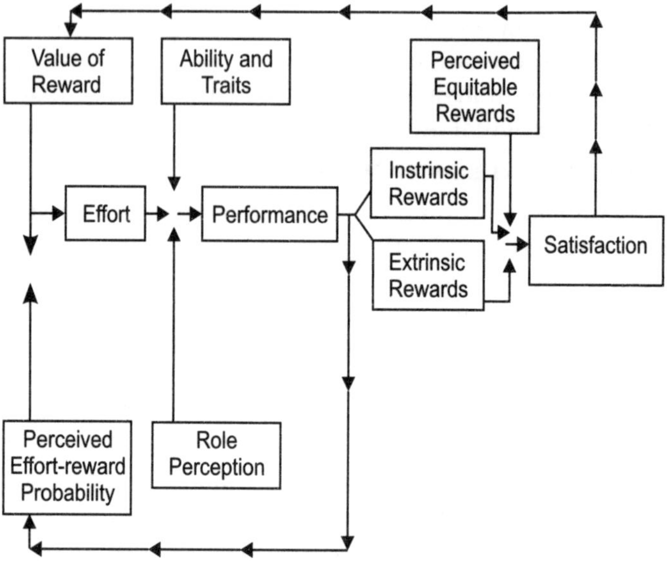

The Porter-Lawler Motivation Model

Key Variables in the Model

1. Effort. Effort refers to the amount of energy exerted by an individual on a given task. It will not directly lead to a specific level of performance. It is the result of attractiveness of the reward and the way in which the individual perceives the linkage between (i) effort and (ii) reward. If an employee places a high value on a reward and if he perceives a high probability that his effort will lead to this reward, then he will exert great quantity of effort. Motivation is seen as the force of an employee to expend effort.

2. Performance. Motivation leads to an observed level of effort by an employee. Effort alone is not enough. Performance results from a combination of effort that an individual puts forth and the level of ability which he has and the way he perceives the role he should take. Effort and performance can not be equated. Quite often a similarity between (i) efforts, and (ii) performance may result.

> Most of the students who burn the midnight oil fail to obtain a satisfactory grade due to lack of ability to understand things properly, or misdirect effort due to the bad planning and eventually turn losers than winners.

3. Rewards. The model clearly shows that performance leads to rewards: (i) intrinsic, and (ii) extrinsic.

Intrinsic rewards are given to a person by himself for good performance. They include feeling of having accomplished something worthwhile. Porter and Lawler believed that intrinsic rewards are subject to fewer disturbing influences and thus are directly related to good performance. This connection is shown in the model by semi-wavy line.

Extrinsic rewards (pay, promotion, job security, status) are given by organisational because they are imperfectly related to performance. Also, the perceived equitable rewards virtually affect the performance–satisfaction relationship. This variable refers to the amount of reward an individual feels he should receive as a result of his performance.

> If Ahmad and Javid are paid Rs. 500 for similar job. But Ahmad feels that he does the job better than Javid. Ahmad may not be satisfied with the reward he is receiving from organisation.

Porter and Lawler viewed satisfaction as a deficiency measure. Thus where:

Actual rewards > Perceived rewards = Satisfaction results in

Actual rewards < Perceived rewards = Dis-satisfaction results in.

4. Satisfaction. Satisfaction is derived from the extent to which actual rewards (i) fall short, (ii) meet, or (iii) exceed the individual's perceived equitable level of rewards. If actual rewards (i) meet, or (ii) exceed perceived equitable rewards, an individual feels satisfied. If these are less than equitable rewards, he will feel dis-satisfied. Thus, it provides two implications:

(a) Satisfaction is only determined by actual rewards.

(b) Satisfaction is more dependent on performance than performance is on satisfaction.

Significance of the Porter and Lawler Model

Porter and Lawler's model is of great significance to managers. Since it makes them sensitive to focus attention on the following to keep their employees motivated:

1. Put the right person on the right job, i.e., match (i) abilities, and (ii) traits of individuals to the requirements of the job.
2. Carefully explain to employees what their role is, and make sure they understand it.
3. Prescribe in concrete terms the actual performance expected of the individuals (output quantity, number of customers to be serviced, number of customers complaints that will be tolerated); and
4. Make sure that the rewards dispended are valued by the employee i.e., find out what rewards are attractive to the employee and see if such rewards can be given to them.

7. Goal Setting Theory

Goal setting is one of the most effective and widely practiced theories of motivation in organisations. Goals are the immediate or ultimate objectives that employees are trying to accomplish from their work effort. Goal setting is the process of motivating employees and clarifying their role perceptions by establishing performance objectives. Actually goal setting potentially improves employee performance in two ways, viz.:

- by stretching the intensity and persistence of effort; and
- by giving employees clearer role perceptions so that their efforts are channeled towards behaviour that will improve work performance.

Goal setting is widely used to motivate employees. Some companies apply goal setting through a formal process known as Management by Objectives (MBO). The MBO process starts with goal setting, when managers and employees define and focus on job goals rather than on (i) rules, (ii) activities, and (iii) procedures. The goal setting stage involves identifying specific areas of job responsibility, developing the standards for measuring performance and even formulating a work plan for achieving the goals. Certain guidelines should be provided to the managers and the team leaders on how to set goals. These will include:

- State what is to be done in the form of a job description.
- Be specific about what parameters will be used to measure performance.
- Specify what is to be the performance standard.
- Clearly indicate the time period in which the goals are to be reached.
- Prioritise the goals in terms or order of (i) importance, and (ii) difficulty.

Effective Goals: Characteristics

Goal setting is more complex than simply telling someone to "do your best". Instead, organisational behaviour scholars have identified five conditions, shown below that are necessary to maximize task effort and performance:

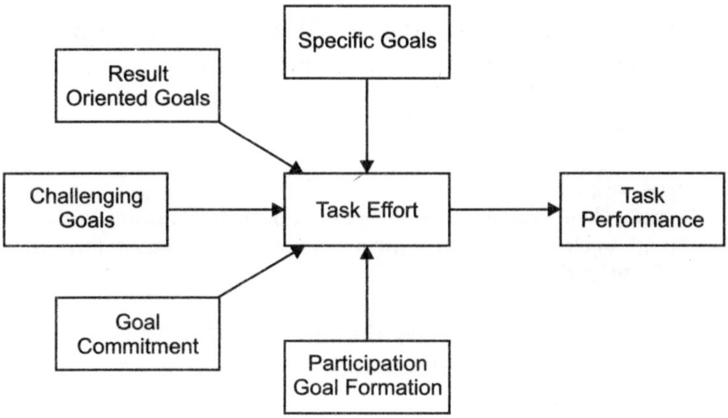

Characteristics of effective goal setting

Specific Goals

Employees put more effort into a task when they work towards specific goals rather than "do your best" targets. Specific goals have measurable level of change over a specific time, such as, reduce scrap rate by 7 per cent over the next six months. Specific goals communicate more precise performance expectations, so employees can direct their effort more (i) efficiently, and (ii) reliably.

Result Oriented Goals

Result oriented goals improve work performance more than process oriented goals. A result oriented goal is one that directly refers to the person's job performance, such as, the number of customers served per hour. Process oriented goals refer to the work processes used to get the job done.

> An example of a process oriented goal would be finding one way to reduce the time for customers to describe their problems.

Research indicates that these process oriented goals encourage employees to think about difficult way to get the job done, but they seem to block them for choosing one method and getting on with the job. Therefore, results oriented goals tend to be more effective.

Challenging Goals

Employees tend to have more (i) intense, and (ii) persistent work effort when they have challenging rather than easy goals. Challenging goals also fulfil a person's need for achievement or growth needs when the goal is achieved.

> Some organisations, such as General Electric and Daimler Cryssler, like to use, "Stretch" goals–goals that are challenging enough to stretch the employee's abilities and motivation towards peak performance.

Stretch goals are effective if employees receive the necessary resources to accomplish them and do not become over-stressed in the process.

Goal Commitment

Of course, there are limits to challenging goals. At some point, a goal becomes so difficult that employees are no longer committed to achieve it. At that point, work effort falls dramatically.

Another influence on goal commitment is an employee's self-efficiency. As we know that self-efficacy employees have a "can do" attitude. They are confident that they can perform the tasks facing them. There are evidences that high self-efficacy employees are more likely to accept their goals because they believe they can choose successful strategies to reach those goals. Those with low self-efficacy, can the other hand, tend to be in a panic when given a unique goal where the means to achieve that goal is not obvious.

Participation in Goal Formation

Another way to build or maintain commitment to goals is to ensure that employees are involved in the goal setting process. Participation in goal formation tends to increase goal commitment because employees take ownership of the goal, compared to goals that are merely assigned by supervisors. In fact, today's workforce increasingly expects to be involved in goal setting and other decisions that affect them.

Participation may also improve goal quality, because employees have valuable information and knowledge that may not be known to these who initially formed the goals.

> Some organisations have employees throughout a work area review the unit's future goals.

This process ensures that employees are busy in those goals and have the competencies and resources necessary to accomplish them.

Goal Feedback

Feedback is another necessary condition for effective goal setting. As we know feedback is a powerful source of learning. In terms of goal setting, feedback lets us know whether we have achieved the goal or are properly directing our effort towards it. Feedback is also an essential ingredient in motivation because our growth needs cannot be satisfied unless we receive information on goal accomplishment.

CASE STUDY

What Do They Want?

Mike Riverer is Vice President of manufacturing and operations of a medium size pharmaceutical firm in the Midwest. Mike has a Ph.D. in Chemistry, but has not been directly involved in research and new product development for twenty years. He is from the "school of hard knocks" when it comes to managing operations, and he runs a "tight ship". The company does not have a turnover problem, but it is obvious to Mike and their key management personnel that the hourly people are only putting in their eight hours a day. They are not working anywhere near their full potential. Mike is very upset with the situation because, with rising cost, the only way that the company can continue to prosper is to increase the productivity of its hourly people.

Mike called on his personnel manager and laid it on the line. "What is it with our people, anyway?" Your wage surveys show that we pay near the top in this region, our conditions are tremendous and our fringes choke a horse. Yet these people still are not motivated. What in the world do they want? The personnel manager replied, "I have told you and the President time after time that money, conditions and benefits are not enough. Employees also need other things to motivate them. Also, I have been conducting some random confidential interviews with some of our hourly people, and they tell me that they are very discouraged because, no matter now hard they work, they get the same pay and opportunities for advancement as their co-workers who are just scraping by." Mike then replied, "Okay, you are the motivation expert, what do we do about it? We have to increase their performance."

DISCUSSION POINTS

1. Explain the "motivation problem" in this organisation in terms of the content models of Maslow, Alderfer and Herzberg. What are the "other things" that the personnel manager is referring to in speaking of things besides money, conditions and fringe benefits that are needed to motivate employees?

2. Explain the motivation of the employees in the company in terms of one or more of the process models. On the basis of the responses during the confidential interviews, what would you guess are some of the expectancies, valances, inequities and attribution of the employees in this company? How about Mike? Do you think he is internally or externally controlled?
3. How would you respond to Mike's last question and statement if you were the personnel manager in this company?

QUESTIONS

- Define motivation. Why is it a critical issue of interest to managers in organisations? Identify the difference among motives, motivating and motivation.
- Compare and contrast:
  (a) Maslow's Theory of Motivation.
  (b) Alderfer's ERG Theory of Motivation.
  (c) Herzberg's Two Factor Theory of Motivation.
- Examine:
  (a) Carrot Stick Approach Theory of Motivation.
  (b) Theory X, Theory Y, and Theory Z of Motivation.
- Give a detailed account of:
  (a) Vroom's Expectancy Theory of Motivation,
  (b) Porter and Lawler Expectancy Theory of Motivation, and
  (c) Goal Setting Theory.
- "High achievers often strike others as being unfriendly and 'loners'. They are very quiet and never talk about their accomplishments. They are realistic about their abilities and do not allow other people to get in the way of their goal accomplishment." Discuss in the light of MeClalland's basic characteristics of high achievers.
- Name two outcomes in your job or classroom that have negative valance for your personality. How does

knowledge of these helps you while trying to motivate people?

- Elaborate some organisational problems you may come across. What different motivation models you may use to resolve the same? Discuss the potential problems in using these models.
- Describe the difficulties that are encountered when managers use motivation theories (e.g., equity and expectancy), that rely on subjective employee responses. What do you suggest under such a situation?
- Do you agree that the negative or fear of motivation produce lasting positive effects on behaviour and morale? Support your reasons.
- The basic premise of need theories is that human motivation is caused by:
  (a) Goal deficiencies;
  (b) Reinforcement;
  (c) Need definitions;
  (d) Satisfaction;
  (e) Rewards.
- High need achievers:
  (a) Want immediate and specific feedback.
  (b) Tend to select goals of extreme difficulty.
  (c) Offer no reluctance to delegate responsibilities.
  (d) Select goals that are unattainable.
  (e) Frequently take jobs in areas like research and development.

Job Stress

6

Learning Objectives

- Meaning and Definitions of Stress
- Factors Causing Stress
- Causes of Stress
- Consequences of Stress
- Coping Strategies of Job Stress
- Stress and Job Performance

STRESS–MEANING

Stress, as per the medical explanation of the term, is the body's general response to environmental situations i.e. stress is anything that changes our (i) physical, (ii) emotional, or (iii) mental state while encountering various stimuli in our environment. It is, usually, thought in negative terms caused by something bad.

1. A loved one is seriously ill.
2. The boss gives a formal reprimand for poor performance.

This is a form of distress. But there is also a positive and pleasant side of stress caused by good things.

An employee is offered promotion at another location.

This is a form of eustress. This term was coined by the pioneers of stress research from the Greek 'eu' which means good.

Stress is viewed by many people in a number of different ways, viz.:

Stephen P. Robbins defines stress as:

"*A dynamic condition in which an individual is confronted with an (i) opportunity, (ii) constraint, or (iii) demand related to what he or she desires and for which the outcome is perceived to be both (i) uncertain, and (ii) important.*"

Fred Luthans defines stress thus:

"*An adaptive response to an external situation that results in (i) physical, (ii) psychological, and/or (iii) behavioural deviations for organisational participants.*"

According to T.A. Beehr and J.E. Newman, stress is:

"*A condition arising from the interaction of people and their jobs and characterised by changes within people that force them to deviate from their normal functioning.*"

It is also important to know what stress is not.

1. Stress is not Simply Anxiety

Anxiety operates solely in the (i) emotional and (ii) psychological sphere, whereas stress operates there and also in the physiological sphere. Thus, stress may be accompanied by anxiety, but the two should not be equated.

2. Stress is not Simply Nervous Tension

Like anxiety, nervous tension may result from stress, but the two are not same. Unconscious people exhibit stress, and some people keep it "bottled up" and not reveal it through nervous tension.

3. Stress is not Necessarily Something Damaging, Bad or to be Avoided

Eustress is not damaging or bad and is something people should seek out rather than avoid. The key, of course, is how a person handles the stress. Stress is inevitable, distress may be prevented or can be effectively controlled.

STRESS–FACTORS

Before we go into the factors determining the stress in individuals, it would benefit if we are familiar with the term 'fight or flight response" which comes as a part of a reaction.

Fight or Flight Response

Numerous changes occur in the human body during a stress reaction. Breathing and heart rates alter, brain wave activity goes up and hearing and sight become momentarily more acute when faced with stressed situations or environment, the natural reaction would be the fight (attack back) or flight (flee from the scene). Such natural body reactions are known as the fight or flight response. However, this term may not be very apt in work situations.

> A subordinate is asked to do an unpleasant work assignment at any cost. As per the fight or flight response, the employee may prefer to physically assault his boss or make a noiseful and nasty exit from the office, either of which will be inappropriate actually. In reality, the subordinate inspite of not liking the assignment, will be expected to calmly make a good job of it.

There are primarily four factors which may make individuals feel stressful as shown in the below given figure:

The Effect of Stressor(s) on Stress at the individual level

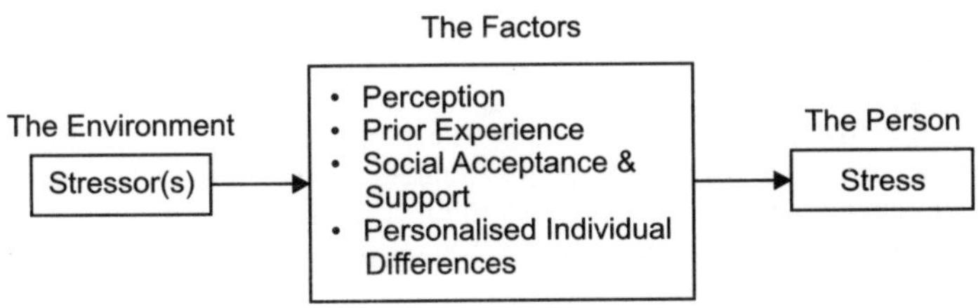

Perception

We know perception is a psychological process by which a person or employee selects and organises environmental information into a concept of reality. Employee perceptions of a situation can influence how (or whether) they experience stress.

> Two employees (under probation) who joined the concern together, one day receive notification from their managers to work on two different assignments. The first employee perceives this assignment to be a challenging one and is happy about the management's confidence in him. In contrast, the second employee perceives that the management is unhappy with his performance and hence has given a difficult assignment.

Prior Experience

A person may perceive a situation as more or less stressful, depending on how familiar that person is with the situation and prior experience with the particular stressors involved. Prior experience or training may allow some employees in an organisation to deal (i) calmly and (ii) competently with stressors that would greatly intimidate (i) less experienced or (ii) inadequately trained employees. The relationship between (i) experience and (ii) stress is based on reinforcement. Positive reinforcement or previous success in a similar situation can reduce the level of stress that a person experiences under certain circumstances, punishment or past failure under similar conditions can increase stress under the same circumstances.

Social Acceptance and Support

The presence or absence of other people (may be colleagues, superiors, etc.), can have influence on the way an individual experiences stress at workplace and reacts or responds to the stressors.

> If a person is happy working with his coworkers or colleagues, their presence may increase his confidence enabling him to cope effectively with the stressful situation. Conversely, if a person is uncomfortable working with his colleagues, their presence may work on his nerves, disturbing him and thereby making him incapable of coping with the situation.

Personalized Individual Differences

Individual differences in (i) motivation, (ii) attitudes, (iii) personality, and (iv) abilities also influence whether employees experience stress and if they do, how they respond to it. Simply stated, people are different. What one person considers a major source of stress, another may hardly notice. Personality characteristics, in particular, may explain some of the differences in the ways that employees experience and respond to stress.

> If we were to discuss the personality factor labeled 'Agreeableness' it can be said that this factor will indicate the individual responses to various stressors at the workplace. The person who is at one extreme (warm, tactful, considerate), can cope better to work stressors than an unpopular person because he displays traits which may be at the other extreme (cold, independent, rude).

STRESS–CAUSES

The antecedents of stress, or the so-called "stressors" impacting on employees are shown hereunder. These causes come from both (i) outside and (ii) inside the organisation. These come from the (i) groups and (ii) employees themselves.

1. Extra Organisational Stressors

Most analysis of job stress ignore the importance of outside forces and events that have a tremendous impact on employees. Taking an open system perspective of an organisation (i.e. the organisation is greatly affected by the external environment), it is clear that job stress is not just limited to things that happen inside the organisation during working hours. Researchers identify extra organisational stressors such as (i) societal, (ii) family, (iii) economic, (iv) financial, and (v) residential conditions, etc.

A person's family has a big impact on personality development. A brief crises in the family such as (i) the illness of a family member or (ii) long strained relations with the spouse can act as a significant stressor for employee.

Sociological variables such as (i) race, (ii) sex, and (iii) class can also become stressors. Sociologists have noted, over the years, that "have nots" may have more stressors than "haves". More recently, research has found that women competing in a male dominated environment, in most organisations, are under constant stress than men. The same is true of the local community or regions that one comes from.

2. Organisational Stressors

Besides the potential stressors that occur outside the organisation, there are also stressors within the organisation itself. Though, the organisation is made up of (i) individuals and (ii) groups, there are also more macro-level dimensions, unique

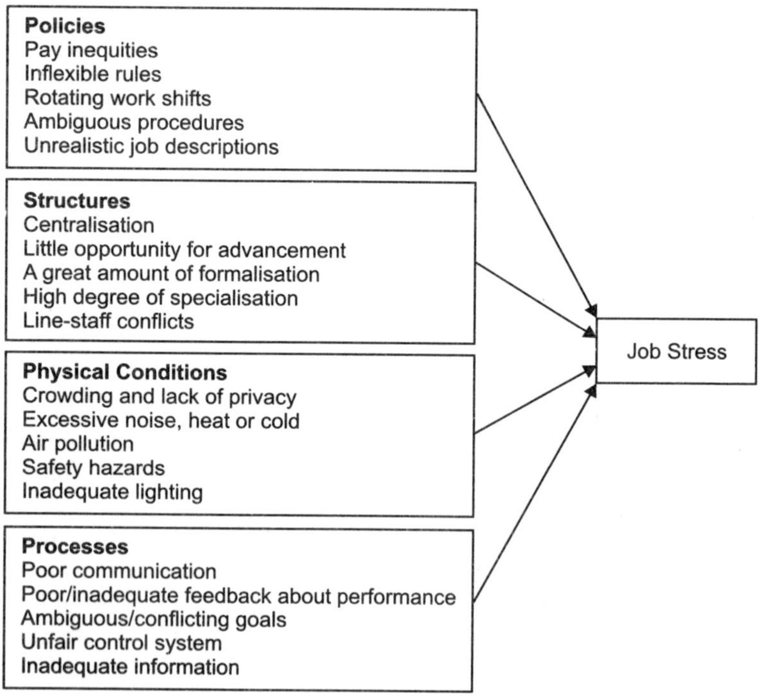

to the organisation, that contains potential stressors. These macro-level stressors can be categorised into:

3. Group Stressors

The group can also be a potential source of stress. These group stressors can be categorised into three areas. It has become empirically clear from flow studies also.

(a) Lack of Group Cohesiveness

Empirically, it has become very clear (from Hawthorne studies) that cohesiveness, or "togetherness" is very important to employees, especially at the lower levels of organisations. If an employee is denied the opportunity of cohesiveness because of

- the task design;
- the supervisor wishes to prohibit or limit it;
- the members of the group want the person out,

this can be very stress producing.

(b) Lack of Social Support

Employees are greatly affected by the support of (i) one or (ii) more members of a cohesive group. By sharing their (i) problems and (ii) joys with others, they feel much better. If this type of social support lacks for an individual, it can be very stressful.

(c) Interindividual, Interpersonal and Intergroup Conflicts

Conflict is very closely linked to stress. Conflict is normally associated with incompatible or hostile acts between interindividual dimensions, such as (i) personal goals or (ii) motivational needs between individuals (i) within a group and (ii) between groups. It can be said that such conflicts can lead to considerable stress for individuals.

4. Individual Stressors

The other stressors (extraorganisational, organisational and group) all eventually get down to the individual level. There is also more research and agreement on individual level stressors. Although there are many possible individual stressors, three areas are mentioned above recognised more than others.

Role Characteristics

Individual employees have multiple roles (family, work, professional, religious, community, etc.), and these often make (i) conflicting demands and (ii) create conflicting expectations. They can experience such role related stresses, viz.:

- Role Conflict
- Role Ambiguity
- Role Overload

(a) **Role Conflict.** Role conflict is experienced when two or more executives in the organisation expect different things to be done by the individual.

> If Mr. Siva's immediate supervisor wants him to credit the day's receipts to one particular account and the department manager wants Siva to credit it to another account, Mr. Siva would experience role conflict since there are conflicting expectations from his two bosses.

(b) **Role Ambiguity.** Role ambiguity results from inadequate information or knowledge to do a job. This ambiguity may be due to (i) inadequate training, (ii) poor communication, or (iii) deliberate withholding of information by a coworker or superior.

(c) **Role Overload.** Role overload refers to that an individual is expected to do many things as part of daily routine.

> If Mr. X is expected to perform the duties of a (i) supervisor, (ii) receptionist, (iii) public relations person. He is likely to experience a lot of stress from the several roles he has to play during the working day. Though he may be able to manage the various roles for a short period, if expected to continue like this for a long period, he is likely to fall sick or quit.

5. Job Stress

The nature of the job performed by the individual can often cause stress. If a job is too (i) routine, (ii) dull, and (iii) boring, or there are frequent transfers which limits the time that can be spent together with the family, the individual is likely to experience stress. Some jobs are (i) hazardous or (ii) morally conflicting to the individual who interfaces with it, such as working in an explosives manufacturing factory for the individual who is advocate of peace. For lack of other job opportunities, the individual is forced to work in this environment and this might be a constant source of severe stress and anguish to the person.

There are certain stressors at the workplace which may cause stress for the employees, they are known as work stressors. Such forms of work stressors are mentioned here under:

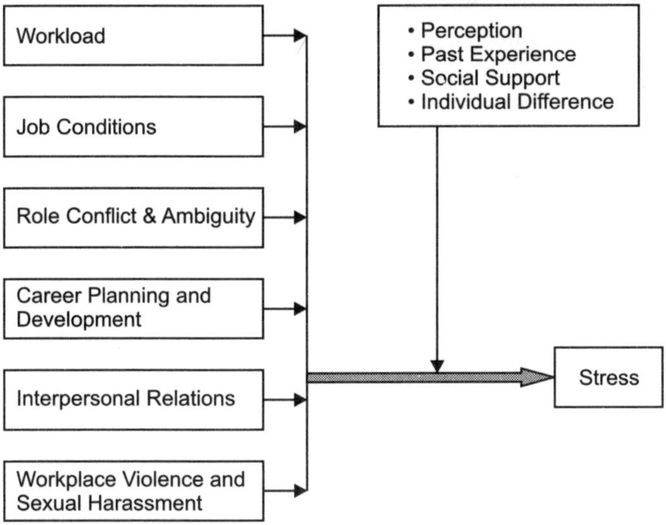

Workload

For many people, having too much work to do and not enough time or resources to do it can be stressful. Role overload exists when demands exceed the capacity of a manager or employee to meet all of them adequately. For stress is the human body's general response to any demand made on it. Many stressful jobs may be in a continuous condition of role overload. Surveys commonly identify work overload or "having to work too hard" as a major source of stress.

Having too little work to do also creates stress. Managers sometimes are guilty of trying to do their subordinates' work, or micro-manage, when their jobs are not challenging enough. Micro-managing might reduce the manager's stress caused by boredom, but it is likely to increase subordinates' stress as he is likely to be constantly under their boss's eye.

Job Conditions

Poor working conditions represent another important set of job stressors. Temperature extremes, loud noise, too much or too little lighting, radiation and air pollution are but a few examples of working conditions that can cause stress in employees. Job performance deteriorates, sometimes markedly, when these environmental stressors are present. Moreover, their effects are cumulative overtime. An associated problem is the requirement of having to travel long distances to reach the place of work. With city and town extensions, a very common sight is that today people are forced to travel long distances in order to reach their place of work. The long distances commuting coupled with long hours of work can also prove to be stressful for the employees.

Role Conflict and Ambiguity

Differing expectations of or demands on a person at the workplace produce role conflict. Role ambiguity occurs when an employee is uncertain about assigned job duties and responsibilities. Role conflict and role ambiguity are particularly significant sources of job related stress. Many employees suffer from role conflict and ambiguity, but conflicting expectations and uncertainty particularly affect managers. Having responsibility for the behaviour of others and a lack of opportunity to participate in important decisions affecting their jobs are other aspects of employees roles that may be stressful.

Career Planning and Development

The past liberalisation scenario in India has seen many of the business organisations going for reorganisation and downsizing to keep in line with the industry demands. Such restructuring of jobs, work teams, departments or entire organisations can have many career related (especially career planning and development) concerns for the employees. One shall be able to perform competently in the new job situation. Is one's new job secure? What are ones future job prospects in terms of career growth? And so on. Typically, employees find these concerns stressful.

Interpersonal Relations

Groups and teams have a major impact on the behaviour of people in organisations. Good working relationships and interactions with (i) peers, (ii) subordinates, and (iii) superiors are crucial aspects of organisational life, helping people achieve (i) personal and (ii) organisational goals. When relationships are poor, they can become sources of stress.

> A study of clerical employees indicated that intrusions by others–interruptions from noisy coworkers, ringing telephones and other people walking into and around their work stations–were a principal source of stress.

A high level of political behaviour, or "office politics" may also create stress for managers and employees. The nature of relationship with coworkers may influence how employees react to other stressors. In other words, interpersonal relationships can be either (i) a source of stress or (ii) social support that helps employees cope with stressors.

Workplace Violence and Sexual Harassment

Aggressive behaviour that causes actual physical or psychological harm to an employee is classified as workplace violence. Extreme cases may end with physical combat resulting in assaulting, ignorance of safety rules and accidental deaths. Such display of workplace violence (especially in heavy industries), may not only result in low productivity but will be a major source of work stress for the employees that needs to be understood and managed.

The second form of overly aggressive behaviour in the workplace is sexual harassment. Sexual harassment is unwanted contact or communication of a sexual nature. Research reveals that 30 per cent of female employees reported that they had been the object of unwanted sexual advances, prepositions or discussions at work. As with workplace violence, this problem seems to be growing. Management clearly has a strong responsibility to do everything in its power to prevent sexual harassment from occurring. When it does occur, it needs to be dealt with firmly. Some practical suggestions for managers who have to deal with this disruptive issue include the following:

- Take all complaints about sexual harassment seriously.
- Publish a policy strongly condemning sexual harassment.
- Inform all employees of their (i) rights and (ii) responsibilities under the policy.
- Develop a proactive complaint procedure that provides means for filling a complaint.
- Immediately respond to any complaint and investigate it with (i) objectivity, (ii) confidentiality, and (iii) due process.
- Discipline managers and employees involved in sexual harassment.
- Keep thorough records of (i) complaints, (ii) investigations, and (iii) actions taken.

STRESS–CONSEQUENCES

The problems due to high levels of stress can be summedup into three general categories, viz.:

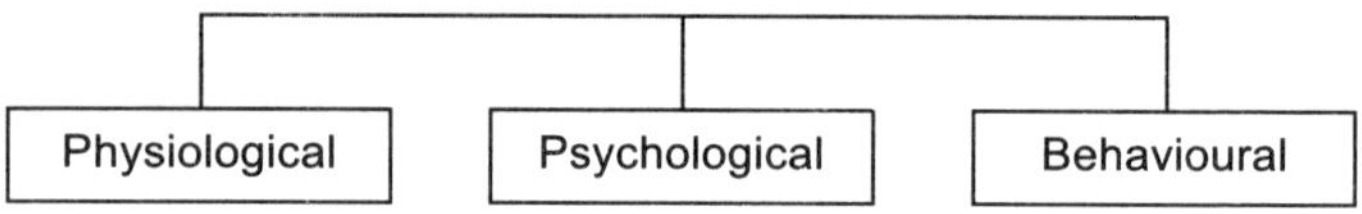

1. Physiological Problems

The basic research over the years, have been devoted to the impact that stress has on physical health. A high level of stress is accompanied by (i) high blood pressure, (ii) heart diseases, (iii) ulcers, etc. There may be even a link between stress and cancer.

Obviously, such serious physical ailments have adverse effect on the individual, not always so obvious, but just as serious are the effects that physical problems such as heart disease can have on the organisation. However, stress can contribute to this dreaded disease and to other physical problems as well.

2. Psychological Problems

Stress can cause dissatisfaction. Job-related stress can cause job-related dissatisfaction. Job dissatisfaction, in fact is the simplest and most obvious psychological effect of stress. But stress shows itself in other psychological states–for instance (i) anger, (ii) anxiety, (iii) depression, (iv) irritability, (v) tension, and (vi) boredom.

Research indicates that when people are placed in jobs that make (i) multiple and conflicting demands or (ii) in which there is lack of clarity in duties, authority and responsibility, both stress and dissatisfaction are increased. Moreover, jobs that provide a low level of (i) variety, (ii) significance, (iii) autonomy, (iv) feedback, and (v) identity to employees create stress and reduce satisfaction and involvement in the job.

3. Behavioural Problems

Behavioural analysis are helpful in analysing the effects of job stress. Behaviourally related stress symptoms include changes in (i) productivity, (ii) absence, and (iii) turnover. They also include undereating or overeating, sleeplessness, increased smoking and drinking.

There has been a significant research investigating the stress–performance relationship.

One company had the problems of on-the-job drinking and it brought a breath-alcohol meter to test its employees.

Like the physiological and psychological problems resulting from stress, the behavioural problems can be (i) prevented and (ii) controlled by the individual and the organisation.

JOB STRESS–COPING STRATEGIES

Generally speaking there are two major types of coping strategies for dealing with job stress, viz.:

- Individual Coping Strategies
- Organisational Coping Strategies

1. Individual Coping Strategies

Today, when (i) self-help remedies, (ii) do-it-yourself approach, (iii) weight loss clinics and diets, (iv) health food, and (v) physical exercise are being given so much attention in the mass media and when people are taking responsibility for their own wellness, individual coping strategies for dealing with stress make sense.

An individual can take personal responsibility for reducing his stress level. Some specific techniques that individuals can use to (i) eliminate or (ii) effectively manage inevitable stress include the following:

(a) **Exercise.** Today, it is not whether we win or lose, but whether we get some good exercise or not. People of all ages, are (i) walking, (ii) jogging, (iii) swimming, or (iv) riding bicycles in order to get some exercise to combat stress. This seems to make a great deal of sense, and many lay people and physicians confirm it firmly. There is still no evidence that exercise will directly reduce the chances of heart disease. But there seems little doubt that it can help people to cope with stress.

(b) **Relaxation.** Individuals can teach themselves to relax through techniques such as (i) take it easy, (ii) meditation, or (iii) bio-feedback. The objective is to reach a state of "deep relaxation", where one feels physically relaxed, somewhat detached from the immediate environment and detach from body sensations. Fifteen or twenty minutes a day of deep relaxation releases tension and provides a person with noticeable sense of peacefulness. Whether it can have a practical impact on job stress is yet to be determined.

(c) **Behavioural Self-control.** Behavioural self-control refers to, "those behaviours that an individual deliberately undertakes to achieve self-selected outcomes. The individual employee selects the goals and implements the procedures to achieve these goals".

> Sales Managers who have regular customer complaints could change the antecedents by having an assistant who would allow only exceptional complaints to reach them. They could also manage the consequences by rewarding themselves with an extra break when they remain calm after interacting with an angry customer. Besides managing their own behaviour to reduce stress, they can avoid (i) people or (ii) situations that they know will put them under stress.

In other words, this strategy involves individuals controlling the situation instead of letting the situation control him.

(d) Networking. A recent finding that has come out of social psychology research is that people will benefit from social support. Applied as a strategy to reduce job stress, this would involve having (i) friends, (ii) family, or (iii) work colleagues who are good listeners and confidence builders who provide support when stress levels become excessive. Today, if such connections are developed, they are called networks.

The relationship between "social support" and "stress reduction" appears complicated. There is some research evidence that a networking strategy may be able to help people to cope with stress. It will be more effective and successful for managers.

2. Organisational Coping Strategies

Organisations coping strategies are designed by management to eliminate or control organisational level stressors in order to prevent or reduce job stress for individual employees. The organisational stressors (i) policies, (ii) structures, (iii) physical conditions, and (iv) processes follows that these areas would be the focus of attention in developing organisational coping strategies.

In addition to working on each specific organisational stressors mentioned above, more generalized strategies might include the following:

(a) Create a Supportive Organisational Climate. Most large organisations, today, have highly formalized structures accompanied by inflexible impersonal climates. This can lead to job stress. A coping strategy would be to make the structure more (i) decentralized and (ii) organic, with participative decision-making and upward communication. These (i) structural and (ii) process changes would create a more supportive climate for employees and would reduce their job stress.

(b) Enrich the Design of Tasks. Enriching jobs either by improving job content factors such as (i) responsibility, (ii) recognition, and (iii) opportunities for achievement, advancement and growth or by improving core job characteristics such as (i) skill variety, (ii) task identity, (iii) autonomy, and (iv) feedback may lead to reduce stress, because these factors give the employee greater control over work and lessen dependence on others.

But not all employees want enriched jobs because (i) low growth needs or (ii) fear of failure will lead him to increased stress. However, careful managing of task design may be an effective way to cope with job stress.

(c) **Reduce Conflict and Clarify Organisational Roles.** Role conflict and ambiguity are major individual stressors. It is upto the management to reduce the conflict and clarify organisational roles so that this cause of stress can be reduced. Each job should have clear information and support so that employees are not left with ambiguous understanding of what he is to do. A specific role clarification strategy would be that the person occupying a role should obtain a list of expectations from each role sender. This list should be compared with the person's expectations and any difference would be openly discussed to clarify ambiguities and negotiated to resolve conflict.

(d) **Plan and Develop Career Paths and Provide Advice.** Organisations have shown only passing interest in career (i) planning and (ii) development of their employees. Individuals are left to decide career moves and strategies themselves and get paternalistic advice once from a supervisor. This situation is similar to the students at a large university where only their names exist on adviser's computer printout sheet, which contains the names of hundreds of advices, without knowing (i) what their next move is or (ii) how they are going to make it. This obviously can be a source of (i) uncertainty and (ii) stress for both the students and professors.

An organisational coping strategy to reduce this type of stress would be to set up a career (i) planning and (ii) development process. This could range all the way from a (i) total, (ii) comprehensive, (iii) organisational entry-to-exit approach at one extreme, to a self-guided workbook at the other.

STRESS AND JOB PERFORMANCE

While examining the relationship between stress and job performance it can be said that there are both (i) positive, and (ii) negative effects. A typical relationship between performance and stress is displayed in the below mentioned figure:

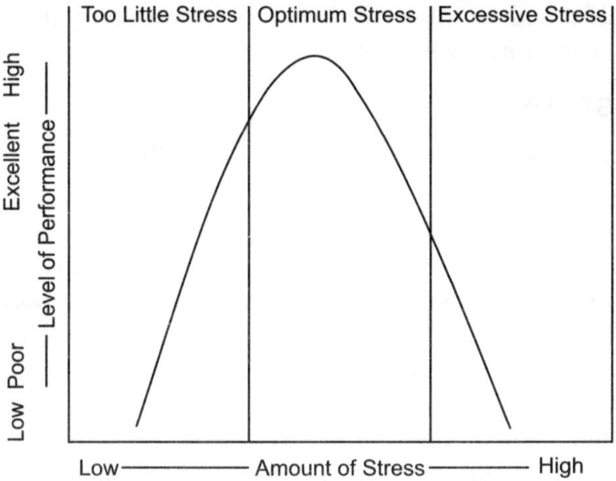

Typical Relationship between Performance and Stress

The figure depicts that at low levels of stress, employees may not be sufficiently (i) alert, (ii) challenged, or (iii) involved to perform at their best. As the curve indicates, increasing a low amount of stress may improve performance–but only upto a point. An optimal level of stress probably exists for tasks. Beyond that point, performance begins to deteriorate. At excessive levels of stress, employees are too (i) agitated, (ii) aroused, or (iii) threatened to perform at their best.

Generally, managers often want to know the optimum stress points for both themselves and their subordinates. This information, however, is difficult to pin down accurately.

> An employee may be absent from work frequently because of boredom (too little stress) or because of overwork (excessive stress).

Also the curve in figure changes with the situation, that is, the curve varies for different people and different tasks, i.e. the stress experienced while performing a particular task by an individual may vary when he is required to perform another task. Thus, ideally the superior must identify the level of stress required for each individual employee to perform well and then motivate him to perform accordingly. Also it is necessary for (i) superiors and (ii) subordinates to identify ways to reduce the magnitude and number of stressors in order to increase the overall team's performance.

CASE STUDY

Sorry, No Seats are Left; Have a Nice Flight

Jim Miller has been a ticket agent for Friendly Airlines for the past three years. This job is really getting to be a hassle. In order to reduce the mounting losses that Friendly has suffered in recent months, management have decided to do two things: (i) overbook their flights so that every seat possible will be filled and (ii) increase their service to their customers and live up to their name. Jim, of course, is at the point of application of this new policy. When checking in passengers, he is supposed to be very courteous and friendly, and he has been instructed to end every transaction with the statement. "Have a nice flight."

The problem, of course, is that sometimes there are more passengers holding confirmed reservations checking in than there are seats on the plane. Rightfully, these people become extremely upset with Jim and sometimes scream at him and even threaten him. During these confrontations Jim becomes "unglued". He breaks into a sweat and his face turns bright red. The company guidelines on what to do in these situations are very vague when Jim called his supervisor for advice. He was simply told to try to book passengers on another flight, but be friendly.

DISCUSSION POINTS

1. Is Jim headed for trouble? What would be some physical, psychological, and behavioural outcomes of this type of job stress?
2. What could the company do to help reduce the stress in Jim's job?

3. What individual coping strategies could Jim try in this situation?

QUESTIONS

- Define the term stress. Discuss the causes and consequences of job stress. What are its coping strategies?
- Differentiate between:
  (a) distress and eustress.
  (b) role ambiguity and role conflict.
- Bring out the impact of stress on (i) performance and (ii) satisfaction.
- Explain in detail the physiological, psychological and behavioural responses to stress.
- "Mild stress is desirable and essential for individual and organisational performance." Discuss.
- How does responsibility for people become a source of stress? Would this stress be reduced if employees were made more responsible for their own activities? Support your answer.
- Indicate the correct responses against the following multiple choice questions:
  - Performance, absenteeism and turnover are examples of:
    (a) stress,
    (b) attitude,
    (c) behaviours,
    (d) cognitions,
    (e) intentions.
  - A task demand factor that may cause organisational stress is:
    (a) conflict,
    (b) ambiguity,
    (c) overload,
    (d) personalities,
    (e) temperature.

PART III

Group Dynamics

7

Learning Objectives

- Definition, Features and Importance of Groups
- Meaning of Group Dynamics
- Theories and Model of Group Formation
- Types of Groups and Group Relevant in Organisation
- Understanding of Group Versus Work Teams
- Types of Work Teams
- Components for Creating Effective Work Teams

GROUPS–DEFINITION

In general, a number of people together at a given (i) place and (ii) time are considered as a group. People in a bus or students in a class are all known as groups. However, from organisational point of view, a group has a different meaning and definition.

Marvin Shaw opines:

"*A group consists of two or more persons who interact with one another in such a manner that each person (i) influences and (ii) is influenced by one another.*"

This definition has two key elements which deserve clarification:

– the "interaction" among group members:

> Coworkers work side by side on related tasks, but if they do not interact with each other, in organisational sense, they are not a group.

- the influence of one member on other group members. This means that the group members are mutually dependent with respect to the attainment of common goals.

Stephen P. Robbins defines the term group as:

"*Two or more individuals, interacting and interdependent, who have come together to achieve particular objectives.*"

Homans, G.C. defines the term group as:

"*Any number of people who share goals, often communicate with each other over a period of time, and are few enough so that each individual may communicate with all the others, person-to-person.*"

With this background, we define the term group:

"*Group is the combination of (i) two or (ii) more people with a purpose of achieving their common and shared goals through their integrated effort.*"

GROUPS–FEATURES

Analysis of the definitions provide us the following features of groups, viz.:

- Combination of two or more individuals.
- Individuals are motivated to come closer (i) physically, and/or (ii) virtually.
- They come closer to achieve their common and shared goals.
- Group members achieve their common goals through integrated efforts.
- Perceive the group as a unified unit.
- Members contribute different inputs (like skills, knowledge and efforts) in different amounts towards the achievement of group goals and
- Reach agreements and disagreements through various forms of interaction.

In the modern days of information technology, people come together physically and/or virtually for several purposes or due to various forces. In addition, people join groups to get various kinds of benefits.

GROUPS–IMPORTANCE

There is no single reason, why individuals join groups. Since most people belong to a number of groups, it is obvious that different groups provide different benefits to their members. The popular reasons for joining a group are related to our needs for:

Security	Self-esteem	Affiliation	Power	Goal Achievement

1. Security

"*There is strength in numbers.*" By joining a group, employees can reduce the insecurity of "standing alone". They feel (i) stronger and are (ii) more resistant to threats. New employees join groups for (i) guidance and (ii) support. They get reassurance from interacting with others and being part of the group.

If management creates an environment in which employees feel insecure, they usually make unions to reduce their feeling of insecurity.

2. Self-esteem

Groups can provide people a feeling of self-worth. That is, in addition to convey status to those outside the group, membership can also give increased feelings of worth to the group members themselves. Our self-esteem increases, when we are accepted by a highly valued group.

> Being assigned a task whose purpose is to (i) review and (ii) make recommendations for the location of the company's new head office can fulfil one's needs for (i) competence, (ii) growth, and (iii) status.

3. Affiliation

Groups can fulfil our social needs. People enjoy regular interaction with group members. For many people, interaction on the job are their primary source of fulfilling their affiliation needs. For almost all people, work groups significantly contribute to fulfilling their needs for (i) friendship and (ii) social relations.

4. Power

One of the appealing aspects of groups is that they represent power. What often cannot be achieved individually becomes possible through group action. Of course, this power should not be used to make demands on others. It may be described merely as a counter measure. In order to protect themselves from unreasonable demands by management, individuals align with others.

Informal groups provide opportunity to individuals to exercise power over others. For individuals who desire to influence others, groups can offer power in the organisations. So, for people with a high power needs, groups can be a vehicle for fulfilment.

5. Goal Achievement

> A three person team studying how they can cut their company's transportation costs which have gone up over 30 per cent a year for several years now, so the corporate controller choose representatives from (i) cost accounting, (ii) shipping, and (iii) marketing to study the problems and make recommendations.

This task group was created to achieve a goal that seems difficult if pursued by a single person. There are times when it takes more than one person to accomplish a particular task. There is a need to pool (i) talents, (ii) knowledge, or (iii) power in order to get a job completed. In such instances, management will rely on the use of a formal group.

GROUP DYNAMICS–MEANING

Groups are inevitable as a norm and part of working in organisations and as a significant unit of sociology contributes immensely to the understanding of organisational behaviour. Hence, while using the concept of a group in organisational behaviour, the focus will be upon the dynamics of the (i) formal and (ii) informal group members in an organisation.

The man responsible for popularizing the term '*group dynamics*' was Kurt Lewin way back in the 1930's. There are several views, which essentially interpret this differently. Few of such significant perspectives on group dynamics are mentioned hereunder:

- The normative view interprets group dynamics as an attempt to describe, "*how a group should be organised and conducted*". As per this view democratic leadership, member participation and overall cooperation are emphasized.
- Another view contributes as a set of techniques and equates it with (i) role playing, (ii) leaderless groups, (iii) group therapy, (iv) sensitivity training, (v) team building, (vi) transactional analysis, and (vii) Johari window.
- Yet another view is from the perspective of the internal nature of groups, how they are formed, their structures as well as processes, how they work and impact individual members, other groups and the organisation.

GROUPS–FORMATION

Why do individuals form into groups? Or why people affiliate with one another? There are many factors that influence the formation of the group.

The basic theory explaining affiliation is 'propinquity'. This interesting word simply means that:

"Individuals affiliate with one another because of (i) spatial or (ii) geographical proximity."

> The students in a class sitting next to one another are more likely to form groups than students sitting at opposite ends of the room.

The theory predicts that in an organisation, employees who work in the same (i) plant, (ii) office, or (iii) managers with offices close to one another would probably form into groups than those who are not physically located together. There is some research evidence to support the propinquity theory and on that ground it has a great deal of merit for explaining group formation.

A more comprehensive theory of group formation than mere propinquity comes from George Homans. This theory is based on (i) activities, (ii) interactions, and (iii) sentiments. These three elements are directly related to one another.

The more activities persons share, the more will be their interactions and stronger will be their sentiments. This theory lends a great deal to the understanding of group formation and process.

The major element is "interaction". Persons in a group interact with one another, not because of physical propinquity sense, but also to (i) solve problems, (ii) attain goals, (iii) facilitate coordination, and (iv) reduce tensions. In an organisation participants interacting in this manner tend to form powerful groups.

Another theory of group formation is 'balance theory' proposed by Newcomb. The Theory states that:

"*Persons are attracted to one another on the basis of similar attitudes towards common relevant (i) objects and (ii) goals.*"

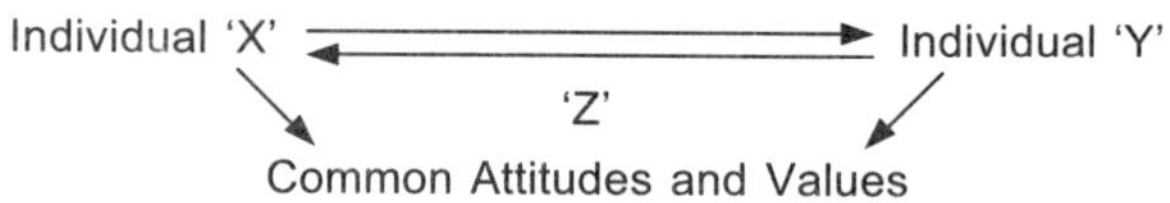

- Religion
- Politics
- Lifestyle
- Marriage
- Work
- Authority

Individual 'X' will interact and form relationship/group with individual 'Y' because of common attitudes and values (Z).

Once this relationship is formed, the participants strive to maintain a balance between the (i) attractions and (ii) common traits. If an imbalance occurs, an attempt is made to restore the balance. If the balance cannot be restored, the relationship dissolves. Both (i) propinquity and (ii) interaction play a role in balance theory.

Exchange Theory. This theory works on the reward-cost outcome interactions. According to this theory a minimum positive level (which means that reward should be greater than costs) of an outcome must exist for attraction or affiliation to take place. Rewards from interaction will satisfy needs, whereas costs will incur (i) anxiety, (ii) frustration, (iii) embarrassment, or (iv) fatigue.

GROUPS–TYPES

From an organisational behaviour viewpoint, there are basically two types of groups:

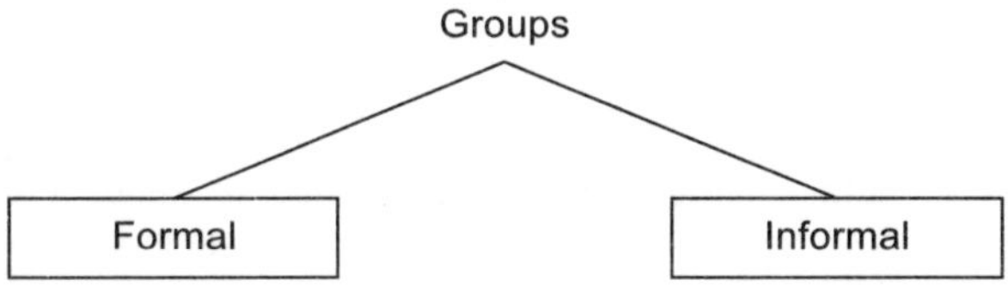

1. Formal Groups

A group is formal when it is consciously and deliberately designed to accomplish an organisational objective or task. It is created by a formal authority for some defined purpose. Group of Production Manager, Materials Manager and Quality Control Manager of a company is an example of formal group.

2. Informal Groups

Informal Groups are created in the organisation because of (i) social and (ii) psychological forces operating at the work-place. They emerge naturally in response of the common interests of organisational members. They exist outside the formal authority system and without general rules and regulations of the organisation.

> Three employees from (i) production department, (ii) marketing department, and (iii) finance department gather in the company's meeting hall and discuss current economic issues. This is an example of informal group.

Besides above mentioned types of groups, there are many designated groups in the modern organisations.

3. Command Group

A Command Group consists of a manager and his/her subordinates. The (i) membership and (ii) structure of command group are formally determined and are represented on the organisation chart. The manager is granted formal authority over the other members of the Command Group.

4. Task Group

The Task Group is formally designed to work on a specific (i) project or (ii) job. Its interaction and structure are formally designed to accomplish the task. However, a task group's boundaries are not limited, it can cross command relationships. It should be clear that all command groups are also Task Groups.

> Human Resource Manager, Finance Manager and Production Manager form a negotiation group in order to settle a salary dispute of factory workers. This negotiation group is an example of Task Group.

5. Interest Groups

People who may not be similar to common (i) Command, or (ii) Task Groups may attain a specific objective with which each is concerned. Besides persons are attracted to one another on the basis of similar attitudes towards common relevant (i) objects, and (ii) goals. This is an Interest Group.

6. Friendship Groups

Groups often develop because the individual members have (i) one or (ii) more common characteristics. We call these formations Friendship Groups. Often, formal organisational arrangements do not satisfy the important social needs. Organisations participate (i) join and (ii) form friendship groups in order to satisfy their needs for affiliation.

> Two employees from Production and Marketing Department with a common character of work avoiding, making friendship and form a group to defend each other's behaviour is called a Friendship Group.

7. Primary Groups

If the individuals with a feeling of comradeship, loyalty and a commonsense of values form into a group, such a group is called a Primary Group.

> Group of family members viz., father, mother, brother and sister is an example of Primary Group.

8. Coalitions

Individuals from different groups form into an ad hoc group in order to achieve a specific task or goal. Such groups are called Coalitions. The individuals have dual membership, i.e., one in the original group and another in the coalition. The coalition gets dissolved after the goal for which it is formed is attained. The characteristics of coalition include:

- Interacting group of individuals.
- Deliberately constructed by the members for a specified purpose.
- Independent of the formal organisation's structure.
- Lacking a formal internal structure.
- Mutual perception of membership.
- Issue oriented to advance the purpose of the members.
- External forms.
- Concerted member action, act as a group.

GROUP DEVELOPMENT–STAGES

From the mid-1960's, it is believed that groups pass through a standard sequence of five stages. These five stages are:

Forming	Storming	Norming	Performing	Adjourning

1. Forming

The first stage, forming, is characterized by a great deal of uncertainty about the groups (i) purpose, (ii) structure, and (iii) leadership. Members are "testing the waters" to determine what type of behaviour is acceptable. This stage is complete when members begin to think of themselves as part of a group.

2. Storming

The storming stage is one of intra-group conflict. Members accept the existence of the group, but there are constraints that the group imposes on individuality. There is conflict over who will control the group. When this stage is complete, there is clear hierarchy of leadership within the group.

3. Norming

The third stage is one in which close relationships develop and the group demonstrates cohesiveness. There is now strong sense of group (i) identity and (ii) friendliness. This norming stage is complete when the group becomes solid and understand completely a common set of correct member behaviour.

4. Performing

The fourth stage is performing. The structure of this point is fully (i) functional and (ii) accepted. Group energy moves from (i) getting to know and (ii) understand each other to perform the task.

For permanent work groups, performing is the last stage in their development. However, for temporary task groups that have a limited task to perform, there is an adjourning stage.

5. Adjourning

The final stage in group development is adjourning. In this stage, the group prepares for break up. High task performance is no longer the group's top priority. Instead, attention is directed towards wrapping up activities. Responses of group members vary in this stage.

Many interpreters of the five stage model have assumed that a group becomes more effective as it progresses through the first four stages. While this assumption may be generally true, what makes a group effective is more complex than this model acknowledges. Under some conditions, high levels of conflict are conducive to high group performance.

Impact of Groups on Individual Employee Effectiveness

The impact of groups on individual employee effectiveness:

- Helps in learning about the (i) organisation and (ii) its environment.

- Helps in learning about oneself.
- Provides help in gaining new skills.
- Obtaining valuable rewards that are not attainable by oneself.
- Satisfying important personal needs, especially needs for (i) social acceptance, and (ii) affiliation.

Impact of Groups on Organisational Effectiveness

The impact of groups on organisational effectiveness is thus:

- Accomplishing tasks that could not be achieved by employees themselves.
- Bringing a number of (i) skills and (ii) talents together to achieve (i) complex and (ii) difficult tasks.
- Providing a vehicle for decision-making that permits (i) multiple and (ii) conflicting views to be aired and considered.
- Providing an efficient means for organisational control of employee behaviour.
- Facilitating changes in organisational (i) policies and (ii) procedures.
- Increasing organisational stability by transmitting shared (i) beliefs and (ii) values to new employees.

GROUP VERSUS WORK TEAMS

For our purpose, a group is any number of people who share goals, often communicate with one another over a period of time, and are few enough so that each individual may communicate with all the others, person-to-person.

(Homans, G.C.)

Often there is a tendency to use the terms 'groups' and 'teams' inter-changeably. But they are not the same. But since these terms are used in organisational context, both have a particular role to play.

A team may be defined as a small number of employees with complementary competencies (abilities, skills and knowledge) who are committed to common performance goals and working relationships for which they hold themselves mutually accountable.

(Henry, J.E.)

From the organisational perspective, work team is a group that interacts chiefly to share information and also make decisions so as to enable each member to perform his role with a pre-designated area of responsibility. Thus, it can be inferred that a work group's performance is a simple addition of the efforts of all its individual members (i.e., positive energy) or collective effort. The collective dynamism of the team will enhance the level of performance resulting in better results and higher effectiveness.

WORK TEAMS–TYPES

There are different types of teams in organisations:

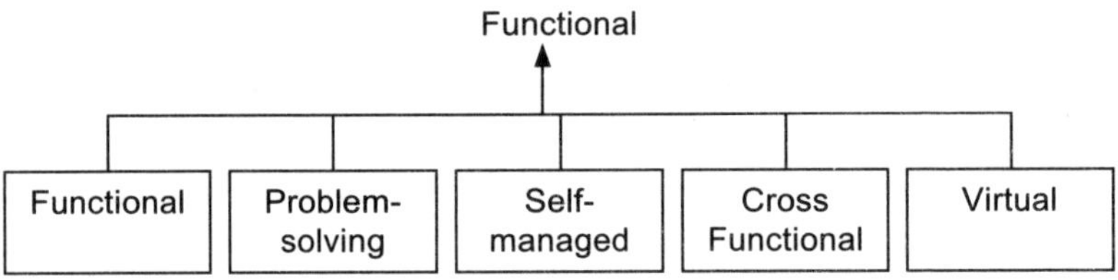

(a) Functional Teams

Such teams usually represent individuals who work together daily on a cluster of ongoing and interdependent tasks. Functional teams often exist within functional departments–marketing, production, finance, auditing, human resources, etc. Within the human resource department, one or more functional teams could operate within the recruiting, compensation, benefits, safety, training and development, affirmative action, industrial relations, and similar functions.

(b) Problem-solving Teams

Such teams focus on specific issues in their areas of responsibility, develop potential solutions and often are empowered to take actions within defined limits. Such teams frequently address quality or cost problems. Their members usually are employees from a specific department who meet at least once or twice a week for an hour or two. Teams may have the authority to implement their own solutions if they do not require major procedural changes that might adversely affect other operations or require substantial new resources. Problem-solving teams do not fundamentally reorganize work or change the role of managers. In effect, managers delegate certain problems and decision-making responsibilities to a team. This approach contrasts with delegating specific tasks and authority to individuals.

(c) Self-managed Teams

Such work teams normally consist of employees who must work together effectively daily to manufacture on an entire product, or service. These teams perform a variety of managerial tasks, such as:

- Scheduling work and vacations by members.
- Rotating tasks and assignments among members.
- Ordering materials.
- Deciding on team leadership.
- Setting key team goals.
- Budgeting.
- Hiring replacements for departing team members.
- Sometimes even evaluating one another's performance.

Each member may even learn all the jobs that have to be performed by the team. Also a sense of high level team empowerment is often created through self-managed teams.

(d) Cross Functional Teams

Such teams bring together the knowledge and skills of people from various work areas to (i) identify and (ii) solve mutual problems. Cross functional teams draw members from several specialities or functions and deal with problems that cut across departmental and functional lines to achieve their goals. U.S. Airways had designed this concept and their typical U.S. Airways team had consisted of flight crew, mechanics, ramp personnel, dispatch and reservation agents. Such across-boundary teams have the ability to solve complex problems. As companies such as Toyota, Ford and Nissan have used such teams to successfully accomplish non-conventional and huge tasks. Another company Motorola had made such functional teams comprising personnel from across the globe for its Lridium Project to develop a huge network containing 66 satellites.

(e) Virtual Teams

Functional, problems-solving, cross functional and even self-managed teams are slowly operating as virtual teams. In this age of information technology everything is gaining virtual dimensions with teams preferring to work from one computer screen to another computer screen.

> Virtual teams comprise groups of individuals, either from the same organisation or multiple organisations, who will collaborate through various information technologies on one or more projects and may be stationed at two or more locations.

Today the technology edge has enabled companies to use facilities such as the WAN (Wide Area Network), which facilitates communication with each other. Apart from WAN, video conferencing and electronic mail are the other technological aids which are being used by firms to connect across nations. Such virtual teams can make collective decisions, think together or simply solve a problem together. The core features of virtual teams include:

- There should be clear, precise and mutually agreed upon goals between virtual team members.
- All the persons involved in a virtual team need to be autonomous, self-reliant while simultaneously working collaboratively with others.
- The virtual team to function effectively needs to use technology based links such as desk top video conferencing systems, collaborative software systems and internet/intranet systems.

INFLUENCES ON TEAM EFFECTIVENESS

The influences on team and group effectiveness can be put broadly under four general categories, viz.:

Components Leading to Effective Team Performance

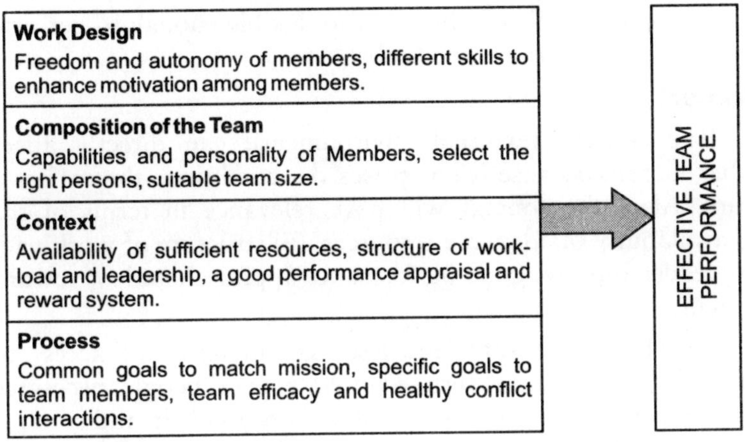

Work Design

The work design must be such that it motivates team members. It should enhance as well as increase the team's effectiveness. Such work designs should ideally enhance the freedom and autonomy of the members, provide opportunity to make use of different skills and talents, the right atmosphere to enable completion of the said task in time and working on a task or project which will have an impact on the other people.

Composition of the Team

While working on the composition of the team members, the organisation has to address the following issues:

- The capabilities of the team members in terms of (i) technical expertise, (ii) problem-solving and decision-making abilities, and (iii) good interpersonal skills.
- Personality of the team members in terms of matching the traits mentioned in Big Five Personality Model.
- Selecting members possessing the individual strengths required for performing the diverse or multiple roles in the team.
- Developing a team whose size will be suitable to allow (i) interaction, (ii) cohesiveness, (iii) commitment, and (iv) mutual authority and accountability.

- At times permitting the members to select their own team members who are also flexible enough to perform the various assigned jobs.

Context

The context (external environment), can directly affect other factors because it comprises the conditions that affect a team. Also, the context will have relevance in terms of the (i) availability of adequate resources, (ii) structure of workload, (iii) leadership, (iv) good performance appraisal, and (v) reward system.

Availability of sufficient resources in terms of access to timely information, modern technology, good people, necessary encouragement and right post, administration help and so on is very crucial and necessary if the teams have to be effective and succeed in achieving their goals.

It is very necessary for the organisation to see that the workload is shared equally among all members, the schedules are worked out keeping in mind the necessary skills required, how team has to workout and make decisions with goal leadership to integrate the individual member skills and organisational goals. The organisation also should have suitable reward system which will be based on evaluating and awarding meritorious individual contributions by considering group based appraisals. These could take the form of profit sharing, gain sharing, group incentives, etc., which will reinforce team efforts and commitment.

Process

There are also certain process variables which can contribute towards effective performance. These process variables include:

- A common goal and purpose for all the team members.
- Specific goals for each team member.
- Team efficacy so as to build up confidence amongst team members to achieve the specific and common goals.
- Healthy conflict interactions among team members will help to develop team effectiveness.

CASE STUDY

The Schoolboy Rookie

Kent Sikes is a junior at State University. He has taken a summer job in the biggest factory in his hometown. He was told to report to the warehouse supervisor the first day at work. The supervisor assigned him to a small group of men who were responsible for loading and unloading the boxcars that supplied the materials and carried away the finished goods of the factory.

After two weeks on the job, Kent was amazed at how little work the men in his crew accomplished. It seemed that they were forever standing around and talking or, in some cases, even going off to hide when there was work to be done. Kent often found himself alone unloading a boxcar while the other members of the crew were off messing around someplace else. When Kent complained to his co-workers, they made it very plain that if he did not like it, he could quit, but if he complained to the supervisor, he would be sorry. Although Kent has been deliberately excluded from any of the crew's activities such as taking breaks together or having a Friday afternoon beer after work at the tavern across the street, yesterday he went up to one of the older members of the crew and said, "What gives with you guys, anyway? I am just trying to do my job. The money is good and I just don't give a hang about this place. I will be leaving to go back to school in a few weeks and I wish I could have just trying to do my job and I wish I could have gotten to know you all better, but frankly I am sure glad I am not like you guys." The older worker replied, "Son, if you had been here as long as I have, you would be just like us."

DISCUSSION POINTS

1. Using some of the theories, explain the possible reasons for the group formation of this work crew. What type of groups exist in this case?
2. What are the major informal roles of the crew members and Kent? What status position does Kent have with the group? Why?

3. Why has not Kent been accepted by the group? Do you agree with the older worker's last statement in the case? Why or why not?

QUESTIONS

- What is a group? Discuss the various types of groups and their characteristics.
- What are the team building interventions? Describe the different stages of group formation and development.
- Differentiate between:
  (a) formal groups and informal groups.
  (b) group cohesiveness and group effectiveness.
- Explain in detail:
  (a) advantages and consequences of group cohesiveness.
  (b) advantages and disadvantages of committees.
- Elaborate:
  (a) work norms that the workers are expected to abide by.
  (b) group increases an individual's sense of power.
- "Group task influences group performance and satisfaction." Substantiate the statement.
- Priorities the issues you must address while managing a team and what steps you would initiate to build trust within a group in your organisations?
- Do you agree that some groups are more successful than others? What guidelines would you suggest for using committees and tasks groups more effectively?
- Group organised around a common interest of the members are:
  (a) relatively permanent and formal.
  (b) relatively permanent and informal.
  (c) relatively temporary and formal.
  (d) relatively temporary and informal.
  (e) formal and informal.

- When comparing a homogeneous group to a heterogeneous group a homogeneous group is likely to have more:
  (a) interaction.
  (b) conflict.
  (c) difficulty communicating.
  (d) differences of opinion.
  (e) none of the above.

Intergroup Behaviour and Conflict

8

Learning Objectives

- Meaning, Features and Significance of Conflict
- Changing Views/Approaches of Conflict
- Functions and Dysfunctions of Conflict
- Types of Conflict
- Conflict Management
- Styles of Conflict Management
- Managerial Implications

CONFLICT–MEANING

Conflict is a very (i) comprehensive and (ii) complicated concept. It can range from a mild disagreement between two individuals to a world war; often, it is couched in such colourful expressions like (i) controversy, (ii) strife, (iii) battle, and (iv) clash, etc.

There has been no shortage of definitions of conflict. But despite the divergent meanings the term has acquired an added significance. Conflict thus may mean different things to different persons. Let us consider some of them.

S.P. Robbins defines conflict as:

"*A process in which an effort is purposefully made by one person or unit to block another that results in frustrating the attainment of the others' goals or the furthering of his or her interests.*"

"*The conditions of objective incompatibility between (i) values and (ii) goals, as the behaviour of deliberately interforming with another's goal achievement, and emotionally in terms of hostility.*"

In short, it is not possible to compress the essential ingredients of conflict in a precise definition because it occurs in many different settings and may take several forms.

(a) An enemy to be defeated.

(b) A moral dilemma to be resolved.

(c) A contract to be signed.

(d) A production quota to be beaten.

CONFLICT–FEATURES

1. Conflict occurs when two or more parties pursue mutually exclusive (i) goals, (ii) values, or (iii) events. It is based on the assumption that there are two or more parties whose interests or goals appear to be incompatible.
2. Conflict arises out of two perceptions.

   > If 'X' perceives his goals to be incompatible with those of 'Y' and 'X' has no opportunity to frustrate the goal attainment of 'Y' there is no conflict.

3. Conflict refers to deliberate behaviour.

   > If 'X' deliberately tries to prevent 'Y' from attaining his (Y's) goals. If interference is accidental, there is no conflict.

4. Conflict can exist either (i) at the latent or (ii) overt level, but generally speaking, conflict is a term that is limited to overtacts.
5. Conflict is different from competition. In conflict one side sees an opportunity to interfere with the other's opportunity to acquire resources or perform activities. In competition both sides try to win, but neither side actively interferes with the other.

CONFLICT–SIGNIFICANCE

Conflict is a basic fact of life in (i) groups, and (ii) organisations. It is an inevitable feature of organisational life. The very nature of organisations guarantees the emergence of conflict. Conflict is inherent in human life. Even individuals face the problems of conflict. However, in organisational setting conflict becomes much more (i) complicated and (ii) frequent because of a number of factors:

- Organisations contain people with different (i) personalities, (ii) perceptions, (iii) attitudes, and (iv) values.
- People in organisations are assigned jobs that have (i) contrasting characters, (ii) enjoy unequal degrees of status, and (iii) frequently faster competition.
- Organisations contain groups that often have conflicting views and that must compete for scarce resources they need to achieve their goals.

Thus, conflict is an inescapable aspect of social interactions, an inevitable consequences of the interactions and inter-dependence between organisational participants.

The effective manager must understand the nature of conflict that is beneficial to the organisation and conflict that is not. He must deal with conflict in ways that promote both (i) individual and (ii) organisational goals. The conflict management is an essential prerequisite to sound human relations.

CONFLICT–CHANGING VIEWS

Attitudes towards conflict in organisations have changed considerably in the last forty years. Table that follows brings out the contrast between the traditional and modern views of conflict.

Shift in Views on Conflict

Traditional	Modern
Conflict leads to loss of individual and group temperaments, energies etc.	Conflicts encourage competition. They result in enhancing competency of individuals, groups and organisations.
Conflicts are the result of improper policies, unreasonable goals and dreams.	Conflicts are the result of the natural course of living of people, existence of teams and organisations. Therefore, they are the result of challenging goals which is the order of the day of global competition.
Conflicts impose ceiling on human potentialities as they effect the human psychology and hurt the feelings of individuals.	Conflicts tap the unused human potentialities, natural resources, etc., by creating challenge.
Conflicts destroy assets and waste the resources and erode the value of existing assets. They lead to decline in organisational and country's effectiveness.	Conflicts create the value, enhance the value and create assets. They lead to organisational and country effectiveness.
Conflicts are undesirable. Therefore, they should be avoided.	Conflicts to a moderate extent are highly desirable. Therefore, they should be encouraged to a moderate extent.

Dr. P. Subba Rao, *Management and Organisational Behaviour*, First ed., 2004.

The traditional view, relevant during the 1930s and 1940s, was that conflict in organisations was unnecessary and harmful. Early managers and management writers generally believed that the appearance of conflict was a clear signal that there was something wrong with the organisations. They thought that conflict would develop only if managers failed to apply sound management principles in directing the organisations or if managers failed to communicate to employees the common interest that bend management and employees together. If these failures were corrected, according to the traditional view, the organisations should operate smoothly.

> Taylor believed that if the principles of Scientific Management were applied, the age-old conflict between management and labour would disppear.

The traditional view of conflict started to change as organisational behaviour researchers and management writers began to identify causes of organisational conflict independent of management errors and as the advantages of effectively managed conflict started to be recognized.

The current view, also called the interactionist view, is that conflict in organisations is inevitable and even necessary, no matter how organisations are designed and operated. This view still suggests that much conflict is, in fact, dysfunctional, it can harm individuals and impede the attainment of organisational goals. But some conflicts can also be functional because it may make organisations more effective. Conflict can lead to search for solutions. Thus, it is an instrument of organisational innovation and change.

CONFLICT–APPROACHES

Over the years, three distinct philosophies that refer to different managerial attitudes towards conflict have been identified:

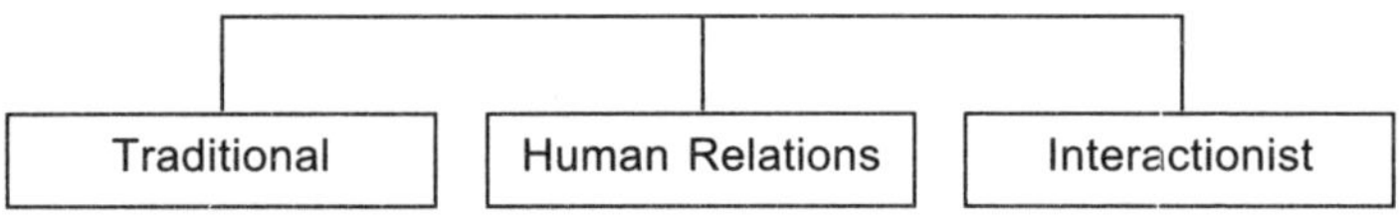

1. Traditional Approach

The traditional approach to conflict assumed that all conflict was bad. Conflict was viewed negatively. It was used synonymously with such terms as (i) anger, (ii) resentment, (iii) confusion, and (iv) lack of cooperation, etc. It was based on the following assumptions:

- conflict is by definition avoidable,
- conflict is caused by trouble makers,
- conflict disrupts the organisation and prevents optimal performance,
- the task of management is to eliminate conflict.

Management, traditionally relied on (i) formal authority, and (ii) classical organisations restructuring to solve their conflict problems. The traditional view of conflict was that it is (i) unnecessary and (ii) harmful. Conflict was considered as a clear signal of weak management.

2. Human Relations

The human relations position argued that conflict was a natural occurrence in all (i) groups and (ii) organisations. Since conflict is inevitable, the human relations school advocated acceptance of conflict. They accepted its existence. They advocated it cannot be eliminated and there are even times when conflict may benefit a group's performance.

3. Interactionist

While the human relations approach accepted conflict, the interactionist approach encourages conflict on the grounds that a (i) harmonious, (ii) peaceful, (iii) tranquil, and (iv) cooperative group is likely to become (i) static and (ii) non-responsive to needs for (i) change and (ii) innovation. The major contribution of the interactionist approach, therefore, is encouraging group leaders to maintain an ongoing minimum level of conflict enough to keep the group (i) viable, (ii) self-critical, and (ii) creative.

This approach is based on some assumptions, viz.:

- conflict is inevitable and unavoidable,
- conflict is determined by many factors including organisational structure, perceptions, values and goals,
- conflict is inherent in the nature of change,
- a minimum level of conflict is optimal.

CONFLICT–FUNCTIONS AND DYSFUNCTIONS

Conflict is inherently neither (i) good nor (ii) bad. However, depending upon its management, conflict can lead to (i) positive or (ii) negative consequences. It is important for a manager to understand both the (i) functions and (ii) dysfunctions of conflict. He has to stimulate the functional conflict and resolve the dysfunctional conflict.

Functions

Most experts, today, view conflict as a potentially useful aspect of organisations. Conflict prevents (i) stagnation, (ii) stimulates interest and curiosity. It is said that an organisation without constructive conflict is an organisation without creative (i) excitement, (ii) dynamism, and (iii) viability. The following are some positive consequences of conflict:

1. Conflicts provide opportunities to (i) individuals and (ii) groups to think again and take a more concrete view of the situation.
2. These lead to innovation as conflicting situations always present threats to the working. In order to overcome this threat, the (i) individuals, and (ii) groups have to find out new ways of working.
3. Conflicts bring cohesiveness in groups. This happens more in case of intergroup conflicts.
4. Conflicts provide challenging working environment as these develop high degree of competition.
5. As conflicts develop among various (i) individuals and (ii) groups, these indicate the shortcomings in the existing system of organisational functioning. Thus, management's attention can be drawn for overcoming such shortcomings.
6. Conflict may be used as a device to overcome many problems (i) frustrations and (ii) tensions. People may express their frustration by means of conflicts. Thus, they are relieved from utter mental tension.

Dysfunctions

The following are the negative consequences of conflicts:

1. Conflict Creates Stress in People. Intense conflict generates feeling of (i) anxiety, (ii) guilt, (iii) frustration, and (iv) hostility. It affects (i) mental and (ii) physical health of the conflicting parties. Winners try to injure the feelings of the defeated. Losers feel defeated and demeaned. The gap between people increases. A climate of (i) suspicion and (ii) mistrust develops.

2. Diversion of Energy. Group members divert their (i) energy, (ii) resources, and (iii) time towards winning the conflicts; rather than achieving the organisational objectives. Parties focus on their own narrow interests and tend to put their aims above those of the organisations. Too much (i) time and (ii) energy is drained off in trying to put out the 'fires'.

3. Instability and Chaos. Under intense conflict (i) coordination and (ii) cooperation across (i) individuals, (ii) groups, and (iii) departments decreases or vanishes. It often leads to communication breakdowns. The normal work flow is disrupted and the whole system is skewed out of balance.

4. Distortion of Perception. Group members perception of their (i) own group and (ii) opposing groups become distorted. They regard their own (i) skills and (ii) performance superior to those of other groups. They also rationalize or dismiss their own shortcomings and emphasize those of competitors.

5. Rise of Negative Stereotypes. As each side belittles the others ideas, the differences between the groups are seen greater than they actually are, while the difference with each group are seen as less than they actually are.

6. Decreased Communication. Conflict usually results in communication breakdown between groups. This can be extremely dysfunctional for the performance of the groups. The decision-making process can also be disrupted.

To conclude, conflict may have either (i) positive or (ii) negative impact on organisational performance, depending upon the nature of the conflict and how it is managed. For every organisation, there is an optimal level of conflict that can be considered highly functional, because it helps to generate positive performance. When the conflict level is too low, performance can suffer. Innovation and change are difficult on the other hand, if the conflict level becomes too high, the resulting chaos can threaten the organisation's survival.

CONFLICT–TYPES

Conflict has been categorized into different types on the basis of different criterion. However, on the basis of organisational level, conflict can be divided into following four categories, viz.:

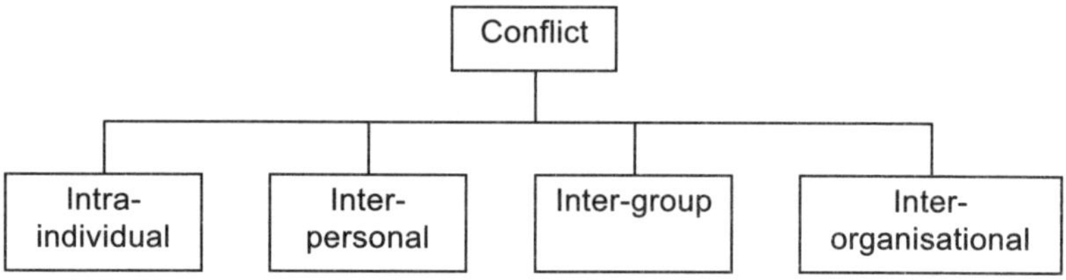

1. Intra-individual Conflict

Intra-individual conflict refers to a situation where there is an internal conflict within an individual. It is one of the most difficult and fundamental types of conflicts. It is, generally, hidden within the personality of an individual. To some extent, it is the root cause of all organisational conflicts. Intra-individual conflict could be further sub-divided into three types, viz.:

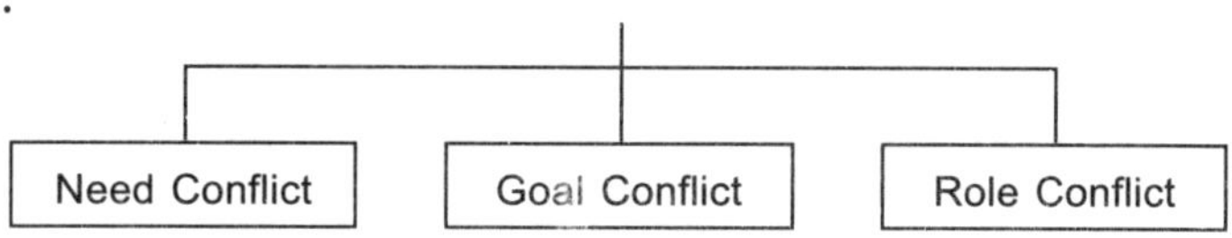

(a) Need Conflict

It is a well-known fact that each individual has a large number of (i) needs and (ii) motives. Needs lead to tensions, which in turn force a person to action or drive. Now, this action may or may not lead to the satisfaction of a particular need. Often, an individual employee is not able to satisfy a particular need, inspite of his best efforts. This situation can generate (i) frustration or (ii) conflict within an individual. Frustration can take different forms like (i) aggression, (ii) withdrawal, (iii) fixation, and (iv) compromise. Frustration occurs due to (i) overt (outward or physical) or (ii) covert (inward or mental) barriers, in the way of need satisfaction. A frustrated individual is highly prone to (i) internal and (ii) external conflicts and stress. Diagram that follows depicts the process of conflicts due to frustration.

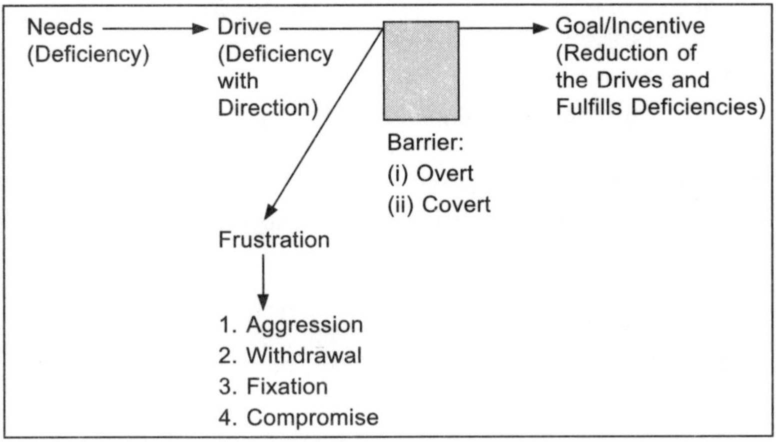

In certain situations, frustration can lead to (i) positive or (ii) negative organisational behaviour. However, in general, a major goal of management should be to eliminate the barriers that are, or will be, frustrating to employees.

(b) Goal Conflict

Another common source of conflict for an individual is a goal which has both (i) positive and (ii) negative features, or two or more competing goals. Whereas in frustration, a single need is blocked before the goal is reached. In goal conflict (i) two or (ii) more goals block one another. For ease of analysis, three separate types of goal conflicts are, generally, identified, viz.:

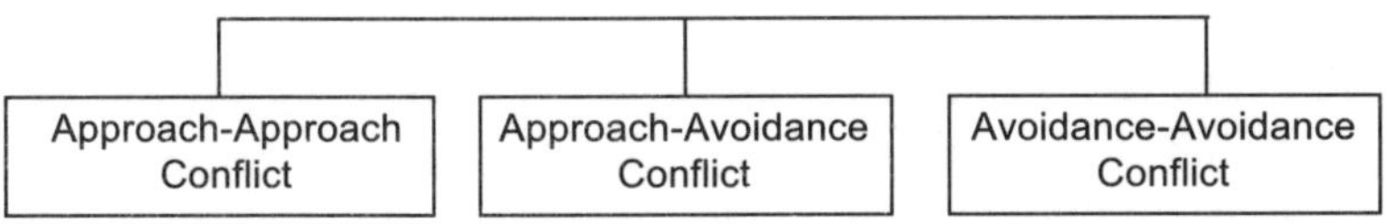

(i) **Approach-Approach Conflict.** This type of conflict may rise about making a choice between two positive goals.

> A new college graduate who is faced with two excellent job opportunities.

> An executive who has the choice between two attractive offices in which to work.

Such situations often cause the person some anxiety but are quickly resolved. This type of goal conflict probably has the least impact on organisational behaviour.

(ii) **Approach-Avoidance Conflict.** In this form of goal conflict, the person attempts to achieve a goal that has both (i) positive and (ii) negative aspects. He is attracted by the positive dimensions but dislikes and wants to avoid the negative aspects.

> Managers, usually, are engaged in long range planning typically very confidential for the future. As time gets near to implement the plan, the negative consequences seem to appear much greater.

Manager in such a situation may reach the point where approach equals avoidance. The result is a great deal of internal (i) conflict and (ii) stress, which may cause (i) indecision, (ii) ulcers, or (iii) depression.

(iii) **Avoidance-Avoidance Conflict.** Under this conflict, an individual faces the situation where he is "*between the devil and the dead sea*". In other words there are two goals before him, both of which he dislikes, but he has to choose one out of the two.

> A worker may dislike his present job, but the alternative of (i) leaving and (ii) looking for another job may be even less attractive.

(c) Role Conflict

A role is a set of expectations people have about the behaviour of a person. It is an expected mode of behaviour. An individual has multiple roles (family, work, professional, religious, community, etc.), and these often make (i) conflicting demands and (ii) create conflicting expectations. However, several other types of role conflicts may be noted.

(i) **Person-role Conflict.** This type of conflict arises when the expected behaviour is incompatible with a person's own basic (i) values and (ii) attitudes.

> Some jobs are (i) hazardous or (ii) morally conflicting to the individual who interfaces with it, such as working in an explosive manufacturing factory for an individual who is advocate of peace. For lack of other job opportunities, the individual is forced to work in this environment.

(ii) Inter-role Conflict. This type of conflict is the result of facing multiple roles. It occurs because different roles may demand conflicting behaviours.

> If Mr. X is expected to perform the duties of a (i) supervisor, (ii) receptionist, (iii) public relations person, he is likely to experience conflict from the several roles he has to play during the work day. Though he may be able to manage the various roles for a short period, if expected to continue like this for a long period, he is prone to fall sick or quit.

(iii) Intra-sender Role Conflict. This occurs when an individual is expected to perform a task within specified limits but it is not possible to behave in a manner consistent with role assignment.

(iv) Inter-sender Role Conflict. This conflict is experienced when two or more executives in the organisation expect different things to be done by the individual.

> If Mr. Siva's immediate supervisor wants him to credit the day's receipts to one particular account and the department manager wants Siva to credit it to another account, Mr. Siva would experience conflict since there are conflicting expectations from his two bosses.

2. Inter-personal Conflict

Besides the intra-individual aspect of conflict, the inter-personal aspect of conflict is also an important dynamic of interactive behaviour. Inter-personal conflict involves two or more individuals rather than one individual.

> – Two boys fighting for one cinema ticket.
> – Two managers competing for the same promotion.

Conflict between individuals in the same organisation is frequently seen as being caused by personality differences.

Inter-personal conflicts usually result in such cases where each person is trying to possess a scarce resource, which may be (i) material thing or (ii) immaterial state, such as (i) status, (ii) prestige, (iii) fame, (iv) power, or (v) money. The most commonly cited reasons for inter-personal conflicts are:

(a) Personality Differences

Some people have difficulty in getting along with others. This is purely a psychological problem and it has nothing to do with their (i) job requirements or (ii) formal interactions.

(b) Perceptions

The factors like varied (i) backgrounds, (ii) experiences, (iii) education, and (iv) training result in individuals developing different perceptions of similar realities. The result being an increase in the likelihood of inter-personal conflict.

> The belief that somebody else is out to eat away our share of resources may create ill feelings between us and that person.

(c) Clashes of Values and Interests

Conflict that commonly develops between (i) engineering and (ii) manufacturing personnel shows how differences in values might underlie conflict.

(d) Power and Status Differences

Inter-personal conflicts arise from unequal distribution of (i) power and (ii) status.

> Conflict may result in when low status employees try to give orders to high status employees.

(e) Scarce Resources

Interpersonal conflict is almost automatic. If anytime there is scarcity, conflicts over scarce resources are exceedingly common in organisations.

> If three qualified individuals aspire for superior positions in the organisation and there is only one such position, inter-personal conflict may develop to an unmanageable level.

3. Intergroup Conflict

Intergroup conflict arises out of the interaction of various groups. There are many factors in the organisation which determine the intergroup relationships. These factors can influence relations between (i) two or (ii) more groups.

Conflict occurs in groups whenever one group perceives that its attempts to accomplish its goals have been frustrated by another group. Intergroup conflicts over (i) authority, (ii) jurisdiction, and (iii) resources are exceedingly common. Every group is in at least partial conflict with every other group it interacts with. Most of the departments in the organisation compete for the allocation of (i) scarce resources and (ii) power. They differ in (i) goals, (ii) work activities, (iii) power, and (iv) prestige. The seeds of intergroup conflict are sown in their differences.

Research findings generally confirm the following types of intergroup conflict, viz.:

(a) Hierarchical Conflict

There may be conflict on the various levels of the organisation. The board of directors may be in conflict with top management, middle management may be in conflict with supervisory personnel or there may be general conflict between (i) management and (ii) workers.

(b) Functional Conflict

There may be conflict between the various functional departments of the organisation.

> If two groups in the organisation depend on one another in (i) a mutual way or (ii) even one way, there tends to be more conflict than if groups are independent of one another.

> Salesmen who depend upon their commission as a reward for their efforts may promise their customers certain quantity of the product and delivery times which the manufacturing department may find it impossible to meet, causing conflict between the two units.

(c) Line-staff Conflicts

Today line and staff differences are the most common type of intergroup conflict. This conflict is basically a clash of domains caused by dividing (i) expertise, (ii) authority, and (iii) roles. Empirical study of line and staff conflict highlighted the following sources:

- Line Managers dislike to take advice from younger staff specialists. They fear being 'shown up'.
- Line Managers label "staff" as agents on trial. The staff in turn, views himself as an expert.
- Line Managers feel that staff oversteps its authority.
- Line people resent staff's highly (i) academic and (ii) untested ideas.
- Staff feel that Line Managers are bull headed and resist new ideas.

(d) Formal-Informal Conflict

There may be conflict between the (i) formal and (ii) informal groups within an organisation.

> The informal groups may generate rumours about formal groups, which are detrimental for the organisation.

Intergroup Conflict–Characteristics

Empirical studies revealed the following characteristics of groups in conflict:

(a) There is a clear distinction and comparison between (i) "we" (the in-group) and (ii) "they" (the out-group).

(b) A group that feels it is in conflict with another group becomes more (i) cohesive and (ii) solid front to defeat the other group.

(c) The positive feelings within the in-group do not transfer to the members of the out-group. The members of the out-group are viewed as the enemy rather than neutrals.

(d) Threatened group members feel superior. They over-estimate their strength and underestimate that of members of other groups.

(e) The communication between conflicting groups decreases. When there is communication, it is characterized by negative comments and hostility.

(f) If a group is losing in conflict, the members' cohesion decreases and they experience increased tension among themselves.

(g) The intergroup conflict is not the result of sensitive tendencies on the part of individual members. This seems to be a product of group interaction, even when individuals in the group are (i) normal and (ii) well adjusted.

4. Interorganisational Conflict

The phenomena in inter-organisational conflict are much the same as those arising within an organisation. The basis of interorganisational conflicts are essentially the same as the bases of intergroup conflict. Most commonly cited reasons for interorganisational conflicts are like (i) incompatible objectives, (ii) conflicts over status, (iii) prestige, and (iv) money are present in interorganisational conflict also. However, inter-organisational conflict is more extensive, more diffuse than the conflict among (i) persons or (ii) groups.

Interorganisational conflict means a situation, where there is conflict going on between two or more than two organisations. Conflict with outside organisation usually can serve four purposes, viz.:

- It promotes closer bonds of unity among individuals within the organisation.
- It builds new life into organisational objectives and values.
- It makes the organisational members dynamic and active.
- It acts as an agency of social control.

Stagner and Rosen have identified five types of inter-organisational conflict. They are:

(a) Management-Government

Conflicts over political contributions (i) bribery, (ii) anti-trust actions, (iii) fair trade, (iv) consumer protection, (v) environmental pollution, etc., are some of the examples of conflicts between (i) organisations and (ii) government.

(b) Intermanagement

Managements of organisations may compete against each other in ways that they believe will enhance their position in the industry.

> Disputes over patents, fulfilment of contracts, price wars are common.

(c) Inter-union

Unions may compete for (i) members or (ii) jobs, as in jurisdictional disputes.

(d) Union-Government

The unions will be scrutinized by agents of government for illegal activities like (i) criminal activities, (ii) illegal strikes, etc.

(e) Union-Management

Conflict is essential for survival of the union; lack of conflict would weaken it. Conflict between (i) labour and (ii) management is expressed in many forms like (i) strikes, (ii) grievances, (iii) negotiations, (iv) absenteeism, etc.

CONFLICT MANAGEMENT

Conflict may be harmful to an organisation, but there are times when it is useful. It is for this reason that managers must learn to recognize the differences between (i) constructive and (ii) destructive conflict situations.

Since, conflict has (i) constructive and (ii) destructive consequences, it must be (i) analysed and (ii) managed carefully. The manager should seek a level of conflict appropriate to the existing conditions. There are basically two approaches to deal with conflict in an effective way:

- To create and stimulate constructive conflict.
- To resolve destructive conflict.

Conflict Stimulation

Conflict is not always negative. Conflict, like fire, can be a useful force when properly handled. Situations in which conflict is too low generally involve people who are afraid of 'rock the boat'. They passively accept things the way they are. When inter-group conflict is too low, it requires stimulation to generate action. Conflict stimulation techniques include:

(a) Bringing in Outsiders

A commonly used method of 'shaking up' a stagnant unit or organisation is to bring in people whose (i) background, (ii) attitudes, and (iii) managerial styles vary significantly from existing employees. This is to ensure a diversity of viewpoints and generation of change.

(b) Going Against the Book

Excluding (i) individuals or (ii) groups from communication to which they are officially entitled or adding new groups to the information network, may redistribute power in the organisation and this stimulates conflict.

(c) Restructuring the Organisation

Changing the structure of an organisation is an excellent way of creating conflict. Breaking up old work groups and departments to reorganize them so that they have new (i) employees or (ii) responsibilities will create uncertainties that call for readjustment immediately. Conflict that develops during this period may ultimately lead to improved methods of operation as members try to adjust to new circumstances.

(d) Encouraging Competition

Offering (i) bonuses, (ii) incentive pay, and (iii) awards for outstanding performance will stimulate competition. Such incentives, when administered properly, foster a competitive spirit among individuals and groups. Conflict will be productive as one group struggles hard to out do the other.

(e) Selecting Appropriate Managers

Some work-groups may be even passive because their managers are too authoritarian and do not allow opposing viewpoints to be raised. Other groups may need an active manager to shake them out of their lethargy. Finding the right manager for the particular group can encourage useful conflict where none exists.

(f) Communication

Managers can manipulate message in such ways as to stimulate conflict. Ambiguous or threatening messages encourage conflict. Such information can stimulate functional conflict in a department and improve performance. Carefully planted rumours also can serve a useful purpose. Playing "devil's role" in inter-personal communication can also stimulate conflict.

Conflict Resolutions

Conflict resolution is generally required when the conflict level is very high in the organisation and it is producing dysfunctional behaviour. There are three types of conflict resolution methods, viz.:

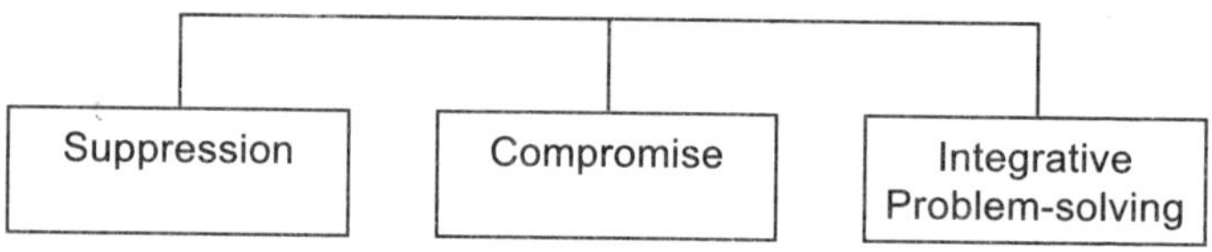

1. Dominance and Suppression

Dominance and suppression methods usually have two things in common:

- They repress conflict rather than settle it.
- They create a win-lose situation.

> Quite often managers use positional authority to fire a lower ranking subordinate they consider to be a trouble maker. The fired subordinate ends up (i) disappointed and (ii) hostile.

Suppression and dominance can be expressed in following ways:

(a) **Forcing.** The use of (i) authority and (ii) power may be the oldest and most frequently employed method for resolving intergroup conflict. Using this method management resolves the conflict as it sees fit.

It usually works in the short run. Such autocratic suppression will often lead to (i) hidden and (ii) destructive expression of conflict.

> Many professors in (i) colleges and (ii) universities have lost promotion and tenured re-appointments because they could not get along well with their respective chairpersons of the departments and had conflicts with them.

(b) Smoothing. Smoothing is a more diplomatic way of suppressing conflict. It emphasizes the common interests of the conflicting groups and deemphasizes their differences. The basic belief behind smoothing is that stressing shared viewpoints facilitates movement towards a common goal.

(c) **Avoidance.** Another method of overcoming conflict is its avoidance, i.e. parties in conflict may either (i) withdraw from the conflict or (ii) conceal the incompatibility. Withdrawal may be observed when one party leaves the field so that other party may win by being in sole possession of the goal in dispute.

Example: A person is trying to just ignore a conflict and avoiding others with whom he disagrees.

(d) **Majority Rule.** Trying to resolve group conflict by a majority vote can be effective if members regard the procedure fair. But it does not cure the root cause of conflict. Minority members still feel disappointed.

(e) **Identifying a Common Enemy.** Groups in conflict may temporarily resolve their differences and unite to combat a common enemy.

> The threat of Hitler produced an alliance between the (i) Western powers and (ii) Russia, that fell apart as soon as the common threat disappeared.

However, it is only a short-term solution of real conflict.

2. Compromise

This is a traditional method of resolving conflicts. There is no distinct (i) winner or (ii) loser because each party is expected to give up something of value for a concession.

> Sometimes employees accept a raise of Re. 1 an hour rather than Rs. 2, to acknowledge partial agreement with a specific viewpoint, and to take partial blame for an infraction.

Through compromise, managers try to resolve conflict by finding a middle ground between (i) two or (ii) more positions. From an organisational viewpoint, however, compromise is a weak conflict resolution method because it will not usually lead to a solution that will best help the organisation to achieve its goals. Special forms of conflict include:

(a) **Separation.** Under this method, opposing parties are kept apart until they agree to a solution. Physical separation may also force the parties to have an objective view of the conflict or to minimize the intensity of the conflict. Separation, sometimes may be the only solution to (i) inter-personal, or (ii) organisational conflicts.

(b) **Arbitration.** Under this method, conflicting parties submit to the judgement of a third party and the decision of the third party is binding on the conflicting parties.

(c) **Resort to Rules.** Under this method, the deadlock rivals agree to "*go by the book*" and let the rules decide the conflict outcome.

(d) **Bribing.** In case of bribing, one party accepts some compensation in exchange, for ending up the conflict.

None of these methods is very likely to leave all parties to the conflict fully satisfied nor to yield creative solutions.

3. Integrative Problem-solving

With this method, intergroup conflict is converted into a joint problem-solving solution that can be dealt with through problem-solving techniques. Parties to the conflict together try to solve the problem that has arisen between them. Instead of suppressing conflict or trying to find a compromise, the parties openly try to find a solution acceptable to all. There are several types of integrative problem-solving techniques, viz.:

(a) **Consensus.** The conflicting parties meet together to find the optimal solution to their problem, rather than trying to achieve a victory over other group. Group consensus is offered by any one individual.

(b) Confrontation. In this technique, the opposing parties express their respective views directly to each other. The reason for conflicts are examined and the methods of resolving them are sought out.

(c) Super Ordinate Goals. The establishment of super ordinate goals can also be a conflict resolution method. These goals and objectives cannot be attained without the cooperation of groups involved.

(d) Expansion of Resources. A major cause of intergroup conflict is limited resources. Groups within the organisation vie for budget funds, space, supplies, etc. Expanding resources is a very successful technique for solving conflicts in many cases. In reality, however, resources usually are not easily expandable.

(e) Membership Rotation. Exchange of people between interdependent departments creates an atmosphere where the newcomer can exchange his views with others. It helps him to see the real picture and his role in it.

(f) Reduce Interdependence. The potential for conflict is very great in situations where two departments have to work in an interdependent fashion. One way to resolve such conflict is to reduce interdependence by providing departments with resources that are independent of those provided for other departments.

(g) Liaison Groups. To arbiter differences between two conflicting groups a full time integrator can be appointed, who can speak the language of both the parties.

(h) Altering the Human Variable. Altering the human variables involves trying to change the behaviour of group members. The method focuses on the causes of the conflict and on the attitudes of the people involved. While this method is certainly difficult, it does centre on the causes of conflict.

CONFLICT MANAGEMENT–STYLES

There are five conflict management styles, viz.: (i) competition, (ii) collaboration, (iii) compromise, (iv) avoidance, and (v) accommodation. These five styles are presented below.

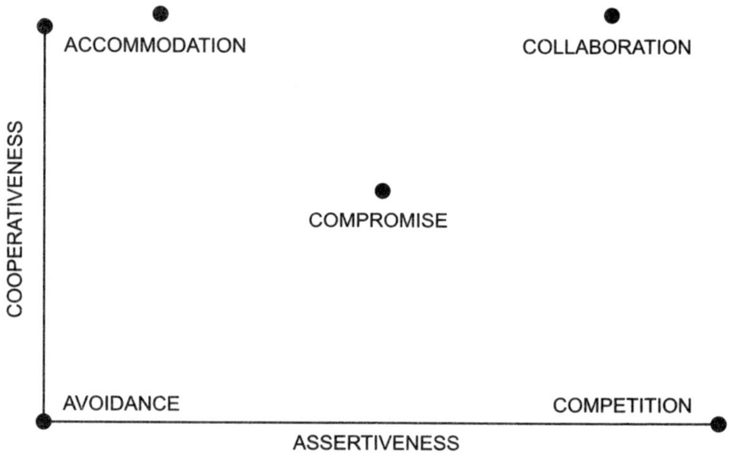

The figure classifies each style as some combination of a person's:

Cooperativeness: Desire to satisfy the other person's concerns.

Assertiveness: Desire to satisfy one's own concerns.

As is clear, only the collaboration approach scores high on both dimensions. Hence, this approach is highly effective to resolve conflict.

Table that follows outlines specific situations where each conflict resolution behaviour is more appropriate.

When to Use the Five Conflict-Handling Orientation

Conflict-Handling Orientation	Appropriate Situations
Competition	• When quick, decisive action is vital. • On important issues where unpopular actions need implementing. • On issues vital to the organisations' welfare and when you know you are right. • Against people who take advantage of non-competitive behaviour.

Conflict-Handling Orientation	Appropriate Situations
Collaboration	• To find an integrative solution when both sets of concerns are too important to be compromised. • To do when your objective is to learn. • To merge insights from people with different perspectives. • To gain commitment by incorporating concerns into a consensus. • To work through feelings that have interfered with a relationship.
Avoidance	• When an issue is trivial, or more important issues are pressing. • When you perceive no change of satisfying your concerns. • When potential disruption outweighs the benefits of resolution. • To let people cool down and regain perspective. • When gathering information supersedes immediate decision. • When others can resolve the conflict more effectively. • When issues seem tangential or symptomatic of other issues.
Accommodation	• When you find you are wrong to allow a better position to be heard to learn and to show your reasonableness. • When issues are more important to others than yourself to satisfy others and maintain cooperation. • To build social credit for later issues. • To minimize loss when you are outmatched and losing. • When harmony and stability are especially important. • To allow subordinates to develop by learning from mistakes.
Compromise	• When goals are important, but not worth the effort or potential disruption of more assertive modes. • When opponents with equal power are committed to mutually exclusive goals. • To achieve temporary settlements to complex issues. • To arrive at expedient solutions under time pressure. • As a backup when collaboration or competition is unsuccessful.

Source: K.W. Thomas, "Towards Multi-dimensional Values in Teaching: The Examples of Conflict Behaviour", *Academy of Management Review*, July 1997, p. 487.

MANAGERIAL IMPLICATIONS

At the outset a manager must understand that conflict is inevitable, nay desirable, from the point of employees (i) performance and (ii) satisfaction. Such activities as (i) hiding information, (ii) making misleading statements, (iii) postponing meetings, and (iv) advising organisational members "*not to rock the boat*" and "*to be a company man*", on the part of managers so that they need not face conflict do no good for furthering the interest of the organisation.

Realising the inevitability of conflict is not enough, managers must play a positive role to stimulate conflict. Recent developments in conflict management stress both (i) conflict stimulation and (ii) conflict reduction techniques. While the resolution strategies were discussed earlier, the stimulation techniques are stated here. Before that, signs which point out the need for conflict stimulation need to be mentioned. Following are the indicators:

- The organisation is filled with "yes men".
- Employees are afraid to admit ignorance.
- Compromise is stressed in decision-making.
- Managers put too much emphasis on (i) harmony and (ii) peace.
- People are afraid of hurting the feelings of others.
- Popularity is considered to be more important than technical competence.
- People exhibit resistance to change.
- New ideas are not forthcoming.
- There is an unusually low rate of employee turnover.

Once the need is identified, managers may adopt one or more of the following approaches to stimulate conflict:

- Encourage individualistic thinking.
- Increase individual competition.
- Provide threatening information such as reduction in profits or the loss of a competitive edge in market.
- Create role conflict.
- Change the organisational structure.

CASE STUDY

Drinking up the Paycheck

James Emery is the father of four children. He was raised in a hard working immigrant family. His needs for achievement and power were developed while he was growing up. Now he finds himself in a low paying dead end assembly like job with a large manufacturing firm. It is all he can do to get through the day, so he has started day dreaming on the job. On pay day he often goes to the tavern across the street and generally spends a lot of money. The next day he is not only hung over but also very depressed because he knows that his wife cannot make both ends meet and his children often go without the basic essentials.

Now he cannot take it any longer. At first, he thought of going to his boss for some help and advice, but he really does not understand himself well enough and he certainly does not know or trust his boss enough to openly discuss his problems with him. Instead, he went to his union steward and told him about his financial problems and how much he hated his job. The steward told James exactly what he wanted to hear. "This darn company is the source of all your problems. The working conditions are not suited for a slave, let alone us. The pay also stinks. We are all going to have to stick together when our present contract runs out and get what we deserve better working conditions and more money."

DISCUSSION POINTS

1. Explain Jame's behaviour in terms of the frustration model.
2. Cite a specific example of role conflict in this case.
3. What type of conflict resolution strategy is the union steward suggesting? Do you think the real problem facing James are working conditions and pay? Why or why not?
4. What, if anything, can be done to help the James Emery's problems of the world?

QUESTIONS

- Define conflict. What are its functional and dysfunctional consequences?
- Discuss the reasons and strategies for resolving:
  (a) Inter-personal conflict.
  (b) Intergroup conflict.
- What steps you would suggest to reduce and resolve the conflict that is:
  (a) Structural in nature.
  (b) Behavioural in nature.
- What is transactional analysis? Explain various kinds of transactions.
- "Conflict may be harmful to an organisation, but there are times when it is useful." Elaborate.
- What do you mean by "differentiation of groups"? Do you agree that differentiations become the cause of conflict among groups? Elucidate your argument.
- Have you noticed changes in the perceptions, attitudes and behaviours of group members during intergroup conflict in an organisation you are familiar with? What were the changes in relation between groups? Elaborate your response.
- Indicate the correct response against the following multiple choice questions.
  - Conflict stimulation should be used when:
    (a) Groups are comfortable with the status quo.
    (b) Conflict becomes disruptive.
    (c) The focus of the conflict is internal to the group.
    (d) Group consensus is difficult to achieve.
    (e) None of the above.

- Which of the following is true concerning the concepts of conflict and competition?
  (a) Competition and conflict can occur simultaneously.
  (b) Conflict cannot exist without competition.
  (c) Competition cannot exist without conflict.
  (d) Competition and conflict are the same thing.
  (e) None of the above.

Leadership Theories

9

Learning Objectives

- Definition and Characteristics of Leadership
- Comparison Between a Manager and a Leader
- Theories of Leadership:
  - Trait
  - Behavioural
  - Situational
- New Charismatic Theories/Models
- Transformational Leadership Model

LEADERSHIP–DEFINED

The five bases of inter-personal power suggest that power can be defined as the ability to influence another person's behaviour, where one individual attempts to affect the behaviour of a group without using the coercive form of power, this effort is described as leadership. More specifically,

> "*Leadership is an attempt to influence the activities of followers through the communication process and towards the attainment of some goal(s).*"
>
> (Edwain A. Fleishman and James G. Hunt)

This definition implies that leadership involves the use of influence and that all relationships can involve leadership.

A second element in the definition involves the importance of the communication process. The (i) clarity and (ii) accuracy of communication affect the behaviour and performance of followers.

Another element of the definition focuses on the accomplishment of goals. The effective leader may have to deal with (i) individual, (ii) groups, and (iii) organisational goals. Leader effectiveness typically is considered in terms of the degree of accomplishment of (i) single or (ii) a combination of these goals. The Figure (a) represents a model of leadership based upon the above definition.

The model summarizes the key sources and perceived bases of interpersonal power. It also presents some of the possible moderating factors between the sources and perceived basis of power and outcomes (goals). The model suggests that:

- A successful leader is one who is aware of sources of power and the importance of perceived power.

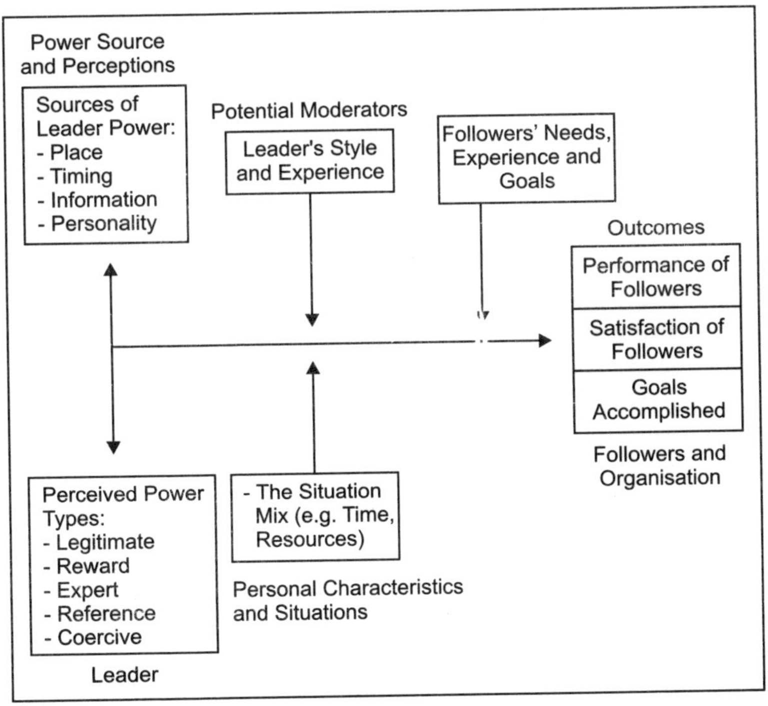

Figure (a): Model of Leadership

- The leader does not rely on coercive power.
- The sources of a leader's power include (i) place, (ii) time, (iii) information, and (iv) personality characteristics and
- The accomplishment of goals depends not only on power sources and perceptions but also on (i) followers' needs, (ii) the situation, and (iii) the experience of the leader.

LEADERSHIP–CHARACTERISTICS

The analysis of the definition of leadership gives certain basic characteristics. These are as under:

1. Leadership is basically a personal quality. This quality motivates the individuals to be with leaders.
2. Leader by exercising his leadership, tries to influence the behaviour of individuals around him to fulfil certain predetermined objectives.
3. Leader tries to influence the individual to behave in a particular way.
4. There is a relationship between (i) leader and (ii) individuals (followers) which arises out of functioning for a common goal.
5. Leadership is a continuous process of influencing behaviour.
6. Leadership is exercised in a particular situation. The situation variable also affect the effectiveness of leadership.

The above characteristics of leadership functions hold good in any organisation whether it be a (i) political, (ii) religious, (iii) business or any other organisation.

Management and Leadership–Distinction

It is a practice of some social scientists to treat "managership" and "leadership" as synonymous. However, a distinction can be made between these two terms. The key difference between these two lies in the word organisation. As a matter of fact, there can be leaders of completely unorganised groups. Leadership may be viewed as the process of influencing behaviour of an individual or group regardless of the reasons. It may be for one's own goals or a friend's goals and (i) may or (ii) may not be congruent with organisational goals. On the other hand, there can be managers only where organised structures create such roles.

Another difference in the two concepts lies in the context of scope of functions performed. A manager has to perform all the five functions of management viz.: (i) planning, (ii) organising, (iii) staffing, (iv) directing, and (v) controlling. Leadership functions come under directing through which behaviour is directed to get maximum use of subordinate's ability. Subordinates are guided by rules and requirements enforced by managerial authority. However, in this process, subordinates may work about 60-65 per cent of their capacity, just enough to satisfy the requirements for holding their jobs. To raise efforts towards total capability, the managers must induce zealous response on the part of efficient subordinates by exercising leadership. Thus, leadership is a part of management but not all of it. This implies that a strong leader can be weak manager because he is weak in planning or some other managerial duty. The reverse is also possible. That is, a manager can be weak leader and still be an acceptable manager, especially, if he happens to be managing people who have strong inner achievement drives.

Kotter draws a clear distinction between the terms leadership and management. According to him, the primary function of a leader is to carve a vision of the organisation and the strategy for attaining it. By contrast, the job of the manager is to implement the vision [see below mentioned Figure (b)].

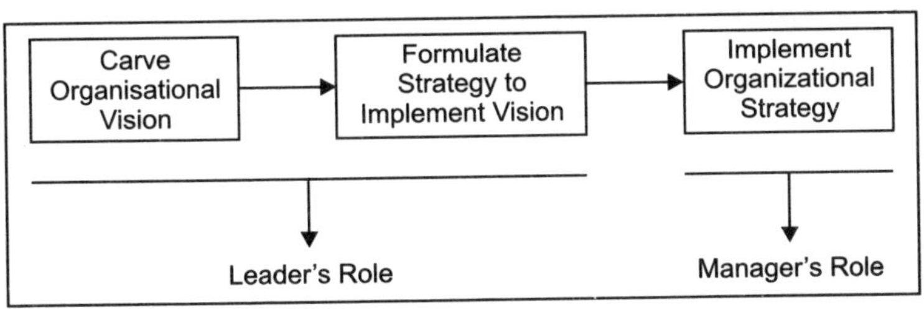

Figure (b): Model

Comparison between a Manager and a Leader

A Manager	A Leader
Thinking Process	
- Takes initiative	- Is originative
- Is more focused on issues	- Is more focused on people
- Prefers looking inward	- Looks outward
- Easily accepts reality	- Believes in investigating reality
Direction of Operation	
- Makes plans operational	- Has a vision for the future
- Tries to improve upon the existing setting	- Tries to create a new future
- Focuses on immediate financials	- Looks out for new markets
Relationship with Employees	
- Tries to gain control	- Prefers to empower people
- Considers employees as subordinates	- Treats employees as associates
- Instructs, directs and co-ordinates the efforts of the employees	- Helps employees to learn through trust and development
Mode of Operation	
- Believes in efficiency	- Believes in effectiveness
- Can deal with complexity by asking the "how" and "when"	- Embraces complexity by asking "what" and "why"
- Can manage change	- Creates change
Decision-Making/Taking	
- Decision method involves policy, rules and procedures	- Decision method involves values and principles
- Relies more on process and system	- Relies more on "ideas" and people
- Strives to achieve what's expected	- Strives to excel

LEADERSHIP–THEORIES

Various research studies, particularly by behavioural scientists, have been undertaken to find out the answer of the question: What makes a leader effective? Is his success due to his personality, or his behaviour, or the types of followers he/she has, or the situation in which he works, or a combination of all these? These researchers, however, could not give a satisfactory answer of the question. Instead these researchers have resulted in various theories or approaches on leadership, the prominent among these being:

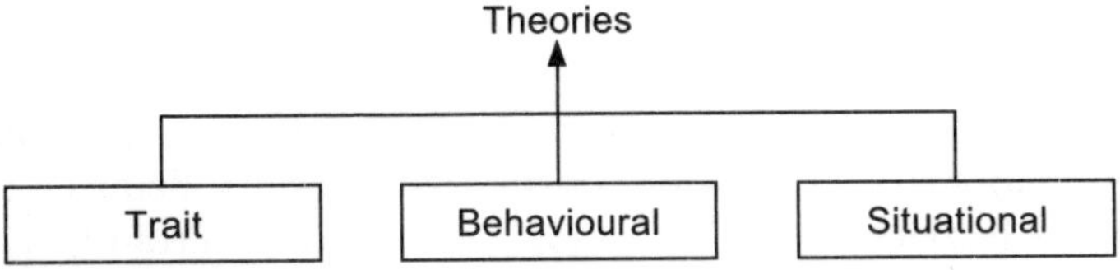

1. Trait Theories

Much of the early work (between 1930 and 1950), on leadership focused on identifying the traits of effective leaders. The approach was based on the assumption that a finite number of individual traits of effective leaders could be found. Thus, most research was designed to identify the following traits of successful leaders, viz.:

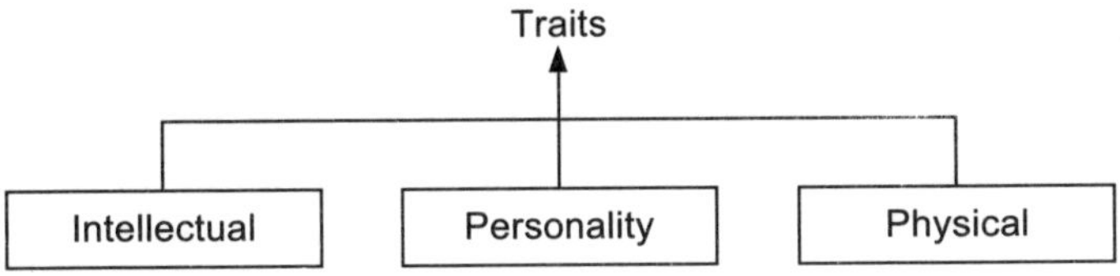

(a) Intellectual Traits

Dimensions of intelligence that have been associated with leadership effectiveness include (i) decisiveness, (ii) judgemental ability, (iii) knowledge, and (iv) verbal abilities. In a review of 35 studies, Stagdill found a general trend indicating that leaders were somewhat more intellectual than their followers, but not exceedingly more so. Extreme intelligence differences tended to be dysfunctional.

(b) Personality Traits

Some researchers suggest that personality traits such as (i) alertness, (ii) originality, (iii) personal integrity, and (iv) self-confidence are associated with effective leadership. Still other investigators identify (i) creativity, (ii) emotional balance, (iii) non-conformity, and (iv) diplomacy. A major difficulty in attempts to relate (i) personality and (ii) leadership has been finding valid ways to measure personality traits. Progress, however, although, slow is being made.

(c) Physical Traits

Studies of the relationship between effective leadership and physical characteristics such as (i) age, (ii) height, (iii) weight, and (iv) appearance provide contradictory results. Being (i) taller and (ii) heavier than the average of a group certainly is not advantageous for achieving a leader position. However, many organisations believe that a physically large person is required to secure compliance from followers. This notion relies heavily on the (i) coercive, or (iii) fear basis of power, on the other hand (i) Truman, (ii) Gandhi, (iii) Napoleon, and (iv) Stalin are examples of individuals of small stature who rose to positions of leadership.

Although traits such as these have, in some studies, differentiated effective from ineffective leaders, many contradictory findings still exist. Consequently, after years of speculation and research, we are not even close to identifying a specific set of leadership traits. Thus, the trait approach, while interesting and intuitively appealing, does not seem to be very efficient for (i) identifying and (ii) predicting leadership potential.

Trait Theory–Critical Analysis

The trait theory is very simple. However, this fails to produce clear-cut results. It does not consider the whole environment of the leadership, of which trait may be only one factor. Moreover, no generalization can be drawn about various traits for leadership as there were considerable variations in traits established by various researchers. Engeine E. Jennings has concluded:

> "*Fifty years of study has failed to produce a one personality trait or set of qualities that can be used to discriminate leaders and non-leaders.*"

In brief, this approach presents the following problems:

1. There cannot be generalization of traits for a successful leader. This was evident by various researches conducted on leadership traits.

2. No evidence has been given about the degree of the various traits because people have the various traits with different degrees.
3. There is a problem of measuring the traits. Though there are various tests to measure the personality traits, however, no definite conclusion can be drawn.
4. There have been many people with the traits specified for leader, but they were not good leaders.

This approach, however, gives indication that leader should have certain personal characteristics. This helps management to develop such qualities through (i) training and (ii) development programmes.

2. Behavioural Theories

In the late 1940's researchers began to explore the notion that how a person acts determines that person's leadership effectiveness. Instead of searching for traits, these researchers examined behaviours and their impact on the (i) performance and (ii) satisfaction of followers. Today, there are a number of well-known behavioural theories of leadership. Let us examine the more prominent among them.

The Lowa Leadership Studies–Lippitt and White or Leadership Styles

The behaviour exhibited by a leader during supervision of subordinates is known as leadership style. There are, probably, as many different styles of leadership as there are leaders. However, three styles are listed below.

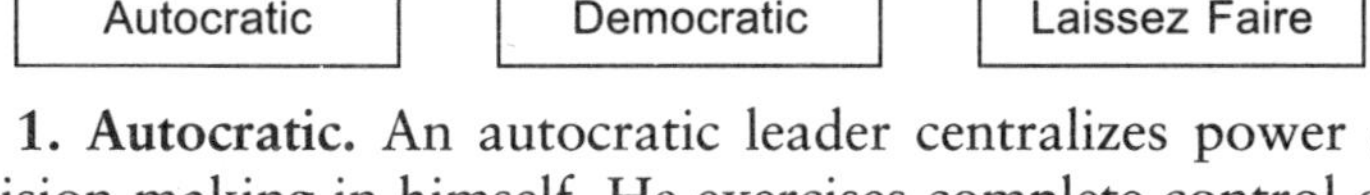

1. Autocratic. An autocratic leader centralizes power and decision-making in himself. He exercises complete control over the subordinates. He freely uses threat of punishment and penalty for disobedience. He sets the group goals and structures the work. He runs his own show. The leader gives orders and the subordinates are to follow them unquestioningly.

The problem with this style is that:

- Subordinates are made aware of (i) what to do but not (ii) why?
- It may be satisfying for the leader to dictate others continuously but for subordinates this may be totally frustrating.
- Subordinates are compelled to follow the leader's directions even though they may be wrong. And when errors creep in, they avoid responsibility since they were merely obeying.

In autocratic leadership frustration, low morale and conflict develop easily. Subordinates are induced to avoid responsibility, initiative and innovative behaviour. Moreover, autocratic leadership can be only as good as the leader is. If the leader is weak and incompetent, the followers will be weak and incompetent.

Autocratic style permits quick decision-making and hence can be applied with success in situations where:

(a) The subordinates lack knowledge of company goals.

(b) The subordinates are inexperienced.

(c) The company endorses (i) fear, and (ii) punishment as disciplinary techniques.

(d) The leader is active and dominant in decision-making, and

(e) there is little room for error in final accomplishment.

Under conditions of stress, or when great speed and efficiency are required, autocratic leadership can yield positive outcome. It can increase productivity.

2. Democratic. The democratic leader practices leadership by (i) consultation and (ii) participation. He is like a 'theory Y' leader and invites decision sharing. Here authority is decentralized. Decisions are arrived at after consultation with followers and participation by them. The participative leader attaches high importance to both work and people. This style improves (i) job satisfaction, (ii) morale of employees,

(iii) recognition of human relations, etc. In fact, no manager can perform effectively over a long period of time without some degree of employee participation.

However, there is no evidence that participation is good for everybody, when subordinates prefer minimum interaction with the leader participative style may not yield positive results. And also, over a period of time group members develop a habit of consultation, when they are not consulted, they feel insulted and become resentful and uncooperative.

Participative leadership style is appropriate where:

(a) The organisation has communicated its goals and objectives to the subordinates. And the subordinates have accepted them.

(b) Rewards and involvement are used as the primary means of motivation and control.

(c) The leader truly desires to hear the ideas of his employees before making decisions.

(d) The leader wishes to develop analytical and self-control abilities in his subordinates.

(e) The subordinates are reasonably knowledgeable and experienced.

(f) The subordinates desire active involvement in matter that affect them.

(g) The time for task completion allows for the participation.

3. Laissez Faire. Laissez Faire leadership is rather complete delegation of authority into the hands of the subordinates so that they must (i) plan, (ii) motivate, (iii) control, and (iv) otherwise be responsible for their own actions. The free rein manager avoids power and relinquishes the leadership position. He becomes, just, another member of the group.

Free rein style would seem to be appropriate under the condition where:

(a) The organisational goals have been communicated well and are accepted by the subordinates.

(b) The leader is interested in delegating decision-making fully.

(c) The subordinates themselves are (i) well trained, and (ii) highly knowledgeable concerning their tasks and are ready to assume responsibilities.

The problem with free rein style is that it tends to permit various units of an organisation to proceed at cross purposes. Hence, it should be the rare exception not a general rule.

Four Systems of Management–Rensis Likert

Rensis Likert and his associates have studied the patterns and styles of managers for many years and have developed certain concepts and approaches important to understanding leadership behaviour. The four systems proposed by Likert are called "*Systems of Management Leadership*". They are:

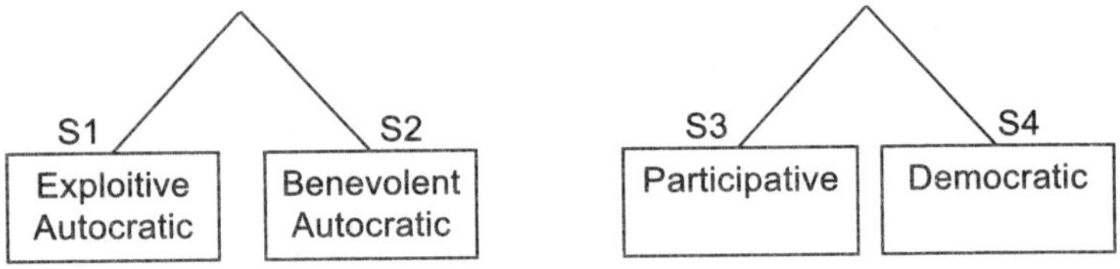

1. Exploitive Autocratic. The manager who operates under system 1 [Exploitive Autocratic] is very authoritarian and actually tries to exploit subordinates.

Leadership Variable	Exploitive Autocratic (S1)
Confidence and trust in subordinates.	Manager has no confidence or trust in subordinates.
Subordinates feeling of freedom.	Subordinates do not feel at all free to discuss things about the job with their superior.
Superiors seeking involvement with subordinates.	Manager seldom gets ideas and opinions of subordinates in solving job problems.

2. Benevolent Autocratic. The manager who operates under system 2 [Benevolent Autocratic] is also authoritarian but in a paternalistic manner. This benevolent autocrat keeps (i) strict control and (ii) never delegates authority to subordinates, but he "pats them on the head" and "does it for their best interests".

Leadership Variable	Benevolent Autocratic (S2)
Confidence and trust in subordinates.	Manager has condescending confidence and trust, such as master has in a servant.
Subordinates feeling of freedom.	Subordinates do not feel very free to discuss things about the job with their superior.
Superiors seeking involvement with subordinates.	Manager sometimes gets ideas and opinions of subordinates in solving job problems.

3. Consultative. The system 3 manager uses a consultative style. This manager receives participative input from subordinates but maintains the right to make the final decision.

Leadership Variable	Participative (S3)
Confidence and trust in subordinates.	Manager has substantial but not complete confidence and trust, still wishes to keep control of decision.
Subordinates feeling of freedom.	Subordinates feel rather free to discuss things about the job with their superior.
Superiors seeking involvement with subordinates.	Manager usually gets ideas and opinions and usually tries to make constructive use of them.

4. Democratic. The system 4 manager uses a democratic style. This manager gives some direction to subordinates and makes decision by (i) consensus and (ii) majority.

Leadership Variable	Democratic (S4)
Confidence and trust in subordinates.	Manager has complete confidence and trust in subordinates in all matters.
Subordinates feeling of freedom.	Subordinates feel completely free to discuss things about the job with their superior.
Superiors seeking involvement with subordinates.	Manager always asks subordinates for ideas and opinions and always tries to make constructive use of them.

Likert, on the basis of intensive research, has shown that high producing departments in several organisations studies are marked by system 4 (democratic). He ascribes this mainly because of (i) participation in management and (ii) supportive relationship.

Michigan Leadership Studies

At about the same time when the Ohio studies were being conducted, a group of researchers from the Survey Research Center at the University of Michigan began their studies to find behavioural characteristics of leaders which relate to measures of performance effectiveness.

The Michigan group came up with two dimensions of leadership behaviour and labeled them as:

1. Employee-oriented. Leaders who are employee oriented stress on inter-personal relations. They take a personal interest in the needs of their subordinates. They accept individual differences among members.

2. Production-oriented. The production-oriented leaders emphasize on (i) production and (ii) technical aspects of the job. Their main concern is to accomplishing tasks and the group members are considered means to that end.

The conclusions given by the Michigan researchers strongly favoured the leaders who were employee-oriented in their behaviour.

Employee-oriented leaders were associated with higher (i) group productivity and (ii) job satisfaction.

Production-oriented leaders were associated with lower (i) group productivity and (ii) job satisfaction.

Ohio State Leadership Studies

The most comprehensive behavioural theories resulted from research that began at Ohio State University in 1945. The researchers tried to identify independent dimensions of leader behaviour. Beginning with over a thousand dimensions, they identified two dimensions called:

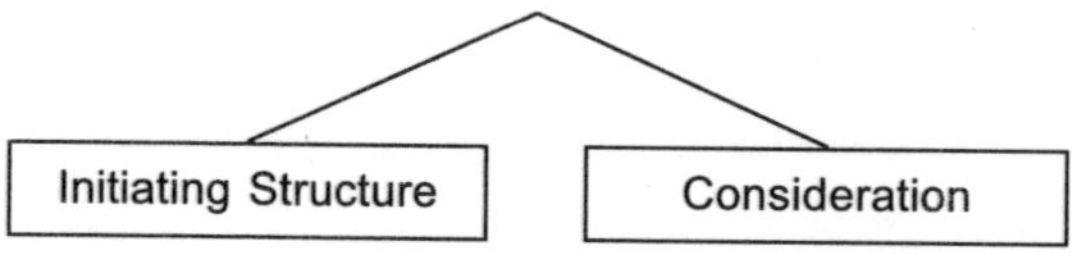

1. Initiating Structures. Initiating structure refers to the leaders, (i) define and (ii) structure the role of subordinates so that organisational goals are accomplished. It includes behaviour that attempts to (i) organise work, (ii) work relationship, and (iii) goals. The leader high in initiating structure could be described as (i) assigns group members particular tasks, (ii) expects workers to maintain definite standard of performance, and (iii) emphasizes the meeting of deadlines.

2. Consideration. Consideration refers to the ability of a leader to establish (i) mutual trust, (ii) respect for subordinates' ideas, and (iii) regard for their feelings. He shows concern for followers (i) comfort, (ii) well-being, and (iii) satisfaction. A leader high in consideration could be described as one who is (i) friendly, (ii) approachable, and (iii) treats all subordinates equally.

During research, the Ohio State scholars developed Leader Behaviour Description Questionnaire (LBDQ), that contains 15 items regarding (i) consideration and (ii) initiating structure to describe the activities displayed by the leader.

The researchers found that (i) initiating structure and (ii) consideration were independent and distinct dimensions. A high score on one dimension does not necessitate low score on the other.

Leader behaviour was plotted, for the first time, on two separate axis rather than on a single continuum. Four quadrants were developed to show (i) initiating structure and (ii) consideration in varying combinations. Figure on next page.

Extensive research, based on these definitions, found that leaders "high" in (i) initiating structure and (ii) consideration (a "high-high" leader) tend to achieve high subordinate

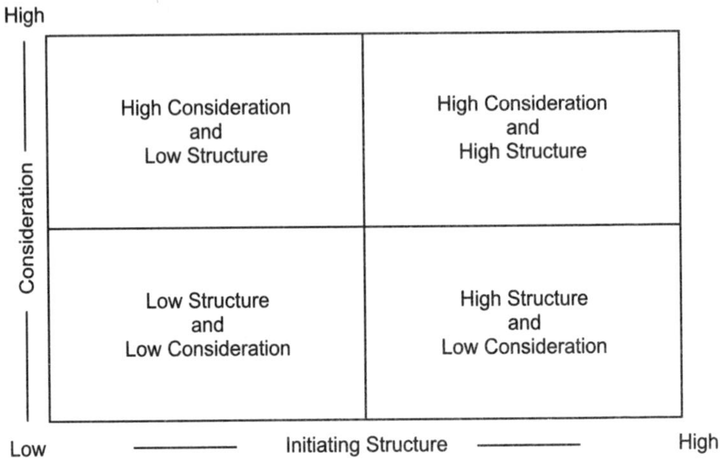

(i) performance and (ii) satisfaction more frequently than those who rated low either on (i) consideration and initiating structure or (ii) both.

In conclusion, the Ohio State Studies suggest that the "high-high" style, generally, resulted in positive outcomes.

Michigan and Ohio State Studies–Similarities

1. Both studies have accepted that leader behaviour is more complex than (i) oversimplified group of tasks and (ii) maintenance-oriented behaviour.
2. Both studies identified and stressed on performance: (i) production emphasis at Ohio, (ii) goal emphasis or high standard of production performance at Michigan.
3. Both studies found that the pattern of effective leader behaviour definitely varied with the situation.

The Managerial Grid

One of the most widely known a two dimensional view of leadership style was developed by Robert Blake and Jane Mouton. They proposed a "Managerial grid" based on the styles of:

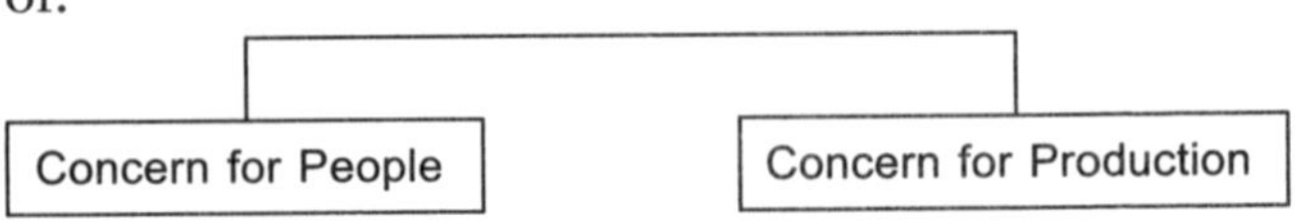

These two dimensions are, of course, equivalent to the (i) consideration and (ii) initiating structure functions identified by the 'Ohio State Studies' and (i) employee centered and (ii) production centered styles used in 'Michigan Studies'.

1. Concern for People. It is not confined to consideration of interpersonal warmth and friendliness. It covers a variety of concerns which include:

- Personal commitment to completing a job for which one is responsible.
- Accountability based on trust rather than force.
- Desire for a sense of security in work.
- Friendship with coworkers leading to a healthy working climate.

2. Concern for Production. Concern for production means the attitudes of superiors towards a variety of things, such as:

- Quality of policy decisions.
- Procedures and processes.
- Quality of staff services.
- Work efficiency.
- Volume of output.

The grid has nine possible positions along each axis, creating 81 different positions in which the leader's style may fall. The grid does not show results produced but, rather, the dominating factors in a leader's thinking in getting results.

The five basic styles identified in the grid represent varying combinations of concern for (i) people and (ii) production.

- The 1,1 or 'impoverished' manager has minimum concern for (i) people and (ii) production.
- The 1,9 or 'country club' manager has (i) high concern for people, but (ii) low concern for production.
- The 5,5 or 'the middle of the road' style of manager's have moderate concern for both (i) people and (ii) production.
- The 9,1 or 'task manager' has (i) high concern for production, but (ii) very little concern for people.

- The 9,9 or 'team manager' has high concern for both (i) people and (ii) production.

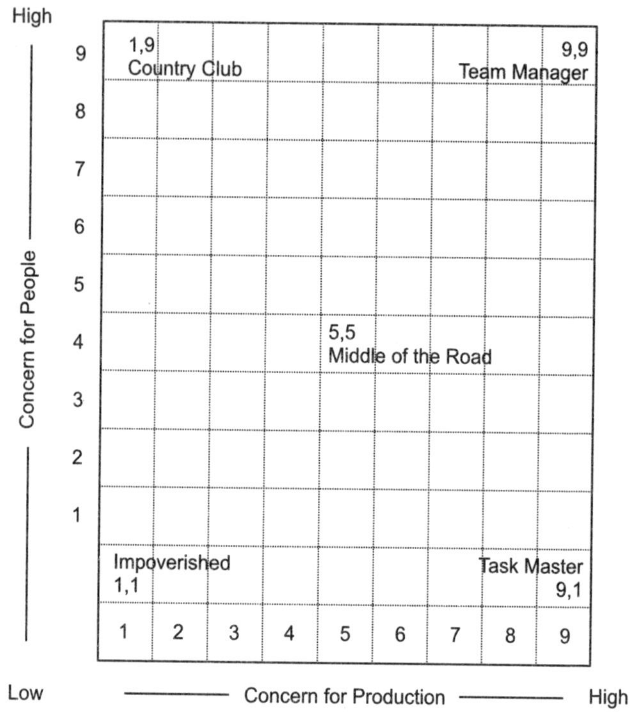

According to Blake and Mouton, managers were found to perform best, in all organisations, and under all situations, under a 9,9 or team management.

Merging 'Grid' with 'Ohio State Studies'. When compared with the Ohio Research of the behavioural analysis of leadership, managerial grid is an (i) attitudinal and (ii) conceptual description of leaders. Managerial grid measures (i) values and (ii) feelings of managers and may be termed as attitudinal model. The Ohio State Studies reflect both (i) attitudinal and (ii) behavioural components. If we single out this major difference and conveniently merge these two leadership theories for comparison, it will be interesting.

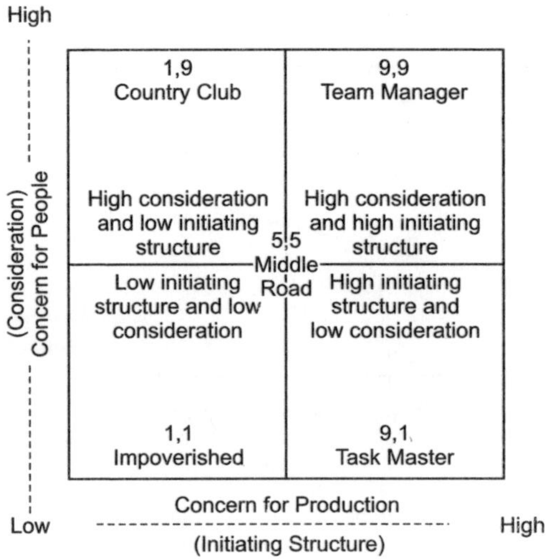

3. Situational Theories. The search for the "best" set of (i) traits or (ii) behaviour has failed to discover an effective leadership mix and style for all situations. What has evolved are situation-leadership theories that suggest that the leadership effectiveness depends on the fit between (i) personality, (ii) task, (iii) power, (iv) attitudes, and (v) perceptions. As the importance of situational factors and leader assessment of forces became more recognized, leadership research became more systematic and contingency models of leadership began to appear in the (i) organisational behaviour and (ii) management literature. There are several (i) publicized and (ii) researched situation-oriented leadership approaches. The most prominent of these are discussed hereunder:

Continuum of Leadership Behaviour. Tannenbaum and Schmidt used a contingency framework to discuss effective leadership patterns taking a situational approach. They identified the range of possible leadership styles and presented them on a continuum journeying from "Boss centered leadership" at one end and "subordinate centered leadership" at the other end.

The figure reveals that the manager is presented with a number of leadership behaviour alternatives. On the left side of the continuum are the leaders who enjoy (i) a high degree of

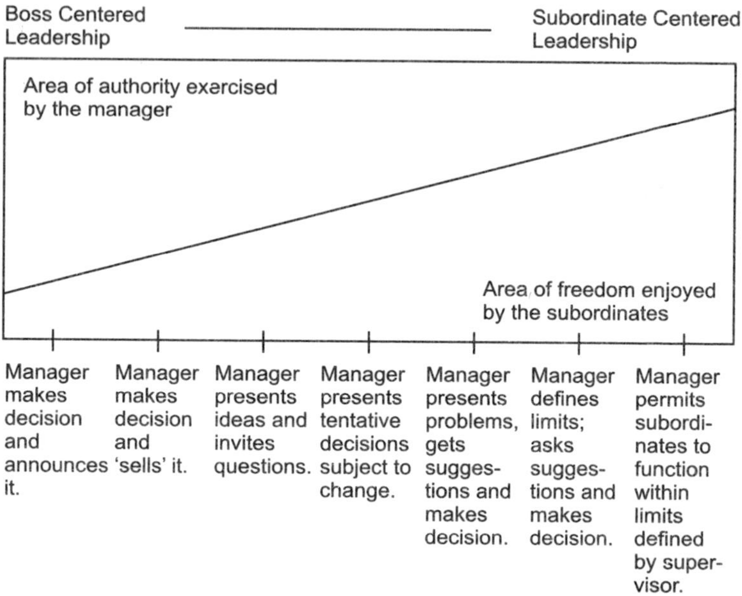

control and (ii) delegate very little authority. At the extreme right, the subordinates enjoy a greater freedom in work related matters.

Now the question arises: how a manager moves along this continuum. This depends upon 3 forces viz.:

1. Forces in the Manager. These forces include the value system of leaders (e.g., the feeling that subordinates should participate in decisions that affect them), confidence in his subordinates, his leadership preferences and tolerance of ambiguity.

2. Forces in the Subordinates. These include (i) the subordinates need for independence, (ii) tolerance for ambiguity, (iii) ready to assume responsibility for decision-making, (iv) understanding and identifying organisational goals, and (v) abilities, knowledge and experience.

3. Forces in the Situation. These include (i) type of organisation, (ii) nature of problem, (iii) group effectiveness, and (iv) time pressure.

Contingency Theories of Leadership. After the (i) trait and (ii) behavioural approach proved to fall short of being an adequate leadership theory, attention turned to the situational aspects of leadership. Social psychologists began the search for situational variables that have impact on (i) leadership roles, skills and behaviour and (ii) followers performance and satisfaction. Various situational variables were identified, but no theory arrived at any conclusion. Then, Fred Fiedler proposed a widely recognized situation based model for leadership effectiveness.

To test the hypothesis Fiedler had formulated from previous findings, he developed a "contingency model". This model contains relationship between (i) leadership styles and (ii) favourableness of the situation. Situational favourableness was described in terms of 3 contingency dimensions:

1. Leader-Member Relations. It refers to the degree of (i) confidence, (ii) trust, and (iii) respect subordinates have for their leader. It indicates the degree to which group members like the leader are willing to accept the leader's behaviour, as an influence on them. If followers are willing to follow because of (i) charisma, (ii) expertise, (iii) competence, and (iv) mutual respect, the leader has little need to depend on (i) task structure or (ii) position power. If the leader is not trustworthy and is viewed negatively by followers, the situation is considered less favourable.

2. Task Structure. Task structure refers to the degree to which the task requirements are clearly defined (clarity of goals).

- The correctness of a decision to be easily verified (verifiability of decisions made).
- Alternative solution to task problems.

3. Leader Position Power. The most obvious manner in which the leader secures power is by (i) accepting, and (ii) performing the leadership role. Position power in the contingency model refers to the power inherent in the leader's organisational position.

It refers to the degree to which the leader has at his disposal various rewards and sanctions, authority over group members and the degree in which this is supported by the organisation.

The next step in the Fiedler model is to evaluate the situation in terms of these three contingency variables.

- Leader-member relations are either (i) good or (ii) poor.
- Task-structure is either (i) high or (ii) low and
- Position-power is either (i) strong or (ii) weak.

Leader-Member Relations	Good				Poor			
Task-Structure	High		Low		High		Low	
Leader Position-Power	Strong	Weak	Strong	Weak	Strong	Weak	Strong	Weak
Cells	I	II	III	IV	V	VI	VII	VIII

Very Favourable ——— Very Unfavourable

A favourable situation is where:

- The leader-member relations are good.
- The task is highly structured.
- The leader has enormous power to exert influence on the subordinates.

The first cell in the Table above is identified with this high degree of favourableness.

At the other extreme, an unfavourable situation is where:

- The leader's power is weak.
- The relations with members are poor.
- The task is unstructured and unpredictable.

The last cell represents this situation.

Fiedler concluded that:

- Task-oriented leader tend to perform better in situations that are very favourable or very unfavourable to them.

– Relationship oriented leaders, however, perform better in situations that are moderately favourable or moderately unfavourable.

Leadership Style. The fundamental question remains as what type of leadership style is to be exercised by the leader in these situations?

To determine the style of leadership, Fiedler introduced a scale called Least Preferred Coworker (LPC). LPC is a set of sixteen objective pairs and is referred to as the "heart" of his research programme. Leaders are asked to think of a person with whom he has worked least well. They are then asked to describe this person on a series of bipolar objective scales as under:

Friendly	8	7	6	5	4	3	2	1	Unfriendly
Enthusiastic	8	7	6	5	4	3	2	1	Unenthusiastic
Cooperative	8	7	6	5	4	3	2	1	Non-cooperative
Helpful	8	7	6	5	4	3	2	1	Frustrating
Interesting	8	7	6	5	4	3	2	1	Boring
Distant	8	7	6	5	4	3	2	1	Close

In this bipolar scale '8' represents the most favourable perception of one's least preferred coworker and '1' the reverse. The leader's responses are measured and then aggregated and arranged.

According to Fiedler, a high score represents that the leader has human relations orientation and low LPC score indicates a task orientation.

Leaders who rate their least preferred coworker in a 'favourable' light derives satisfaction through interpersonal relations. Leaders who rate their least coworkers in a relatively 'unfavourable' light are bound to get satisfaction out of successful performance.

Path-Goal Theory

The path-goal theory of leadership, another popular contemporary perspective, is a contingency approach focusing on the situation and leader behaviours, rather than the fixed traits of the leader. The path-goal theory thus allowed for the possibility of adopting leadership to the situation. The theory was developed in the 1970s by Martin Evans and Roberts House.

Basic Premises

The path-goal theory has its roots in the expectancy theory of motivation. Basically expectancy theory states that an individual's (i) attitudes and (ii) behaviours can be predicted from two interrelated factors.

- The degree to which he or she believes that job behaviour will lead to various outcomes (expectancy).
- The value of these outcomes (valences) to the individual.

Path-goal theory states that subordinates are motivated by the leader to the extent that leader behaviour influences their expectancies. That is, the leader affects the performance of subordinates by clarifying the behaviour (paths) that lead to desired rewards (goals). When the rewards are contingent on effective performance, the cycle is completed. Path-goal theory also suggests that a leader may exhibit several behaviours depending on situational factors.

Leader Behaviours

Path-goal theory identifies four kinds of leader behaviour. These include:

1. **Directive Leadership.** The leader lets subordinates know what is expected of them, gives specific guidance as how to accomplish tasks, schedules work to be done, and maintains definite standards of performance for subordinates.

2. **Supportive Leadership.** The leader is friendly and shows concern for the (i) status, (ii) well being, and (iii) needs of subordinates.

3. **Participative Leadership.** The leader consults subordinates about issues and takes their suggestions into consideration before making a decision.

4. **Achievement-oriented Leadership.** The leader sets challenging goals, expects subordinates to perform at their

highest level and shows a high degree of confidence that the subordinates will put forth effort and accomplish goals.

Unlike Fiedler's contingency theory, path-goal theory assumes that the same leader may display any or all of these leadership styles depending upon the situation.

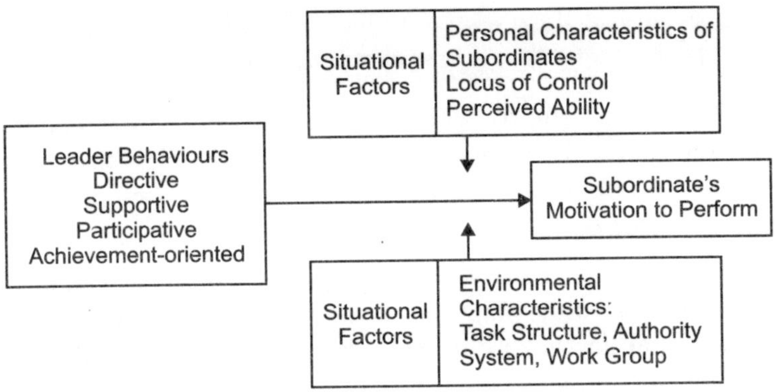

Situational Factors

The theory proposes two types of situational factors that influence the relationship between (i) leader behaviour and (ii) subordinate satisfaction, the personal characteristics of the subordinates and the characteristics of the environment.

Two important personal characteristics of subordinates are: (i) locus of control and (ii) perceived ability. Locus of control refers to the extent to which individuals attribute what happens to them to their own behaviour or to external causes. Research indicates that individuals who attribute outcomes to their own behaviour may be more satisfied with a participative leader, whereas individuals who attribute outcomes to external causes may respond more favourably to a directive leader. The second personal characteristics has to do with the individual's perception of his or her ability with respect to the task. Employees who rate their own ability relatively high are less likely to accept directive leadership.

Important environmental characteristics are task structure, the formal authority system, and the primary work group. The theory proposes that leader behaviour will be motivational if it helps subordinates cope with environmental uncertainty created by these factors. However, in some cases, certain forms of leadership will be redundant, decreasing subordinate satisfaction.

> When task structure is high, directive leadership is less effective.

> When the work group provides the individual with social support, supportive leader behaviour may also be less critical.

Thus the extent to which leader behaviour matches the (i) personal and (ii) environmental characteristics is presumed to influence subordinate motivation to perform.

Scientific Evidence

The path-goal theory was designed to provide a general framework for understanding how (i) leader behaviour and (ii) situational factors influence subordinate's (i) attitudes and (ii) behaviours. But the intention of the path-goal theorists was to stimulate research on the major propositions, not to offer definite answers. Researchers anticipated that a more fully developed, formal theory of leadership might emerge from continued research. That is why it can be mentioned that it is a post-hoc theory and is yet to be extensively tested.

Hersey and Blachard's Situational Leadership Model

Situational leadership model was developed by Paul Hersey and Kenneth Blachard to help people attempting leadership, irrespective of their role, to be more effective in their interactions with others. This model deals with the interplay between:

- The amount of guidance and direction (task behaviour) a leader provides.
- The amount of socio-emotional support (relationship behaviour) a leader gives.
- The readiness level that followers display while performing a specific task, function or objective.

Task behaviour is the extent to which a leader spells out to subordinates (i) what to do, (ii) where to do it, and (iii) how to do it? Leaders who use precise directions and tight controls are engaged in close supervision of their subordinates.

Relationship behaviour is the extent to which a leader (i) listens, (ii) provides support and encouragement, and (iii) involves subordinates in the decision-making process.

Follower readiness is the subordinates ability and willingness to perform the prescribed tasks. Followers have various degrees of readiness as shown in the figure below:

	High	Moderate		Low	
Mature	R4	R3	R2	R1	Immature
	Able and willing or confident	Able but unwilling or insecure	Unable but willing or confident	Unable and unwilling or insecure	

Follower Readiness

As we observe in R1, the followers are either (i) unable or (ii) unwilling to perform the task. Whereas in R4, they are (i) able, (ii) willing, and (iii) confident that they can perform the task. In R2 followers are unable but are willing to perform a task and are confident that they can. In R3, followers are able to do the task but are not confident that they can. According to the situational leadership model, as the readiness level of individuals increases from R1 to R4, a leader should change his or her style from task to relationship behaviours to increase subordinates (i) commitment, (ii) competence, and (iii) performance.

Leadership Styles and Followers

Leadership style will be the behaviour displayed by the leader (including identifying of task and relationship behaviour), as perceived by the followers.

Task behaviour and relations behaviour are separate and distant and can be placed on separate axis of a two dimensional graph with the four quadrants used to identify the four leadership styles as shown in the Figure on the next page. When task behaviour is plotted from low to high on the horizontal axis and the relationship behaviour on the vertical axis, both

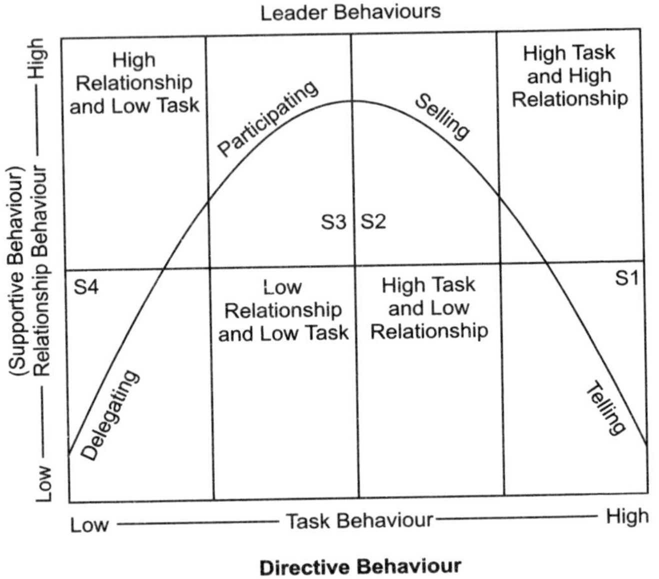

are plotted from low to high, it is possible to describe leader behaviour in four ways or styles.

- A telling style provided clear and specific instructions. Because followers are either unable or unwilling to perform the task, specific directions and close supervision are needed. That is, the leader tells subordinates what to do and how to perform various tasks.
- A selling style is likely to be effective when followers are willing but still unable to carryout their tasks. The selling style provides both task and relationship leader behaviours. This style encourages two-way communication between the leader and followers and helps subordinates build confidence in their ability to perform the tasks.
- A participating style seems to work best when the followers are able but not fully confident of their ability to perform their tasks. This level of follower readiness requires the leader to maintain two-way communication

and to encourage and support followers in the use of the competencies they have developed.

When follower are able and willing to perform their tasks and confident that they can do so, a delegating style of leader behaviour is most appropriate. A delegating style provides little task or relationship behaviours because subordinates are empowered to make decisions. They decide how and when to perform tasks and also know how to perform them.

Implications and Limitations

Hersey and Blanchard's situational model is simple to understand and its recommendations are straightforward. In practice, the readiness level of followers must be checked constantly in order for the leader to determine what combination of task and relationship behaviours would be most appropriate in the situation. An inexperienced employee (low readiness) may perform at as high a level as an experienced employee if given direction and close supervision. If the style is appropriate, it should also help followers increase their levels of readiness. Thus, as a leader develops a team and helps its members learn to manage themselves, the leaders style used should be changed to fit the changing situation.

Limitation. The model says that each person will have a unique readiness level, then the question arises, how will a leader manager in team situations involving many (different) readiness levels of team members?

The model addresses only one "follower readiness" contingency variable ignoring other situational factors such as time and work pressures, etc., which could also effect the leader's choice of behaviour.

The model makes an assumption that a leader can easily adopt a leadership style to suit the situation, which is not always possible.

This model is not sufficiently supported by scientific research although it is being used to help individuals to better their diagnostic abilities.

LEADERSHIP THEORIES–MODERN

The modern theories of leadership include:

Charismatic Leadership Theory

Charismatic leadership involves (i) motivating and (ii) directing followers primarily by developing their strong emotional commitment to a vision and set of shared values. It is said that charismatic leaders obtain power through their followers identification with them. Followers identify with and are inspired by charismatic leaders in the hope that they will succeed.

> The President of India, Dr. A.P.J. Abdul Kalam can be easily referred to as a charismatic leader because of his ability to distill complex ideas into simple message and communication with symbols and anecdotes.

Broad Concept

The broad concept of charismatic leadership suggests that it represents attributes such as the following:

- **Emphasizes Shared Vision and Values**: Leader focuses on creating mental image of a highly desirable future and shareholder values, linking these values to the organisation missions, goals and expected behaviours.
- **Promotes Shared Identity**: Leader focuses on creating common bonds among followers and shared sense of "who we are" and "what we stand for" as an organisation.
- **Models Desired Behaviours**: Leader displays personal commitment to the values, identity and goals that he or she is promoting, engaging in self-sacrifice to show commitment to those values and goals.
- **Reflects Strengths**: Leader displays and creates the impressions of self-confidence, social and physical courage, determination, optimism and innovation.

Restricted Concept

Some leadership experts hold a more restricted concept of charismatic leadership. They contend that charisma exists only when the following five elements are present and operate in combination with each other:

- There is a person with extraordinary gifts and qualities.
- There is a social or organisational crises or situation of desperation.
- There is a radical vision or set of ideas promising a solution to the crisis as proposed by the person.
- There is a set of followers who are attracted to the gifted person (leader) and come to believe in the leaders exceptional powers and radical vision.
- There is the realization (validation) of the person's (leader's) extraordinary gifts and the radical vision by repeated successes in dealing with the perceived crisis.

The restricted concept of charismatic leadership has been summed up in this way.

Charismatic leadership involves more than a set of extra-ordinary characteristics of a person, viz.:

- They exclude self-confidence.
- They have strong convictions in their own beliefs and ideals.
- They communicate high expectations with respect to followers performance.
- They express great confidence in their followers.

Behavioural Components of Charismatic and Non-charismatic Leaders

	Non-charismatic leader	Charismatic leader
Relation to status quo	Essentially agrees with status quo and strives to maintain it.	Essentially opposes to status quo and strives to change it.
Future Goal	Goal not too discrepant from status quo.	Idealized vision which is highly discrepant from status quo.
Likeableness	Shared perspective makes him/her likable.	Shared perspective and idealized vision makes him/her a likable and honourable hero worthy of identification and imitation.

Contd...

Trustworthiness	Disinterested advocacy in persuasion attempts.	Disinterested advocacy by incurring great personal risk and cost.
Expertise	Expert in using available means to achieve goals within the framework of the existing order.	Expert in using unconventional means to transcend and existing order.
Behaviour	Conventional, conforming to existing norms.	Unconventional or counter normative.
Environmental Sensitivity	Low need for environmental sensitivity to maintain status quo.	High need for environmental sensitivity for changing the status quo.
Articulation	Weak articulation of goals and motivation to lead.	Strong articulation of future vision and motivation to lead.
Power Base	Position power and personal power (based on reward, expertise and liking for a friend who is similar to other).	Personal power (based on expertise, respect, and admiration for a unique hero).
Leader-follower	Egalitarian, consensus seeking or directive nudges or orders people to share his/her views.	Elitist, entrepreneur and exemplary. Transforms people to the radical changes advocated.

Source: Richard M. Hodgetts, *Organisational Behaviour*, p. 234.

TRANSFORMATIONAL LEADERSHIP MODEL

Transformational leadership involves anticipating future trends, inspiring followers to understand and embrace a new vision of possibilities, developing followers to be leaders or better leaders and building the organisation or group into a community of challenged and rewarded learners. Transformational leadership may be found at all levels of the organisation: teams, departments, divisions and the organisation as a whole.

As we see in the figure that follows, the transformational model can be said to be built on and an extension of transactional, charismatic and attribution model of leadership. The components in the model relating to followers include:

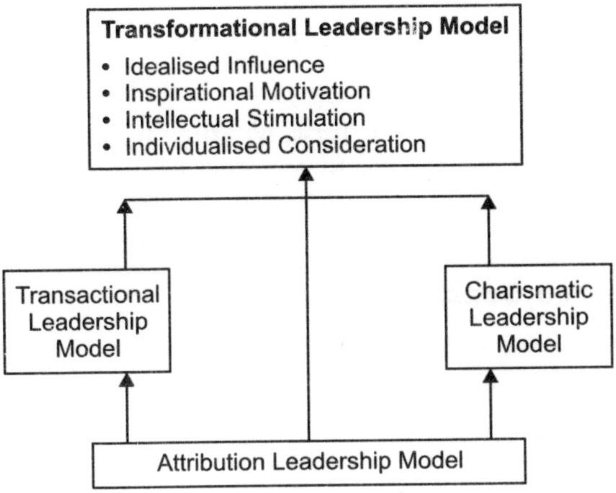

Components of Transformational Leadership Model

Inspirational Motivation

Inspirational motivation refers to the pattern of behaviours and communication that guide followers by providing them with a sense of meaning and challenge in their work. Transformational leaders display great enthusiasm and optimism, which carries over into the lives of followers and fosters a sense of team spirit. Such leaders get followers involved in and eventually committed to a vision of new future state that may be significantly different from the present. Transformational leaders inspire others by what they say and do.

Intellectual Stimulation

Intellectual stimulation is the encouragement given to followers to be innovative. Transformational leaders urge followers to questions and assumptions, explore new ideas and methods and approach old situations with new perspectives. In addition, such leaders actively seek out new ideas and creative solutions from followers. Followers' ideas are not criticised just because they may differ from those of the leader. Leaders have a relatively high tolerance for mistakes made by conscientious followers, who are not publicly criticised for those errors.

Transformational leaders focus on the "what" in problems rather "who" to blame for them.

Idealized Influence

Idealized influence refers to the behaviours of the transformational leaders, which indicates high standards of ethical and moral conduct, which followers strive to evaluate or mirror.

Individualized Consideration

Individualized consideration is the special attention paid by a transformational leader to each follower's needs for achievement and growth. Transformational leader may act as coach, mentor, teacher, facilitator and counselor. Followers and colleagues are encouraged to develop to successively higher levels of their potential. Individual differences are embraced and rewarded to enhance creativity and innovation. An open dialogue with followers is encouraged and "management by continuous engagement" is standard practice. Listening skills are sharp and reflect this observation. It is not what you tell them, it is what they hear. In addition, transformational leaders empower followers to make decision.

Faced with increasing turbulence in their environment, organisations need transformational leadership more than ever and at all levels, not just at the top. The need for leaders of vision, confidence and determination, whether they are leading a small team or an entire organisation, is increasing rapidly. Such leaders are needed to motivate others to assert themselves, to join enthusiastically in team efforts and to have positive feelings about what they are doing. Top managers must come to understand, appreciate and support as never before employees who are willing to make unpopular decisions, who know when to reject traditional ways of doing something, and who can accept reasonable risks. A "right to fail" must be nurtured and be an integral part of an organisation's culture.

TRANSACTIONAL LEADERSHIP MODEL

Transactional leadership involves motivating and directing followers primarily through contingent reward based exchanges.

The transactional leader tends to focus on a carrot (but sometimes a stick) approach, set performance expectations and goals and provide task related feedback to followers.

The three primary components of transactional leadership that are usually viewed as helping followers achieve their performance goals are:

Contingent Rewards

The leader identifies a part that links the achievement of goals to rewards. Clarifies expectations, exchanges promises and resources for support, arranges mutually satisfactory agreements, negotiates for resources, exchanges assistance for effort and provides commendations for successful performance.

Active Management by Exceptions

The leader monitors followers performance, takes corrective action if deviations from standards occur and enforces rules to prevent mistakes.

Passive Management by Exception

The leader intervenes when problems become serious but wait to take action until mistakes are brought to his or her attention.

Transactional leadership is best viewed as insufficient, but not bad, in developing maximum leadership potential.

CASE STUDY

He Sure Looked Good

Mannion Inc. started looked for a new corporate President almost eighteen months ago. The process was slow, for a while, it appeared that none of the applicants would make the final list. However, after interviewing over thirty executives from both inside and outside the company, the selection committee recommended that five people be considered for the position. In its report to the board of directors, the committee said that each of the five finalists was "equal to the task and any one of them can provide us the leadership needed for the twenty-first century".

The board reviewed the list and unanimously agreed that there were two individuals who warranted initial consideration. If either was deemed superior to the other after the interviews, this person would be offered the job and the second would be kept as a backup. Only if both individuals proved unacceptable or could not be hired would the board move on and consider the remaining three candidates.

The first person to be interviewed was Mark Schlaiffer, forty-four had worked for a major competitor for fourteen years. He is currently senior production Vice-President and is considered to be one of the most effective managers in the industry. Based on a strategic plan he developed, his company was able to cut costs by 22 per cent and emerge as one of the low cost producers in the world. It is likely that Mark will be made President of his company if he remains.

The other person was Margaret Hutchins, forty-five, Vice-President of operations at a large high tech company. Although Mannion Inc. is not in the high tech business, Margaret's success in nurturing and developing research and development projects is well-known in the industry and she is considered a first rate leader. Much of the success of her company is attributed, by insiders as well as industry analysts, to Margaret's skills and abilities. She has been offered the presidency of three companies over the last five years and in each case she has declined. However, she has indicated that she would take the job at Mannion if it were offered.

Subsequently, the board met and made its decision. The offer was made to Mark. In explaining why they choose him, there were five reasons that seemed to outweigh the other. They were these:

- He is distinguished looking, he has a "Presidential" look.
- He is tall (6'6") and this helps him convey an image of power and authority.
- He is affable and friendly.
- He is a good public speaker.
- He is extremely intelligent.

There were also many positive comments made about Margaret, including her fine operating performance. However, the board was unanimous in deciding to make the first offer to Mark. If he did not accept, they planned to invite in two more individuals and then choose between them and Margaret in deciding whom next to offer the job.

DISCUSSION POINTS

1. On what basis did the company make its choice?
2. Based on your answer to the above question, did the board make a mistake?
3. What recommendations would you make to them based on their decision and the comments supporting it?

QUESTIONS

- Define leadership. Discuss various sources of power of a leader.
- State the difference between:
  (a) Leader and Manager.
  (b) Leadership and Management.
- Explain trait theories of leadership.
- Compare and contrast different behavioural theories of leadership:
  (a) Lippitt and White Leadership Styles.
  (b) Rensis Likert's four systems of management.
  (c) Michigan leadership styles.
  (d) Ohio State Leadership Studies.
  (e) Managerial grid.
- Discuss different situational theories of leadership:
  (a) Continnum of leadership behaviour.
  (b) Path-goal theory.
  (c) Hersey and Blachard's leadership model.
- Explain modern theories of leadership.

- How does the maturity of the followers determine or impact upon the styles of leadership?
- "A leader is able to influence his followers and followers influence their leaders." Discuss how.
- Do you think that leadership makes any difference to the effectiveness of an organisation? Defend your position.
- What personal characteristics/traits would you look into an individual to be an effective leader?
- Indicate the correct response against the following multiple choice questions:
  - According to the framework of leadership perceptive, the Michigan and Ohio State Leadership Studies maintained a:

    (a) contingent approach and trait focus.

    (b) universal approach and behavioural focus.

    (c) contingent approach and behavioural focus.

    (d) universal approach and trait focus.

    (e) universal approach and contingent focus.
  - Based on the attribution perspective, if a leader attributes a subordinate's poor performance to external factors, a likely response might be:

    (a) a reprimand.

    (b) training.

    (c) dismissal.

    (d) providing negative feedback.

    (e) correcting a poorly designed task.

PART IV

Organisational Communication

10

Learning Objectives

- Definition, Purpose and Significance of Communications
- Functions and Process of Communication
- Barriers to Effective Communication
- Types of Organisational Communication
- Essentials to Effective Communication
- Principles of Effective Listening
- Transactional Analysis

COMMUNICATION–DEFINED

The word communication has been derived from the Latin word, "*communis*" which can be translated as common. It is the process through which two or more persons come to exchange ideas, and understand among themselves. This definition involves two aspects in communication.

- There is something which is transmitted, such as facts, feelings, ideas, etc. It suggests that there must be a receiver if communication is to occur. The sender of the message must consider the receiver while delivering the message. When the receiver is not considered, there is either (i) no response or (ii) wrong response.
- The definition emphasises that the understanding element in the communication sharing of understanding would be possible only when the person, to whom the message is meant, understands it in the same sense in which the

sender wants him to understand. Thus, communication involves something more than (i) mere transmission of the message or (ii) transmission and physical receipt thereof.

Dale S. Beach defines communication as:

"*The transfer of information and understanding from person to person.*"

McFarland opines communication as:

"*A process of meaningful interaction among human beings. More specially it is the process by which meanings are perceived and understanding are reached among human beings.*"

COMMUNICATION–PURPOSE

The purposes of communication in human resources management include:

- Communication is needed to exchange the ideas, opinions, information, etc., with the colleagues, superiors, subordinates, customers, public, etc.
- Communication is needed for designing jobs and human resource planning.
- Employee orientation and socialization programmes become possible mostly through communication.
- Recruitment and selection functions are performed through communication by persuading the prospective employees to apply for a job, knowing the skills and knowledge of the prospective employees.
- Employee's performance is evaluated by getting (i) information, (ii) opinions, and (iii) ratings from the superiors, subordinates and employers.
- Almost all the process of training and executive development are carried out through the communication process. In fact, most of the training and developments are done through teaching and learning process.
- Employee's ventilate their grievances to their superiors through communication. Superiors also redress the

employee grievances and deal with the disciplinary cases through communication.

- Collective bargaining process is mostly carried out through communication process of exchanging the (i) demands, (ii) offering proposals, and (ii) counter proposals, etc.
- Participative management is successful through effective communication process.

COMMUNICATION–SIGNIFICANCE

Communication is important in the organisation for three reasons.

- We know that all functions of management such as (i) planning, (ii) organising, (iii) leading, and (iv) controlling involve the act of communication without which they cannot be performed at all. The process of communication makes it possible for managers to carryout their task responsibilities. Information must be communicated to managers so that they will have basis for planning; the plans must be communicated to others in order to be carried out. Organising requires communicating with others about their job assignments. Leading requires managers to communicate with subordinates so that group goals can be achieved. Written and oral communication are an essential part of controlling. Managers can carryout their management functions by interacting and communicating with others. The communication process is thus the foundation upon which the management function depends.
- Managers devote a major portion of their time to the activity of communication. Actually, a large share of managerial time is devoted to the activity of communication. Rarely are managers alone at their desks thinking, planning or contemplating alternatives. In fact, managerial time is spent largely on face to face or telephone communication with subordinates, peers, supervisors, suppliers or customers. The time spent by

managers on communication and the attention it receives from them speak about the importance of communication.

- For organisations to function successfully, effective communication is a basic requisite. Interpersonal, intra-group and intergroup communication are essential for information to flow, ideas to generate and feelings to be exchanged. What communication does for an organisation resembles what the blood stream does for an organism. The blood stream supplies all the cells of the organism with oxygen; the communication system supplies all the units–departments, people of the organisation with information.

Communication is significant as it serves four major functions within a group or an organisation, viz.:

- Communication helps control member behaviour in more than one way. Organisations have authority, hierarchies and formal guidelines that employees are required to follow.

> When employees are required first to communicate any job related grievance to their boss, to follow job description; or to comply with company policies, communication is performing a control function.

- Communication fosters *motivation* by clarifying to employees what is to be done, how well they are doing, and what can be done to improve performance if it is below standard.
- For many employees, their work group is a primary source for social interactions. The communication that takes place within the group is a fundamental mechanism by which members show their frustrations and feelings of satisfaction. Communication, therefore, provides a release from the *emotional* expression of feelings and fulfilment of social needs.
- Communication provides *information* to individuals and members for taking a decision by identifying and evaluating alternative choices.

COMMUNICATION–FUNCTIONS

No organisation can function without communication. It is an ever present activity among participants in the organisation. Communication in the organisation performs mainly the following functions:

- Information and knowledge are transmitted from one person to another.
- People are motivated and directed only with the help of communication.
- People's attitude and beliefs are moulded and their behaviour is influenced positively with the help of communication, and
- It also performs the function of entertainment and the maintenance of social relations among them. Scott and Mitchell summarized the functions of communication as shown below:

Functions of Communication

Function	Orientation	Objective Sought
Emotive	Feeling	Increasing acceptance of the organisational tasks.
Motivation	Influence	Seeking commitment to organisational objectives.
Information	Technological	Providing data necessary to rational decisions.
Control	Structure	Clarifying duties, authority, accountability.

Since the manager continuously interacts with other people in the organisation, his job mainly involves communication and to do this better, he is required to be skilful in speaking, listening, reading and writing.

COMMUNICATION–PROCESS

Communication is the process through which two or more persons come to exchange ideas and understanding among themselves. The communication process explains how (i) information, (ii) meaning, and (iii) understanding can be transmitted from person to person.

The first widely recognized model that presented communication as a (i) dynamic, (ii) interactive process was developed by David Berlo. This model can be applied to any human communication, from a television network to two person conversing. The components in the model are thus:

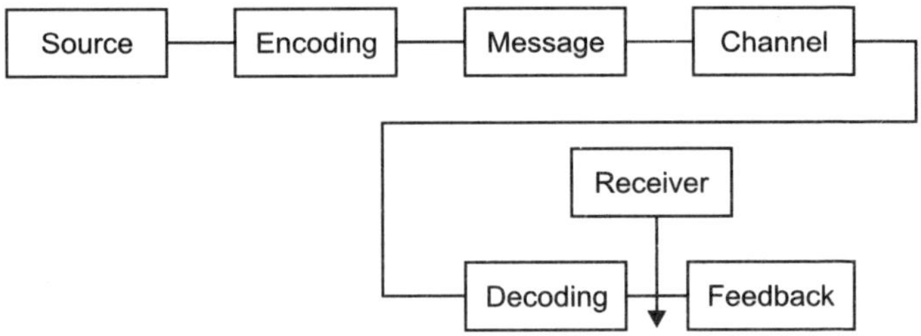

1. Source/Sender

This is the logical beginning of the communication process. The source consists of raw information and includes some (i) thought, (ii) needs, (iii) idea, or (iv) information on the part of the sender.

> Accounting, statistics and computer data are raw information which must be given meaning and purpose in the information source.

2. Encoding

Since the subject matter of communication is (i) abstract, and (ii) intelligible, its transmission requires systematic pattern of (i) signs, (ii) symbols, or (iii) signals. Conversion of the subject matter into these patterns is the process of '*encoding*'.

3. Message

The message is the actual physical product from the source encoding. When we speak, the speech is the message. When we write, the writing is the message. When we gesture, the movement of our arms, the expression of our face are the message. The message represents the meanings; the sender wants to convey to the receiver. It must be understandable to both the parties.

4. Channel

The channel is the medium through which the message travels. It is selected by the source, who must determine which channel is (i) formal or (ii) informal. Formal channels are established by the organisation. They transmit messages that pertain to job related activities of members. They transmit messages that pertain to job related activities of members. They follow the authority network within the organisation. Other forms of messages, such as (i) personal or (ii) social, follow the informal channels in the organisation.

5. Decoding

When the channel brings the message to the receiver, he interprets the message and translates it into information that is meaningful to him.

6. Receiver

The receiver is the (i) individual or (ii) organisation to whom the message is transmitted. Just as the sender is limited by his (i) skills, (ii) attitudes, and (iii) knowledge, the receiver is equally restricted. Just as the source must be skilful in (i) writing or (ii) speaking, the receiver, must be skilful in (i) reading and (ii) listening.

7. Feedback

Feedback is necessary to ensure that the receiver has received the message and understands it in the same sense as sender wants. It is the check on how successful we are in transferring our messages as intended. It determines whether understanding is achieved. It also acts as an energizing factor, thereby changing the course of action in the communication. Better feedback always results in better communication. Without feedback, the communication process is not said to be complete.

EFFECTIVE COMMUNICATION–BARRIERS

The various inadequacies that can be identified through communication evaluation are required to be analysed in terms of various factors–obstructions and barriers–that hinder flow of communication. There might be a number of such barriers that hinder the flow of communication in the organisation, viz.:

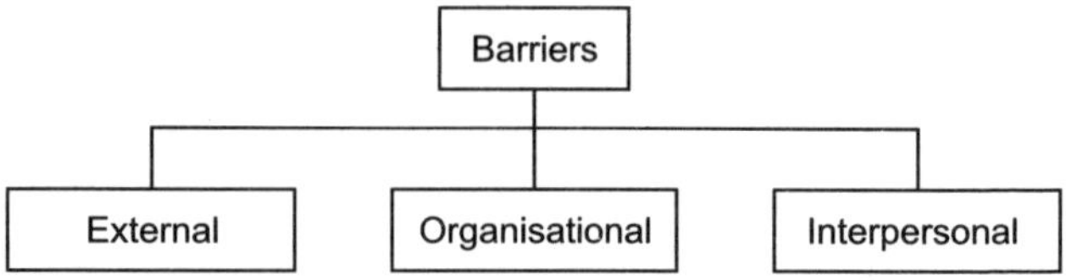

1. External Barriers

Barriers to communication may be either (i) external to the parties involved or (ii) internal to them. External barriers may affect communication in any context, such barriers may be in the following forms:

Semantic Barriers

Semantic barriers are hindrances caused in the process of (i) receiving or (ii) understanding the message. These barriers arise from the language problem of the parties involved. Following are some of the main semantic barriers:

- **Badly Expressed Message**: Lack of clarity and precision in a message makes it badly expressed (i) poorly chosen empty words and phrases, (ii) bad organisation of ideas, and (iii) awkward sentences structure are some common faults found in this case.
- **Faulty Translations**: Early manager receives various types of communication from (i) superiors, (ii) peers, and (iii) subordinates. He must translate information destined for (i) subordinates, (ii) peers, and (iii) superiors into language suitable to each. Hence, the message must be accompanied by an interpretation which will be understood by the receiver.
- **Specialists' Language**: Technical personnel and special groups tend to develop a special, peculiar language of their own. This increases their isolation from others and builds a communication barrier. Whatever be the intention of this special language, it hinders their communication, because of the receiver's ignorance of that type of language.

2. Organisational Barriers

The major organisational barriers are as under:

(a) Organisational Rules and Regulations

Organisational rules and regulations affect the flow of communication by prescribing the subject matter to be communicated and also the channel through which these are to be communicated. The rules may restrict the flow of certain messages and may leave important ones. Communication through proper channel in a specified way prescribed by these rules delays and works against the willingness of persons to convey the message.

(b) Status Relationships

The placing of people in superior-subordinate capacity in the formal organisation structure also blocks the flow of communication particularly in upward direction. Greater the difference between hierarchical positions in terms of their status, greater would be the possibility of communication breakdown.

(c) Complexity in Organisation Structure

In an organisation where there are number of managerial levels, chances of communication getting distorting are more. This is true in case of upward communication, because people, generally do not like to pass up the adverse criticism either of (i) themselves or (ii) their superiors.

3. Interpersonal Barriers

There are many interpersonal barriers that disrupt the effectiveness of communication process. They involve such characteristics of either (i) sender or (ii) receiver that cause communication problems. Some of these are:

(a) Filtering

Filtering refers to intentionally withholding or deliberate manipulation of information by the sender, either (i) because the sender believes that the receiver does not need all information or (ii) it is better for receiver not know all the aspects of a given situation. It is also possible that the receiver is simply told what he wants to hear.

(b) Perception

Perception is the process through which we receive and interpret information from our environment and create a meaningful world out of it. Different people may perceive the same situation differently. Ignoring information that conflicts with what we know can totally distort the content of the message. Some of the perceptual situations that may distort a manager's assessment of people resulting in reduced effectiveness of the communication are:

- A manager may make total assessment of a person based on a single trait.
- A manager may assume that his subordinate's perception about things and situations are similar to his own.
- A manager may perceive to belong one category or another as stereotypes, rather than (i) unique and (ii) distinct individuals.

(c) Emotions

The interpretation of communication also depends upon the state of the receiver at the time when message is received. The same message received when the receiver is (i) angry or (ii) depressed may be interpreted differently than when he is happy. Extreme emotions are most likely to hinder effective communication because rational judgement is replaced by emotional judgement.

(d) Cultural Barriers

The cultural differences can adversely affect the communication process, specially multinational companies and enterprises with multi ethnic work force e.g.:

- Most Jewish people will not work on Saturdays and most Muslims will not work on Friday afternoons.
- Punctuality in some countries is not considered important.

– 'Coke adds life' may be misinterpreted as a device for long life.

Management must identify these cultural differences and attempt to minimize any adverse affects on communication due to these differences.

(e) Senders Credibility

When the sender of the communication has credibility in the eyes of the receiver, the message is taken more seriously. If the receiver has (i) confidence, (ii) trust, and (iii) respect for the sender, then the interpretations of the message will lead to meaning that would be closer to the intended meaning of the sender, contrary if the sender is not trusted, the receiver will scrutinize the message heavily.

ORGANISATIONAL COMMUNICATION–TYPES

There are three primary methods of communicating in organisations. These are:

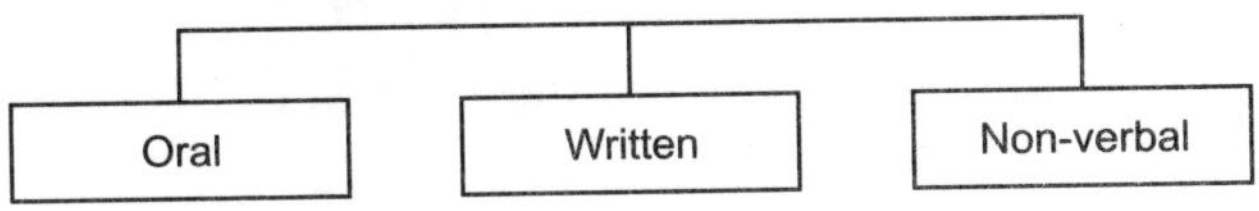

1. Oral Communication

The most prevalent form of organisational communication is oral. It is also known as face-to-face communication. This may be in the form of direct talk and conversation between the speaker and listener when they are psychically present at one place or through telephone conversation. Rumour or grapevine are also popular form of oral communication.

Oral communication is powerful because the receiver not only hears the content of the message but also observes the physical gestures associated with it. The human voice can impart the message more effectively and is an effective way of changing (i) attitudes, (ii) beliefs, and (iii) feelings.

Advantages

Advantages of oral communication are:

- It saves time and cost.

- It is effective media.
- Easy to understand the message due to the possibility of two-way communication.
- Effectiveness of communication can be measured immediately.
- It can be used in emergency situations.
- It involves accuracy and speed.
- Various mechanical devices can be used, and
- Proper control and supervision.

Disadvantages

Despite these advantages, oral communication suffers from various disadvantages. These are:

- It can be disturbed by noise.
- Secrecy and confidentiality cannot be completely maintained.
- Involvement of problem of language.
- Problem of technical and mechanical devices.
- Problem of record and evidence, and
- Sometimes it is costly.

2. Written Communication

A written communication is put in writing. It is generally in the form of (i) instructions, (ii) letters, (iii) formal reports, (iv) policy manuals, (v) information bulletins, etc. These areas are covered in writing for efficient functioning of the organisation. It is effective when communication requires future action, and/or is of general informational nature.

Objectives

The objectives of written communication include:

- To provide the facility for further reference.
- To have a record of evidence.
- To measure the progress.
- To provide necessary information on earlier activities and decisions.

- To reduce mistakes and errors based on the earlier records.
- To provide information for effective decision-making.
- To improve organisational efficiency, and
- To meet the legal requirements.

Advantages

The advantages of written communication are:

- Influence of self-interest and attitude is minimum.
- Written communication is more reliable and one can trust it.
- Written communication does not suffer from the danger of being destroyed.
- It is the best method of communication when the sender and the receiver of the message are located geographically far off.
- It has capacity of being stored.
- It is suitable for lengthy matters to be communicated.
- It is useful where documentary work is involved.
- It will not carry rumour or gossip, and
- This method is useful when secrecy or confidentiality of matters are involved.

Disadvantages

Written communication suffers from some limitations. These limitations include:

- Confusion and misinterpretation.
- Slow movement.
- Absence of personal touch.
- Absence of scope for interaction.
- Absence of two-way communication.
- Absence of grapevine.
- Absence of immediate feedback.

3. Non-verbal Communication

The opposite end of the technically based information theory approach to communication is non-verbal communication. Although verbal communication has long been recognized as being important (non-verbal communication has also recently been given attention in the study of communication).

Sometimes called the "silent language", non-verbal communication can be defined as:

> "*All behaviour expressed (i) consciously or (ii) unconsciously, performed in presence of others and perceived either (i) consciously or (ii) unconsciously.*"

Thus, whether a person says something or does not say anything, communication can still take place.

There are many forms of non-verbal communication. Probably the most widely recognized is body language. Body movements convey meaning and message. This is called "Kinetics" and includes facial expressions and what people do with their (i) eyes, (ii) hands, (iii) feet, and (iv) posture.

Human physical movements and "body language" include both body movements and body position. The table on next page illustrates some common forms of body language.

Besides the types of communication mentioned in the table, other types may be:

1. Formal Communication. Formal communication is an outcome of organisation structure. Such communication passes from a person of one position to a person of other positions. Generally, the superior communicates formally to his subordinates in the form of (i) orders or (ii) instructions. Similarly, the subordinates send their suggestions and feelings to the superiors. Formal communication takes place through (i) meetings, (ii) conferences, (iii) bulletins, (iv) manuals, (v) periodical reports, etc.

Body Language	Interpretation
Facial Expressions	
Frown	Displeasure, unhappiness
Smile	Friendliness, happiness
Raised eyebrows	Disbelief, amazement
Narrowed eyes, pursed lips	Anger
Eye Contact	
Glancing	Interest
Steady	Active listening, interest, seduction
Gestures	
Pointing finger	Authority, displeasure, lecturing
Folded arms	Not open to change, preparing to speak
Arms at side	Open to suggestions, relaxed
Hands uplifted outward	Disbelief, puzzlement, uncertainty
Body Postures	
Fidgeting, doodling	Boredom
Hands on hips	Anger, defensiveness
Shrugging shoulders	Indifference
Square stance or shoulders	Problem solving, concerned, listening
Fidgeting, biting up, shifting, jingling money	Nervousness
Sitting on the edge of chair	Listening, great interest
Slouching in chair	Boredom, lack of interest

Source: *Management Today: Principles and Practice* by Gene Burton and Manab Thakur, p. 403.

2. Informal Communication. Informal communication develops out of personal or group interests of the employees. It is commonly known as "grapevine". It is indirect and flexible. It may be expressed by a (i) gesture, (ii) glance, (iii) smile, etc. It is quite natural that a number of colleagues working (i) side by side, (ii) hours after hours, (iii) days after days, must communicate among one another, irrespective of their positions and formal relationships.

3. Downward Communication. Downward communication is more common which flows from the superior to the subordinate. It moves in a chain from top to bottom. It is a great force for (i) controlling, (ii) influencing, and (iii) initiating activities of organisational members. Communication in this category includes:

- Orders and instructions about job.
- Organisational policies and procedures.
- Feedback of subordinates' performance.
- Reprimands, criticisms, etc.
- Questions inviting upward communication.

In an organisation, people at lower levels have a high degree of (i) fear and (ii) respect towards such communication, which leads to a high degree of acceptance of such communication.

4. Upward Communication. Upward communication flows from a subordinate position to a superior position. It includes information about:

- Subordinates work performance.
- Problems relating to work.
- Performance appraisal of their subordinates.
- Clarification of order.
- Personal and family problems.
- Criticisms.

Upward communication encourages employees to contribute valuable ideas or opinions for improving organisational efficiency. The participative decision-making can develop a great deal of upward communication.

5. Horizontal Communication. It is the flow of information between persons of the same hierarchical level. It is often necessary to save time and facilitate coordination. They are informally created to short circuit the vertical hierarchy and expedite action. It provides means by which managers at the same organisational level coordinate their activities without referring all the matters to their superiors.

IMPROVING COMMUNICATION

The American Management Association has suggested guidelines for improving communication. These are as under:

1. Clarity in Idea. The communicator should be quite clear about what he wants to communicate. The idea to be communicated must be well planned and clearly identified. This will eliminate ambiguity so that the message will not be subject to more than one interpretation.

2. Purpose of Communication. Every communication has some purpose, the basic purpose of any communication is to get behavioural response from the receiver of the communication. However, the ultimate objective may be extended further.

3. Empathy in Communication. The effective way of communication is to be sensitive towards receiver's (i) needs, (ii) feelings, and (iii) perceptions. This is what psychologists call empathy in communication. When the sender of the message looks at the problems from receiver point of view, much of the misunderstanding is avoided.

4. Two-way Communication. Communication is a two-way process. This fact must be realized in communication. Two-way communication brings two minds together which is the basic core of any communication. It involves a continuous dialogue between sender and receiver of the message. Upward communication can become a reality in the organisation if this fact is recognized.

5. Appropriate Language. The subject matter of communication is transmitted by decoding it into some symbols. Such symbols may be in the form of words, either (i) spoken or (ii) written. If the words are used (the language used for communication), it should be such which is understandable by the receiver. Technical terminology may be impressive looking, but that may be troublesome to the listener. One way of making the communication simple is to use repetitive language with which the receiver is quite familiar.

6. Supporting Words with Action. Often, it is said that action speaks louder than words. While communicating, the sender must use the actions to emphasise a point. This enhances the understanding and emphasizes the important point in communication. This will ensure the seriousness in communication.

7. Credibility in Communication. One criterion for effective managerial communication is that it has credibility. The subordinates obey the order of the superior because he has demonstrated through his competence that he is trust worthy. He must also maintain his credibility. Thus, any communication, which is based on credibility, will lead to intended meaning of the sender.

8. Good Listening. A communicator must be a good listener too. By this process, he is not only giving chance to others to speak but he gathers useful information for further communication. By concentrating on the speaker's explicit and implicit meaning, the manager can obtain a much better understanding of what is being said. But here we should know that listening is different from hearing. Hearing is merely picking up sound whereas listening is making sense from what we hear. Hence listening requires paying (i) attention, (ii) interpreting, and (iii) remembering sound stimuli.

Listening–Active and Passive

Effective listening must be active but not passive. In passive listening, the receiver just records the information. Active listening gets the receiver understand the information from the point of view of the sender. The receiver has to concentrate and fully understand the information in the process of receiving the information.

PRINCIPLES OF EFFECTIVE LISTENING

Principle	Good Listener	Bad Listener
Look for areas of interest	Seeks personal enlightenment and/or information, entertains new topics as potentially interesting.	Turns out dry subjects, narrowly defines what is interesting.
Overlook errors of delivery	Attends to meaning and content, ignores delivery errors while being sensitive to any message in them.	Ignores if delivery is poor, misses messages because of personal attributes of the communicator.
Postpone judgement	Avoids quick judgements, waits until comprehension of the core message is complete.	Quickly evaluates and passes judgement, inflexible regarding contrary messages.

Principle	Good Listener	Bad Listener
Listen for ideas	Listen for ideas and themes. Identifies the main points.	Listen for facts and details.
Take notes	Takes careful notes and uses a variety of note taking or recording schemes depending on the speaker.	Takes incomplete note using one system.
Be actively responsive	Responds frequently with nods, "uhhuhs", etc. shows active body state, works at listening.	Passive demeanor, few or no responses, little energy output.
Resist distractions	Resist being distracted, longer concentration span, places loaded words in perspective.	Easily distracted, focuses on loaded or emotional words, short concentration span.
Challenge your mind	Uses difficult material to stimulate the mind, seeks to enlarge understanding.	Avoids difficult material, does not seek to broaden knowledge base.
Capitalise on mind speed	Uses listening time to summarize and anticipate the message, attends to implicit messages as well as explicit messages.	Daydreams with slow speakers, becomes preoccupied with other thoughts.
Assist and encourage the speaker	Asks for clarifying information or examples, uses reflecting phrases, helps to rephrase the idea.	Interrupts, asks trivial questions, makes distracting comments.

Source: David J. Cherrington, *Organizational Behaviour*, p. 577.

The four essential requirements of active listening are:

(a) Intensity.

(b) Empathy.

(c) Acceptance.

(d) Willingness to take responsibility for completeness.

Our brain is capable of handling a speaking rate of about four times the speed of the average speaker. It leaves a lot of time for idle mind. Hence, listeners have to summarize and process the information that they receive. Empathy requires the listener to get into the shoes of the speaker. It means that the receiver should try to understand what the speaker wants to communicate. An active listener should demonstrate acceptance.

Finally, the listener should do whatever is necessary to get the full intended meaning from the speaker's communication.

Developing Effective/Active Listening Skills

The specific behaviours of effective active listeners are:

- Make eye contact: The receiver should maintain eye contact with the sender during the process of receiving information.
- Exhibit affirmative head nods and appropriate facial expressions.
- Avoid distracting actions of gestures: When listening do not do any other work.
- Ask questions: Asking questions during the process of listening provides clarification, ensures understanding and assures the speaker that the receiver is listening.
- Paraphrase: Paraphrasing means restating what the speaker has said in the listener's own words.
- Avoid interrupting the speaker.
- Do not overtalk: Allow the speaker to talk completely and speak only to the extent necessary.
- Make smooth transition between the speaker and listener concentrate on what the speaker has to say rather than what you are going to say.

TRANSACTIONAL ANALYSIS

Transactional Analysis (TA) is a technique of examining the nature of interpersonal communication between two individuals. It analyses whether or not effective communication is taking place.

Every piece of conversation is treated as a transaction, i.e. when I talk to 'X', it is one transaction. When 'X' responds, it is another transaction. Each transaction comes from the (i) parent, (ii) adult, or (iii) ego state of the individuals.

- The parent ego state is authoritarian.
- The adult ego state is rational, and
- The child ego state is impulsive.

Though all of us transact from three ego states from time to time. Each one of us generally tends to have a dominant ego state from which we transact most of the time. Communication is effective when the sender and receiver of the message operate from ego states that match, rather than conflict with each other. Transactions could be:

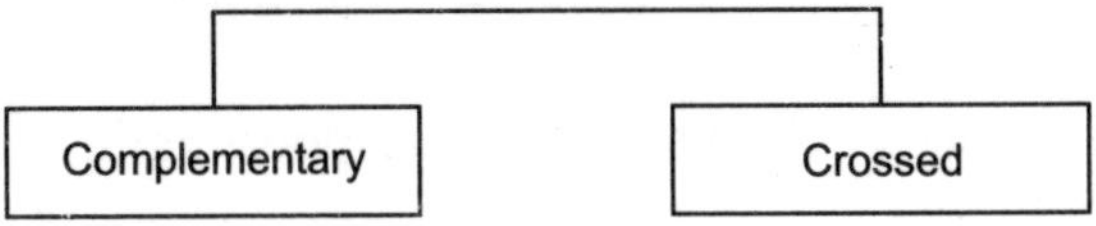

1. Complementary Transaction

There are two types of complementary transactions:

(a) When the boss might talk from his "parent" state to subordinate, to which subordinate may respond from the child state.

> "I don't understand why you are not submitting the reports that you were supposed to."

> "My God. I hate writing those boring reports, but since you need them, I will start working on them right away."

(b) When the two individuals talk from the adult ego state to each other and carry rational conversations.

> The boss might say, "you are probably very busy, Javed, but I would appreciate if you would try to finish the reports as soon as possible."

> "Yes, I am working on this new project which I just finished, I will complete the reports right away."

2. Crossed Transactions

A crossed or non-complementary transaction takes place when people are talking to each other from incompatible ego states.

> If the boss says, "You and I should sit down and discuss why you are not performing as efficiently as before."
>
> "Yes, I would like to do so that I can improve my performance."

Both the two boss and subordinate transact from the adult (rational) state, and communicate effectively with each other.

But, if the subordinate replies, "I do not know why you always blame me for everything that goes wrong in the department."

Then, he has a "child to parent" response rather than adult to adult response.

TA is an intervention technique used by organisations to help people communicate and operate more effectively. In organisations, apart from sending message it is always necessary that, the communicator develop the art of listening, establish rapport with others either (i) verbally or (ii) non-verbally, so that the employees are comfortable and have trust and confidence in them.

CASE STUDY

800 to the Rescue

One of the major trends that has changed American industry over the last five years has been the rise of consumer demands for higher quality goods and services. It is becoming tougher and tougher to place customers, and yet those firms that fail to do so are finding themselves losing market share. How can companies keep up with these demands? One way is by developing strategies that help them communicate with their customers and quickly respond to problem areas.

One of the best examples is provided by the rise in toll free telephone numbers that give the customer 24-hour service. This approach has proven so popular that over the last ten years AT & T's 800 line network has grown from 1.5 billion to 8 billion customers. These lines are extremely important in providing companies with feedback regarding how well they are serving their customers and how they can improve? Take the case of Cadillac, which has added 22 toll free numbers since 1984. As a result of this feedback, the company has eliminated the deductibles on warranties and has become the first American carmaker to institute 24-hour roadside service. In fact, the company's emphasis on service plus improvements in the quality of its cars helped it win the Malcolm Baldridge Award in 1990.

General Electric is another good example. Its 800 number network first installed in 1982 and receiving 1000 calls weekly, now handles 65,000 calls a week. The firm has found this channel of communication to be so important that it recently raised its requirements for the 150 phone representatives that staff these phones. Now they must have a college degree and sales experience. They also have to be able to spot trends in consumer complaints and then alert the appropriate division to take swift action. For example, when the representatives started receiving calls from mothers complaining that the end of the cycle signal on clothes dryers distributed to their napping babies, the company responded by changing the signal so that it now can be turned off by the user.

Colgate Palmolive uses its 800 lines to poll consumers and learn how they feel about the company's products. This helps the firm identify problems and make changes necessary to meet customer needs. As the company president puts it, "*our customers want a specific product that does a specific job, and they are less willing to settle for the happy medium. We must interact with them to fill their needs.*"

DISCUSSION POINTS

1. How important is communication feedback to these firms?
2. In addition to the use of 800 lines, how else can firms improve their communication with customers?
3. What can organisations do to ensure that internal barriers are overcome so that proper action is taken with regard to customer concerns?

QUESTIONS

- Define communication. Discuss the fundamentals and process of communication.
- Comment on the contributions of MIS and information technology to the organisational communication.
- Differentiate between and bring out advantages and disadvantages of:
  (a) Oral, written and non-verbal communication.
  (b) Upward, downward and transactional communication.
- What is listening? Explain the role of effective listening in the communication process.
- "Modern managers prefer and encourage grapevine rather than formal communication." Comment.
- "Ineffective communication is the faculty of sender." Do you agree? Discuss yes or no.
- "Despite of taking all possible care, managers often fail to communicate." Why?
- Describe the barriers you have experienced in the process of effective communication. What essential steps have you initiated to overcome these barriers.
- Observe your own behaviour, and discuss what non-verbal communication habits you typically use. Do you notice some habits that mislead receivers?
- Indicate the correct response against the following multiple choice questions:
  - Providing more or less information is a technique for improving interpersonal communication and focuses on:
    (a) The message
    (b) Symbols
    (c) The medium
    (d) Feedback
    (e) Semantics

- The most prevalent form of organisational communication is:
  (a) Written communication.
  (b) Oral communication.
  (c) Non-verbal communication.
  (d) Facial expression.
  (e) Office memorandum.

Organisational Change

11

Learning Objectives

- Meaning, Nature and Significance of Change
- Causes Pressurizing Change
- Kurt Lewin's Phases of Change
- Resistance to Change
- Managing Resistance to Change
- Management of Change

CHANGE–MEANING

Change is a necessary way of life and we see it all around us–the nature, society and even in biological processes. Then how does one define change? According to Stephen P. Robbins, "change is concerned with making things different". As we know, changes are occurring because of the many developments taking place. Technology development has resulted in sophisticated and newer methods of producing goods and services. As with technology, jobs are also becoming increasingly complex requiring people with higher knowledge and skills to perform on the job. With globalization becoming a trend today, organisations have to change and gear themselves to compete in the world market. Man-made environmental changes are inviting nature's fury, calling for an increased government role to handle air, water and energy crises. Thus, it will be apt to say that all developments have made change inevitable and change pervades, everyone's life.

Organisations also exist in a changing environment and cannot afford to have rigid hierarchies, high degrees of functional specialization, job descriptions having narrow or limited scope, or impersonal and autocratic management. For successful companies managing change is a main focus of their effectiveness.

CHANGE–NATURE

Any alternation that occurs in the overall work environment is called change. Keith Davis beautifully explains the nature of work change by experimenting with an air filled balloon. He contends,

> "*When a finger (which represents change) is pressed against the exterior of the balloon (which represents the organisation), the contour visibly changes at the point of impact. The molecules of air in the balloon represent firm's employees. Repeated pressure at the point may unnecessarily weaken the balloon at that point: (i) pressure, and (ii) motion, that create (i) friction, and (ii) heat. Eventually a rupture occurs and the organisation collapses.*"

But an organisation is much more complex than the illustrated balloon. This comparison is merely intended to emphasize the point that just as molecular equilibrium organisations also seek equilibrium.

An organisation strives to achieve equilibrium of its social structure, i.e. people learn to expect various relationships within their working surroundings. They basically learn (i) how to deal with others, (ii) how to perform their jobs, and (iii) what is expected next.

When equilibrium exists, it becomes easier for people to (i) adjust and (ii) adapt. The essence is that change requires new (i) adjustments and (ii) equilibrium. The nature of work change is so complicated that the management should gain acceptance from the change and restore the group equilibrium and personal adjustments that change upsets.

CHANGE–SIGNIFICANCE

The history of organisations is littered with the corpses of enterprises which failed to respond appropriately to the innumerable demands of the environment for change. Organisations are, of course, learning to cope with the devastating rate of (i) internal and (ii) external changes with the help of some fundamental changes in (i) management philosophy and (ii) organisational technology. Modern organisations are highly (i) dynamic, (ii) versatile, and (iii) adaptive to the multiplicity of changes.

- Change basically results from stimuli from both outside and inside the enterprise. Organisational change refers to the alterations of (i) structural relationships and (ii) roles of people in the organisations. It is largely structural in nature.
- Change takes place in all organisations but at varying rates of speed and degree of significance.
- Change takes place in all parts of an organisation but at varying rates of speed and degrees of significance.
- Finally, the enterprise can be changed in several ways, i.e. (i) its technology can be changed, (ii) its structure, (iii) its people, and (iv) other elements.

CHANGE–FORCES

An organisation is subject to many pressures for change from a variety of sources. But, because the complexity of events and the rapid change in the modern world, it is difficult to predict the types of change that will be most significant in future. However, for ease of study, forces of change can be studied under two broad categories, viz.:

1. External Forces

Organisations are forced frequently to introduce changes in relation to environmental resources. A modern manager is change conscious and is operating in the constantly changing environment. Many external changes bombard the modern organisations and make change inevitable. Some of these are mentioned hereunder:

(a) People. Approximately 56 million people were born between 1945 and 1960. These baby boomers are significantly different from previous generations with respect to their

(i) education, (ii) expectations, and (iii) value system. These differences show up in distinct purchasing patterns that affect (i) product or service innovation, (ii) technological changes, (iii) marketing and promotion activities, etc.

(b) Technology. Technology is the major external pressure of change. It is perhaps the greatest factor that organisations reckon with. According to C. Handy:

> "*The rate of technological change is greater today than any time in the past. Technological changes are responsible for changing the nature of job performed at all levels in the organisation. Knowledge explosion, more particularly the computer technology and automation have made a remarkable impact on the functioning of organisations in the recent times. Organisations with outdated technology are no more in the scene today. Technological advancement is, thus, a permanent fixture in the business world and it continues to demand a manager's attention as a pressure for change.*"

Technological changes have always been equated with the progress in society. Today's technology has outstripped the imagination of the science fiction writers of a generation ago.

Technological change has become increasingly (i) diverse and (ii) complex. Its pace is stepping up, making the executives move and more concerned with the adequacy of organisation structure to (i) meet and (ii) match the needs. Manager here confronts the problems of technological alternations. Each technological alternative results in different organisational requirements.

(c) Competition. Although competition is not a new force for change, it has some significant new twists. Most markets will soon be international because of decreasing transportation and communication costs and increasing export orientation of businesses. And in the future, competition from industrialized countries will take a backseat to competition from the booming industries of developing nations.

Developing nations may sooner offer different, cheaper or high quality products while enjoying the benefits of low labour costs, abundant supplies of raw materials, financial protection by their governments that may not be available in industrialized states. Organisations that are not ready for these new sources of competition will suffer a lot.

(d) **Social and Political.** A firm's fate is also influenced by such environmental pressures as (i) social and (ii) political changes. The relationship between government and business has been improving day by day. The drive for social equality is the current issue that poses new challenges for managers which had not been previously confronted. Many new legal provisions in the corporate sector get introduced every time that affect the organisations. Organisational units have no control over these forces but in order to service they are to adopt to meet changes.

Thus, outside the organisations, environmental conditions are becoming less and less day by day; they are even becoming turbulent. These pressures necessitate the organisations to (i) change and (ii) adopt to meet the new demands and requirements. Organisations cannot afford to be rigid and inflexible in the wake of environmental pressures; they must be, rather, dynamic and viable so that they survive.

(e) **Market Situation.** Changing market situation is a seemingly existing phenomenon. These market changes include (i) rapidly changing goals, (ii) needs, and (iii) desires of consumers, suppliers, unions and stockholders, competition for new products, designs, changes in quality is growing at a high pace. In fact, modern organisations are functioning in a highly competitive terrain. If they are to survive, they must place greater emphasis on this pressure for change also.

2. Internal Forces

Pressures for change which occur within the organisation are discussed hereunder:

(a) **Change in the Managerial Personnel.** Knowledge explosion brought obsolescence in the earlier jobs and calls for dynamism in the managerial personnel. These changes encompass the (i) retirement of the old, (ii) transfer and promotion of managers, and (iii) replacement of old and static managers by a more (i) versatile, (ii) dynamic, and (iii) young lots. The changing personnel certainly act as an important pressure that cannot be neglected or underestimated.

One of the most frequent reasons for major changes in an organisation is the change of executives at the top. No two managers have the same (i) styles, (ii) skills, or (iii) managerial philosophies. Managerial behaviour is always selective so that a newly appointed manager might favour different organisational (i) designs, (ii) objectives, (iii) procedures, and (iv) policies than a predecessor. Thus, the filling of the top vacancies presents strategic opportunity for re-examination of the entire structure and explanation of the changes to the people who are affected.

(b) Certain Deficiencies in the Existing System. Another associated internal pressure that is instrumental to organisational change is the existence of certain loopholes in the system itself. They may be (i) unmanageable span of control, (ii) lack of coordination between the departments, (iii) obstacles in communication, (iv) lack of uniformity in the policies, (v) non-cooperation between line and staff, etc. But normally the need for change in such cases goes unrecognized until some major catastrophe occurs. A rational organisational thinks in terms of change long before it turns to bathos.

(c) Certain other Forces. There are some internal forces that precipitate change in the organisations. They relate to change in (i) machinery, (ii) equipment, (iii) methods and procedures, (iv) work standards, and (v) changes in authority status, etc. The demand for job security by employees is justifiably increased. The other forces may be:

- Employees' desire to share in decision-making.
- Employees' demand for effective organisational mechanism.
- Higher employee expectation for satisfying jobs and work environment.
- Employees' desire for higher wage payment.

(d) The Domino Effect. Another main source of change is the change itself. Domino effect is one in which one change touches off sequence of related and supporting changes.

> Creation of a new department may cause the introduction of new managerial positions, changes in assignments with other departments, reallocation of tasks, etc.

Most of the managers fail to consider the potential domino effects. Such an oversight might lead to the problems of coordination and control. Before any significant change is made, the possible consequences of that change must be evaluated to see whether undesirable chain reactions occur.

PLANNED ORGANISATIONAL CHANGE–PROCESS

Organisational change calls for a change in the individual behaviour of the employees. Organisations survive, grow, decline or die depending on the changing behaviour of the employees. Any organisational change whether introduced through a new structural design or new technology, basically attempts to make employees change their behaviour. It is because unless the behaviour patterns of the members change, the change will have a little impact on the effectiveness of organisation. But behavioural changes are not expected to be brought about overnight, rather they devour more time. A commonly accepted model for bringing about change in people was suggested by Kurt Lewin (Force Field Analysis) in terms of three phase process. Lewin's model provides a useful vehicle for understanding change process in the organisation.

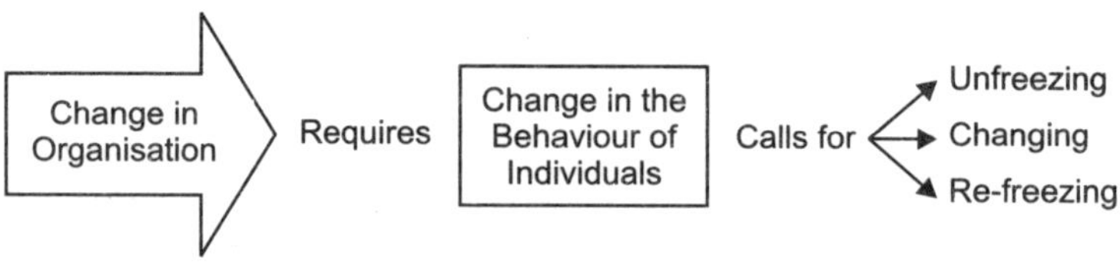

Unfreezing

It refers to making individual aware that the present behaviour is (i) inappropriate, (ii) irrelevant, (iii) inadequate and hence unsuitable to the changing demands of the present situation. The following elements are necessary during this unfreezing phase:

- The physical removal of the individuals being changed from their accustomed routines, sources of information and social relationships.
- The undermining and destruction of social support.
- The humiliating and demeaning experiences to help individuals being changed to see their old attitudes or behaviour as unworthy and think to be motivated to change.
- The consistent linking of reward with willingness to change and of punishment with unwillingness to change.

Unfreezing is, thus, the breaking down of existing mores, old traditions primitive way of doing things, so that the people are ready to accept new alternatives. It involves, discarding the orthodox and conventional methods and introducing a new dynamic behaviour that is most appropriate to the situation.

The essence of this unfreezing phase is that the individual is made to realize that his beliefs, feelings and behaviour are no longer appropriate or relevant to the current situation in the organisation.

Changing

It is the phase where new learning occurs. When the individuals are convinced that their behaviour is inappropriate, they happily come forward to accept the change. In order to change, it is not enough to sense that the current behaviour is inadequate. The necessary condition is that various alternatives of behaviour must also be made available in order to fill the vacuum created by unfreezing phase.

During this phase of 'changing' individuals learn to behave in new ways; the individuals are provided with alternatives out of which to choose the best one. These alternatives are:

(a) Compliance. Compliance or force occurs when individuals are forced to change either by (i) rewards or (ii) punishments.

(b) Internalisation. Internalisation occurs when individuals are forced to encounter a situation that calls for new behaviour.

(c) **Identification.** Identification occurs when individuals recognize one among various models provided in the environment that is most suitable to their personality.

Refreezing

During this phase, individuals internalize the new beliefs, feelings and behaviour learned in the 'changing' phase, i.e. a person accepts the new behaviour as a permanent part of his behaviour. He has to practice and experiment with the new methods of behaviour and see that it effectively blends with his other behavioural attitudes. It is very important for a manager concerned with the introducing change to visualize that the new behaviour is not extinguished soon.

Resistance to Change

One aspect of mankind that has remained more or less constant is his innate resistance to change. It is a fact of life and leadership; people resist change. In a sense, this is positive. It provides a degree of stability and predictability to behave. If there is not some resistance, organisational behaviour would take on characteristics of chaotic randomness. Resistance to change can also be a source of functional conflict.

> Resistance to a change in a product line can stimulate a healthy debate over the merits of the idea and result in a better decision.

It cannot be denied that changes bring challenges, new experiences, new adventures and new rewards and hence a change may be easier to accept when it is accompanied by favourable benefits.

For analytical purposes, resistance of change are grouped into two categories, viz.:

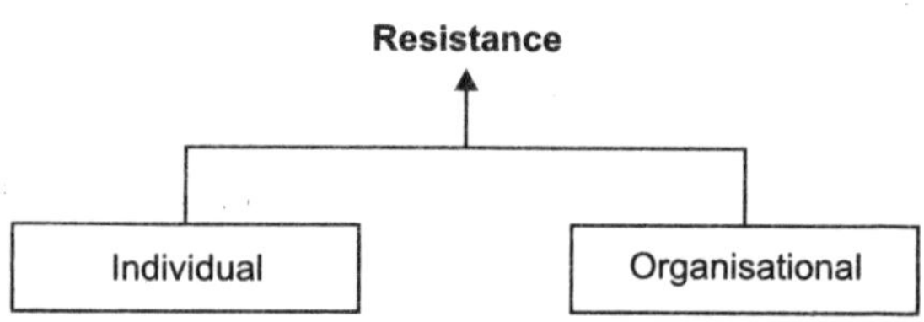

1. Individual Resistance

Individual sources of resistance to change are rooted in basic human characteristics, such as (i) needs and (ii) perceptions. Researchers have identified six reasons for individual resistance to change, viz.:

(a) **Habit.** As human beings, we are creatures of habit. Life is complex enough; we do not need to consider the full range of options from many decisions we have to make every day. To cope with this complexity, we all rely on habits. But when confronted with change, this tendency to respond in our accustomed ways become a source of resistance.

> When an employee is transferred from one branch to another branch across town, it means he is likely to have changed many habits, walking up ten minutes earlier, taking a new set of streets to work, finding a new parking place, adjust to the new office layout, developing a new lunchtime, routine, etc.

(b) **Security.** Some employees like the comfort and security of doing things in the same old way. There is a feeling of constancy and safety in knowing that some things stay the same, despite all the change going on around them. Thus, if a person feels that his security is threatened, he is likely to resist the change.

> Many changes now occurring in jobs, departments and divisions in different organisations have evoked some resistance because they threaten the security of employees.

(c) **Economic Factors.** Another source of individual resistance is concerned that change will lower one's income. Changes in job tasks can arouse economic fears if people are concerned that they won't to able to perform the new tasks especially when pay is closely tied to productivity.

(d) **Fear of Unknown.** Change presents unknown which causes anxiety, whenever people do not know exactly what happens they are likely to resist it. The unknown poses a constant threat and soars them. People fear any untoward and uncomfortable change and its consequences.

> A sales manager may wonder what might happen if he is relocated to company head office in another state. He might ask if his family would like it and if he could find friends. Uncertainty in the situation arises not from the change itself, but from the consequences surrounding the change. To avoid making decisions and fear of unknown, the manager may refuse promotion that requires relocating.

(e) **Lack of Awareness.** Because of perceptual limitations a person may not recognize a change in surroundings and thus may not alter behaviour. People, generally pay attention only to those things that support their viewpoint and do not challenge it. As a result, employees in an isolated regional office may not notice or may ignore directions from head office.

(f) **Social Factors.** People may resist change for fear of what others may think. The group can be a powerful motivator of behaviour. Employees may feel that change will hurt their image, result in ostracism from the group or simply make them "different".

> An employee who agrees to obey work rules established by management may be ridiculed by others who openly disobey the rules.

2. Organisational Resistance

Six major sources of organisational resistance have been identified. These sources are defined as consistently observed relationships in a situation of change.

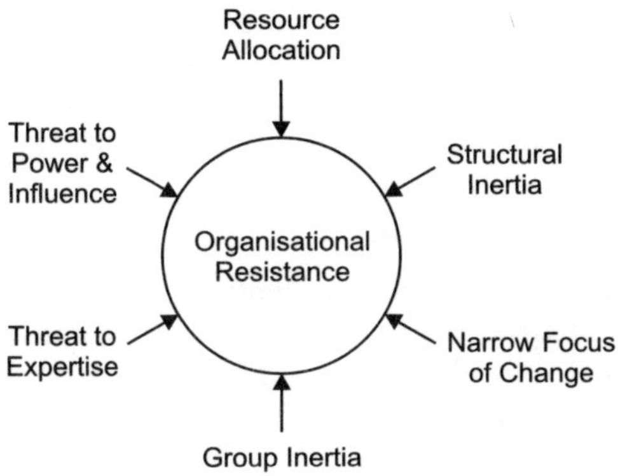

(a) **Structural Inertia.** Organisations have several systems designed to maintain stability.

> To make sure that an employee does the job, the organisation desires, a job candidate must meet specific requirements for the position before being hired; as soon as a person is hired, he is given a job description; the supervisor trains the employee; thereafter the employee's performance is evaluated and finally rewarded.

When an organisation is confronted with change, this structural inertia acts as a counterbalance to sustain stability.

(b) **Narrow Focus of Change.** Organisations are made up of a number of interdependent sub-systems. We cannot change one without affecting the others.

> If management changes the technological processes without simultaneously modifying the organisation's structure to match, the change in technology is not likely to be accepted.

So limited changes in sub systems tend to get nullified by the larger system.

(c) **Group Inertia.** When an employee attempts to change his behaviour, group norms may act as a constraint.

> An individual union member may be willing to accept changes in his job suggested by management. But if union norms dictate resisting any unilateral change made by management, he is likely to resist.

(d) Threat to Expertise. A change in the organisation may threaten the specialized expertise that (i) individuals and (ii) groups have developed over the years. A job redesign or a structural change may transfer the responsibility of a specialized task from the current expert to somebody else, thus threatening the expertise of the specialist.

(e) Threat to Power and Influence. Some people consider change as a potential threat to their position and influence in the organisation. Novel ideas and the new use of resources can disrupt the power relationships and, therefore, are often resisted at organisational level. Specially people who are occupying the top places in the organisation resist some changes because any change might threaten their existing power, i.e. people resist change on the ground that it might affect their position power.

(f) Resource Allocation. Organisations many a time operate under some resource constraints. If the resources with which to operate are available in abundance there will be no problem of introducing change. But the necessary (i) financial, (ii) material, and (iii) human resources may not be available to the organisation to make the needed change. So non-availability of resources also act as a resistance to change.

MANAGING RESISTANCE TO CHANGE

A manager need not always be saddled with the task of change in organisations where resistance is strongly prevalent. He is wedded to some techniques to overcome resistance. One thing he should keep in mind is that he should not underestimate the variety of ways people react to change and the ways they can positively influence specific (i) individuals and (ii) groups during the change process.

Researchers suggested six tactics to deal with resistance to change which are discussed hereunder:

1. Education and Communication

Resistance can be reduced through communicating with employees to help them, see the logic of a change. This tactic basically assumes that the source of resistance lies in misinformation or poor communication. If employees receive the full facts and understand what is to happen, resistance will subside. The manager in this connection should exhibit appropriate leadership styles. Most importantly, a manager should explain:

- What the change is?
- When it is to be introduced?
- How it will be implemented?
- Why the change is needed?
- The basic objectives of change?

Does it work? It does, provided that the source of resistance is inadequate communication and management-employee relations are characterized by (i) mutual trust and (ii) credibility. If these conditions do not exist, the change is unlikely to succeed.

2. Participation and Involvement

In order to overcome resistance a manager may also resort to the technique of participation and involvement, because it is difficult for individuals to resist a change in which they participated. Prior to making a change, those opposed can be brought into the decision process. Assuming that the participants have the expertise to make a meaningful contribution, their involvement can reduce resistance, obtain commitment, and increase the quality of the change decision. Involving employees, however, in the change can be time consuming and must be managed properly.

3. Facilitation and Support

This technique is effective in combating problems arising from (i) desire for security and (ii) fear of the unknown. When employees having difficulty in adjusting to new (i) arrangement or (ii) ways of doing things, a manager may need to arrange for (i) additional training or (ii) provide extra-emotional support while employees become accustomed to the new system. Such facilitation may take some time and effort.

When employees are struggling with a new machine or technique it is very easy for a supervisor to stop their work area and encourage them to work harder, but it takes more time to sit down with them and listen to their problems, because tough and reasoned managers often overlook or ignore this kind of resistance as well as effectively dealing with it. The potential limitations of this method is that it can be expensive, time consuming without any guarantee of success.

4. Negotiation and Agreement

Offering incentives to resistors is another fruitful way of overcoming resistance to change. Where some persons in a group clearly lose out in a change, and where group has considerable power to resist, negotiation and, agreement are helpful. It becomes relatively easy to avoid major resistance through negotiation, because the conflicting parties can be referred back to the negotiated agreement.

5. Manipulation and Cooperation

In situations where other methods are not working or are not available, a manager may resort to the manipulation of information, resources and favours to overcome resistance.

Cooperation is one common form of manipulation. It involves giving individuals a desirable role in design or implementation of change.

One potential benefit of this method is that it can be a relatively quick and inexpensive solution to the resistance. However, one potential danger of this technique is that it can lead to future problems, if people feel they are manipulated.

6. Coercion

Managers do not have other ways, sometimes, than to resort to coercion (i.e. they deal with the resistance coercively). They essentially force people to accept a change by (i) explicitly or (ii) implicitly threatening them (with the loss of their jobs, promotion possibilities, negative performance evaluation, etc.), or by actually firing and transferring them.

This method is commonly applied where speed is essential in implementing change and the change initiator possesses considerable power and definite advantage of this tactics is that it can be speedy and can overcome any kind of resistance. But at the same time, it can be risky if it leaves people wild at the initiators.

MANAGEMENT OF CHANGE–AN OVERVIEW

Management of organisational change is a complex undertaking. Changes in organisations do not take place overnight, instead, they involve formidable exercise on the part of management. Before a particular change is shaped and implemented effectively in an organisation a certain minimum cordinal number of steps need to be followed, viz.:

1. Recognize the Forces Demanding Change

Almost every manager is change-conscious. A manager is not expected to bring radical changes in the organisation instantaneously, rather he proceeds in a logical sequential order. Manager should, first of all, identify the forces demanding change. Change is the reaction to the pressures created both (i) within and (ii) outside the organisation. These forces thus, may be:

(a) **Internal Forces.** Internal forces demanding change include:

- Employee turnover.
- Changing role conflicts.
- Mounting problems from its growing size.
- Any other internal changes.

> Introduction of new department due to expansion in sales, production, etc.

(b) **External Forces.** External forces demanding change include:

- Changing level of technology.
- New marketing strategies in the competitive counterparts.
- New production techniques, sales mixes in the competitive enterprise.

Management of modern organisations is confronting a constantly changing competitive terrain. In the wake of competition, a manager concerned with the change must observe (i) internal and (ii) external forces before introducing change.

2. Recognize the Need for the Change

All forces certainly do not demand change but some do require careful attention on the part of the management. Here the management should isolate the unnecessary forces. This is crucial to the entire change process; manager's decision to act literally depends on this step. Management should identify the discrepancy between what is and what should be. It must analyse the forces that contribute to this gap through (i) evaluation and (ii) performance reports. Management then must commit to discard unnecessary forces and keep a close eye on important pressures that seriously demand change. If the manager feels that forces for change are significant then he moves to the next step in the process known as diagnosis.

3. Diagnose the Problem

Next observable phase in the management of change is a thorough and careful diagnosis of the problem. This involves the identification of the root cause. These diagnostic techniques are employed by the manager or change agent depending on the apparent nature of the problem and capability of the enterprise. Generally, diagnosis is done by a consultant or managers renowned for diagnosing the problem.

The table on next page provides a bird's eye view of the various techniques that are used in the diagnosis, their potential benefits and disadvantages.

The breadth of diagnosis depends on the seriousness of the problem. Sometimes a problem involves only one department, group or individuals and hence diagnosis primarily focuses on the particular area. At other times, if the problem is deep seated, then organisational analysis may be called for. Organisational analysis includes exhaustive study of organisational goals, principles, practices and performance of macro level.

The major decision in this third phase is whether the stimulus for change should be acted upon. Three questions are asked in order to determine this, viz.:

Method	Major Advantages	Potential Problems
Interviews	• Adaptive–allows data collection on a range of possible subjects. Source of rich data. • Emphatic. • Builds report.	• Expensive. • Interviewer can be biased (e.g. he can bias the responses). • Coding/interpretation problems. • Self-report basis.
Questionnaires	• Responses can be qualified and easily summarized.	• Non-emphatic. • Pre-determined questions may miss some issues.
	• Easy to use with big samples. • Relatively inexpensive. • Can obtain large volume of data.	• Data may be over-interpreted. • Response-bias may be there.
Observations	• Collects data on behaviour rather than reports of the behaviour. • Real-time, not retrospective. • Adaptive.	• Interpretation problems. • Sampling problem. • Observer bias. • Costly exercise.
Secondary data/ un-obtrusive measures	• Non-reactive, non-response bias. • High face validity. • Easy for quantification.	• Access/retrieval possibility problems. • Potential validity problems. • Interpretation problems.

– What is the problem as distinct from its symptoms?

– What should be changed to resolve the problem?

– What outcomes are expected and how will these outcomes be measured?

By answering these questions organisations become aware of the problems that suggest the inadequacy of the status quo. Diagnosis also enables the manager to perceive the gap between (i) desired and (ii) actual performance and take necessary actions.

4. Plan the Change

Planning is perhaps the most crucial phase in the management of change. It involves answering three vital problems: (i) what, (ii) how, and (iii) when, to change. Researchers contend that all organisational changes can be classified as changes in:

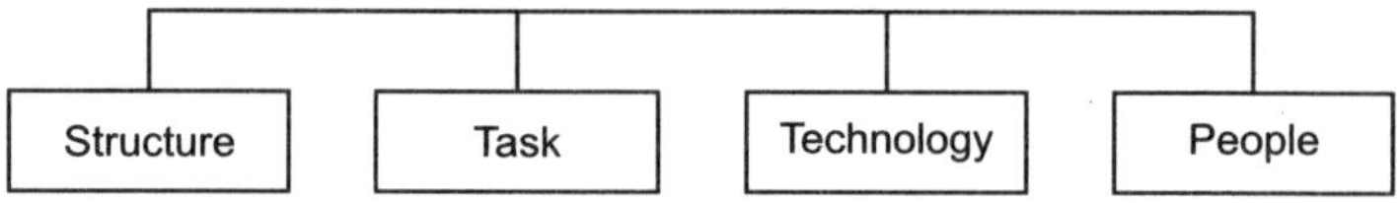

Steps in Planning Change

A change agent must consider the following steps before he plans the necessary change. He should:

(a) Make clear the need for change or provide a climate in which group members feel free to identify such needs.

(b) Permit and encourage relevant group participation in clarifying the needed changes.

(c) State the objectives to be achieved by proposed changes.

(d) Establish the broad guidelines for achieving the objectives.

(e) Leave the details for implementing the proposed changes to the group in the organisation or to the personnel who will be affected by change.

(f) Indicate the rewards to the individuals or groups that are expected to accrue from the change.

(g) Materialize the benefits or rewards, i.e., keep the promise made to those who made the change.

Selection of appropriate strategy is an essential part of planning. In solving organisational change problem, a manager pursues the strategies differently to solve a wide variety of problems.

I. Structure-Focused Change Efforts. These changes primarily include:

- Changing the number of organisational levels.
- Altering the span of management.

- Changing from one base of departmentation to another base.
- Altering the line and staff, and functional authority relationship.

A manager's strategy here, sometimes, is reorganisation. Reorganisation involves entirely a redesign of the structure of the organisation. It also calls for remarkable changes in the departmentation, span of control and coordination. Reorganisation is proved to be effective and most widely used strategy in the case of serious problems.

II. Changing Organisation by Redesigning Tasks. Redesigning tasks is another strategy a manager uses in change. Industrial engineering, scientific management, improvements and creation of highly specialized jobs, etc., all belong to this category of strategy. Jobs vary in scope and depth; and change efforts directed at the task (job) are attempting to alter this scope and depth.

Job scope means the number of operations performed by the job holder and the frequency of the repetition of the job cycle whereas, relative influence of the job holder over the work environment and the degree of self-control in planning and performance of the job determines job depth. The process of upgrading, enlarging or enriching a job by increasing its depth and scope is called vertical job loading and also called job enrichment. Task focused changes include:

- High internal work motivation.
- High quality and work performance.
- Job enrichment.
- Scientific management.
- Industrial engineering, etc.

III. Changing Organisation by Changing Technology. Computerisation is the fashion of the day in today's organisation. The increasing technology and especially computer has profound influence on the organisation and its employees, e.g., it results in more mechanistic organisation structure. Since departments tend to be consolidated, span gets reduced, functional departmentation replaces divisions, resulting in a centralized control. At the lower rungs it results in more routine jobs as well as more compartmentalised jobs in which worker's interaction is less and infrequent.

Computerisation yet, is only one aspect of technological change, other changes include (i) introduction of new production technology, (ii) new employment procedures, and (iii) new performance evaluation programmes, etc.

Technology-focused changes comprise:

- Changing problem, solving and decision-making procedures.
- Introduction of computer to facilitate managerial planning and control.
- Converting from unit production to mass production technology.

IV. Changing Organisation by Changing People. A change in the organisation requires a corresponding change in an individual's personality. Changing personality is a challenging task because the basic personality factors are usually formed and developed in the early childhood of the employee. However, difficult it might be, it is another strategy of change.

There is no dearth of techniques that can be used to change people in an organisation.

- Sensitivity training.
- Transactional analysis.
- Assertiveness training.
- Team building workshops.
- Job training programmes.
- Leadership and supervisory training.
- Management by objectives.

V. Implementation of Change. Having selected the appropriate strategy, the focal points of concentration, the manager's immediate job is to implement the change. Here he confronts the biggest challenge through resistance by the employees. Empirical evidences reveal that creating change is more difficult than it might seem to be. The task of changing behaviour of people in an organisation is a difficult and frustrating endeavour.

Researchers contend that any change encounters three problems in implementation, viz.:

(a) Resistance: First is the problem of resistance to change. Different reasons can be attributed to the resistance mentioned hereunder:

1. Most people prefer (i) stability and (ii) security. Change presents unknown which causes anxiety.
2. People feel that changes imposed on them reduce (i) autonomy and (ii) self-control.
3. People generally develop certain patterns of managing the current behaviour. Change means that they have to find new ways of managing their tasks and environment.
4. People who are in power resist change because they feel change threatens their power.
5. For some ideological reasons also people resist change. They believe that the way things are done currently is better than the proposed change.

Manager in implementing change has to overcome such resistance to change.

(b) Control: The second problem in implementation of change programme relates to control. Change disrupts normal course of events in the organisation. It disrupts and undermines the existing system of management control. During the implementation of change the organisation may easily lose control over certain issues.

(c) Power: The third problem is regarding the power. Any significant change poses the possibility of upsetting or modifying the balance of power among the groups in the organisation. An organisation is a political system made up of different (i) individuals, (ii) groups, (iii) coalitions competing for power.

These problems, their implications and the various action steps are presented in the following table:

Problem	Implication	Action Steps
Resistance	Need to motivate change.	Surface dissatisfy the present state. Participation in change. Rewards for behaviour in support of change. Time and appointments to disengage from resistance. Develop and communicate a clear image of the future.
Control	Need to manage the transition	Use the multiple and consistent leverage points. Develop organisational arrangements for transition. Built-in feedback mechanisms.
Power	Need to shape the political dynamism	Assure the support of key power groups. Use leader behaviour to generate energy in support of change. Use symbols and languages. Build-in stability.

VI. Follow-up on the Change. Management of change is incomplete without proper follow-up organisation must evaluate the effects of change. Objectives must be present and be compared with the performance to see the degree of success in change. End results should be operationally defined and measurements must be done both before and after the implementation of change. This enables the manager or change agent, to compare the performance after the introduction of change with the one prior to it. The manager must make sure that the change is implemented in such a fashion as to maximize the benefits to the organisation by the effective changes.

CASE STUDY

The New Sales Procedures

The Marin Company had more than 100 field sales representatives who sold a line of complex industrial products. Sales of these products required close work with buyers to determine their product needs; so nearly all sales representatives were college graduates in engineering and science. Other product lines of Marin Company, such as consumer products, were sold by a separate sales group.

Recently the firm established a new company-wide control and report system using a large computer. This system doubled the amount of time the industrial sales representatives spent filling out forms and supplying information that can be feed into the computer. They estimate that they now spend as much as two hours daily processing records, and they complain that they now have inadequate time for sales effort. A field sales manager commented, "Morale has declined as a result of these new controls and reports. Sales is a rewarding, gratifying profession that is based on individual effort. Sales representatives are happy when they are making sales, since this directly affects their income and self-recognition. The more time they spend with reports the less time they have to make sales. As a result they can see their income and recognition declining, and thus they find themselves resisting changes."

DISCUSSION POINTS

1. Comment on the sales manager's analysis.
2. What alternative approaches to this situation do you recommend? Give reasons.

QUESTIONS

- Define the term organisational change. Give a detailed account of resistance to change.
- Discuss how resistance to change is beneficial. Why do the employees of the 21st century welcome change?
- Write notes on:
  - (a) Internal forces of change.
  - (b) External forces of change.
- What do you understand by freezing the change? How it can be done?
- "Change is basically positive." Discuss the prose and cons of this statement.

- Have you experienced some benefits of resistance to change in your organisation? Do you think that a low level employee could act as a change catalyst? Explain.
- Argue against the necessity for having vision, charisma and emphasis on double loop learning for a transformational manager to bring about change in an organisation. Do you think these are really needed?
- Indicate the correct response against the following multiple choice questions:

– The most comprehensive type of organisational change is a change of:

  (a) Task Technology

  (b) Structure

  (c) Personnel

  (d) Division of Labour

  (e) Information Flow.

– A type of group and individual change is:

  (a) Collateral Organisational

  (b) Quality of Work Life

  (c) Task Redesign

  (d) Management by Objectives

  (e) Survey-feedback.

Organisational Development

12

Learning Objectives

- Definition and Characteristics of OD
- Objectives and Benefits of OD
- OD Process and OD Interventions / Techniques in Bringing Behavioural Change.

ORGANISATIONAL DEVELOPMENT–DEFINITION

Organisational Development (OD) has inconsistently been defined and used as a convenient label for a variety of activities. In some organisations OD is an old wine but in a new bottle, a new buzzword attached to old activities, viz. organisational planning, personnel or management development. In other organisations OD is employed as a "comprehensive strategy for organisational improvement". In fact, the field of OD is so rapidly changing that in a few years, the label OD may be applied to a somewhat different set of activities. Some of the widely accepted definitions are presented hereunder:

"*Organisational Development is the process of planned change and improvement of organisations through the application of knowledge of the behavioural sciences, such as psychology, sociology, cultural anthropology and other related fields of study.*"

(Ricky W. Griffin, Gregory Moorhead)

"*Organisational Development is a long range effort to improve an organisation's problem-solving and renewal processes, particularly through a more effective and collaborative management of organisation culture with special emphasis on the culture of formal work teams–with the assistance of a change agent or catalyst and the use of the theory and technology of applied behaviour science, including action research.*"

(French and Bell Wendell)

"*Organisational Development is a planned process of change in an organisation's culture through the utilization of behavioural science technology, research and theory.*"

(Bruke W. Warner)

Thus, no single definition of OD is sacred but all emphasize the fact that OD aims at improving the work effectiveness of (i) individuals, (ii) groups, and (iii) organisational system. OD may be taken to refer collectively an assortment of training or therapeutic interventions whose basic aim is to improve the organisation and its members.

ORGANISATIONAL DEVELOPMENT–CHARACTERISTICS

Organisational Development (OD) can be defined as a technique for bringing change in the entire aspect of the organisation, rather than focusing attention on individuals, so that change is easily absorbed. According to Warren G. Bennis, OD has the following characteristics:

1. Long Range Effort

Organisational Development is not designed to solve short-term, temporary or isolated problems. It is a long-term approach meant to elevate the organisation to a higher level of functioning by improving the performance and satisfaction of organisational members. OD programmes generally cover a period of three to five years.

2. Broad-based

Organisational Development is used broadly to describe a variety of change programmes. It essentially deals with a big picture–an organisation. It is a sophisticated attempt to bring about a comprehensive change in the entire organisation. It is concerned not only with changes in organisational design but also with changes in organisational philosophies, skills of individuals and groups.

3. Dynamic Process

Organisational Development includes the effort to guide and direct change as well as to cope with or adapt to imposed change. OD recognizes the fact that the goals of the organisation change and hence the methods of attaining them should also change. OD is thus a dynamic process involving a considerable investment of time and currencies. It is not merely a one shot deal, rather an ongoing, interactive and cycling process.

4. Systems View

Organisational Development utilizes systems thinking. It is based on open, adaptive systems concept. It recognizes that organisations structure and managerial performance are mutually interdependent. The organisation is treated as an inter-related whole and no part of the organisation can be changed without effecting other parts.

5. Research Based

Most of the OD interventions are research based. Change agents do not just introspect the employees and introduce change, rather, they conduct surveys, collect data, evaluate and then take decisions. OD programmes are generally conducted by a special task force and involve the utilization of outside behavioural consultant faculties.

6. Goal Setting and Planning

Since OD is concerned with the entire organisation, the change agent defines the goals of the group and will see to it that together they all work to achieve them.

7. Normative Re-educative Strategy

Organisational Development is based on the principle that "norms form the basis for behaviour and change is a re-educative process of replacing old by new ones".

> Some OD programmes signify major departures from bureaucratic structure of an organisation and calls for changes in managerial leadership styles.

Organisational Development is based on well-established principles regarding the (i) individual and (ii) group behaviours in the organisation and hence it is relatively easy for the OD practitioners to launch and diffuse the required changes by educating them.

ORGANISATIONAL DEVELOPMENT–OBJECTIVES

Organisational Development technology is aimed at developing new organisational learning and new ways of coping and dealing with problems. The primary focus is on improving productivity, morale and satisfaction of employees in an organisation. It is not a difficult exercise to catalogue the other important objectives of OD.

(a) To build and enhance interpersonal trust, communication, cooperation and support among all (i) individuals and (ii) groups throughout the organisation at all levels.

(b) To increase the incidence of confrontation of organisational problems both within groups and among groups in contrast to "sweeping problems under the rug".

(c) To create an environment in which authority of assigned role is augmented by authority based on (i) knowledge and (ii) skill.

(d) To increase the openness of communications (i) laterally, (ii) vertically, and (iii) diagonally.

(e) To increase personal responsibility for planning, implementing the plans and responsible for the consequences. This will build enthusiasm (i) individually and (ii) group-wise and will involve communication, feelings, open competition as well as compromise, conflict resolution, etc. This will increase a sense of self-direction for all people within the organisation.

(f) To find synergistic solutions to problems with greater frequency.

ORGANISATIONAL DEVELOPMENT–PROCESS

Organisational Development is a process rather than a solution to a given problem. OD process involves the following steps:

1. Problem Identification

Understanding and identification of the problem in the organisation is the first step in OD process. The awareness of the problem includes knowledge of the possible organisational problems of growth of human satisfaction and use of human resources and the problem of organisational effectiveness. Having understood exactly what the problem is, OD practitioner can proceed to collect the necessary data to solve problem.

2. Collection of Data

Data gathering is perhaps the most important activity in the process of OD. Personal interviews, personal observations and questionnaires are the most common ways through which the data is collected. Different types of problems require different data and as such the question of "which method" to use depends upon the nature of problem the organisation encounters. Having collected the necessary data, organisation proceeds to analyse it.

3. Diagnosis

There is no cook-book formula for accurate diagnosis. It demands considerable skills of analysis and observation as most of the problems are often expressed by organisation members in ambiguous terms. OD programme may turn out to be a self-defeating exercise if decisions were to be based on such vague information. Before decisions are taken, the information collected must be subjected to a microscopic examination, and, therefore, experience and judgement are critical to this phase.

If organisation leaders show indecent haste to arrive at decisions quickly without considering the pitfalls, dangers, it may prove to be very costly at the end.

Diagnosis should not be limited to a single problem. Often, important factors like attitudes, assumptions, available resources, etc., must be taken into account in the diagnostic phase. For this purpose attitudes surveys can be undertaken through questionnaires wherein the respondents may be asked to evaluate and rate several job related factors like working conditions, pay, etc. Such surveys will help identify the problem clearly as perceived by the organisational members. Diagnosis assists the planners to locate the source of specific problem and see what changes are required in the system, the structure or in people.

4. Planning and Implementation

After diagnosing the problem, the OD expert turns his attention to the planning of change and implementating it. OD interventions come into picture here. Intervention is considered to be the action phase in OD process. Intervention is a set of planned, programmed activities and techniques by which organisations and their clients collaborate in an OD programme. According to French and Bell, "Interventions consist of the long range evolving application of OD techniques targeted for changing individuals, groups or the total organisation."

The range and number of available interventions is not small but extensive. The particular intervention to be used depends on the target group in the organisation. One intervention differs from another in terms of the intensity or depth with which it penetrates into the working of the organisation. An effective OD programme does not consider all interventions, but selects the appropriate one that suits the requirements.

5. Evaluation and Feedback

Probably one of the important stages in OD process is evaluation. As one stage ends, another stage looms, evaluation is helpful to know as to what has been done, whether correctly done or not, and show whether further work is needed before proceeding to the next stage. While evaluating, the change agent carefully observes the decisions taken, and their consequences in an organisation.

Any OD activity is incomplete without proper feedback. Feedback must be carefully handled because sometimes emotional factors set in.

> When mistakes of some of the members are spelled out then emotional factors accompanying the resentment may creep in.

Feedback should be based on the broad array of data and should include the assessment of the change model itself.

ORGANISATIONAL DEVELOPMENT INTERVENTIONS

The number of OD interventions is not small. It is large. But they all vary in the range and depth of their penetration into the organisational system and the purpose they serve. No two interventions are alike and there is no single OD method capable of serving all the likely objectives of organisations. Sometimes several methods of OD are used together.

It is very difficult to classify the OD interventions because of the inter-related and overlapping nature. Different social scientists have used different methods of classification. However, some popular and frequently techniques of OD are mentioned hereunder:

1. Sensitivity Training

One of the popular techniques of OD is sensitive training. It is a method of changing behaviour through unstructured group interaction. Sensitivity training is sought to help individuals towards better relations with others. The primary focus is on reducing inter-personal friction.

In sensitivity training, the actual technique employed is T-group (T stands for training). It is a small group of ten or twelve people assisted by a professional behavioural scientist who acts as a catalyst and trainee for the group. There is no specified agenda. He merely creates the opportunity for group members to express their ideas and feelings freely. Since the trainer has no leadership role to play, the group must workout its own methods of proceedings. A leaderless free group session is on. They can discuss anything they like. Individuals are allowed to focus on behaviour rather than on duties. As members engage in the dialogue, they are encouraged to learn about themselves as they interact with others.

Features

The notable features of sensitivity training are:

(a) The primary objective of sensitivity training is to break through the barrier of (i) intellectualization and (ii) verbalization to facilitate the participants to experience his own behaviour and effect. It says, open your eyes. Look at yourself. See how you look to others. Then decide, what changes, if any, you want to make and in which direction you want to do.

(b) Sensitivity training emphasizes the process rather than the content of the training and focuses upon emotional rather than conceptual training.

(c) It is an experience-based methodology aimed at changing behaviour through unstructured group interaction.

(d) It is not a set of hidden, manipulative process, aimed at brain washing individuals.

(e) It is not intended to suppress conflict, it is not a group therapy and it does not guarantee change.

Research Findings

Research on T-group training is highly inconclusive as it reveals both positive and negative sides.

On the positive side it is empirically found that:

- Sensitivity training can apparently result in more supportive behaviour, more considerate managers and more sensitive people.
- Participants are reported to have become more open and self-understanding.
- Communications are improved a lot and the leadership skills have been reported well.
- It promotes an opportunity to gain insight into personal blind spots, and people become aware of the norms of the group, role flexibility and a sense of belonging to the group.

On the negative side of the coin, research reveals:

- Some individuals report a feeling of humiliation, manipulation, decline in self-confidence and psychological damage.
- T-group training is not only capable of inducting anxiety, but very likely to do so.

- The anxiety may have an unrewarding effect, such as causing the people to be highly frustrated, unsettled, and upset.

2. Team Building

Another important intervention that has received most attention and support in recent years is the team building. In fact, most of the OD practitioners have great faith in team building. Essentially, team building is an attempt to assist the work-group in becoming adept by learning how to identify, diagnose and solve its own problems. It directly focuses on the identification of problems relating to task performance and lays down concrete plans for their elimination. A team building programme deals with new problems on an ongoing basis. It is an effective technique by which members of an organisational group diagnose how they work together and plan changes that will improve their effectiveness.

Team building attempts to improve effectiveness of work groups by allowing the group members to concentrate on:

(a) Setting goals or priorities for organisational groups.

(b) Analysing or allocating the way the work is preformed.

(c) Examining the way a group is working, i.e. to examine group processes. Such as (i) norms, (ii) decision-making, and (iii) communication.

(d) Assessing the relationship among the people doing the work.

Thus, the fundamental aim of team building is to help the group members in examining their own behaviours and developing action plans that foster task accomplishment.

Team Building Cycle

Team building usually follows a logical cycle as:

In team building, employees belonging to some work group gather and discuss problems relating to their task performance. These discussions are generally held away from the regular organisational settings and are as frank and candid as possible. In a typical team building exercise, sessions start with identifying

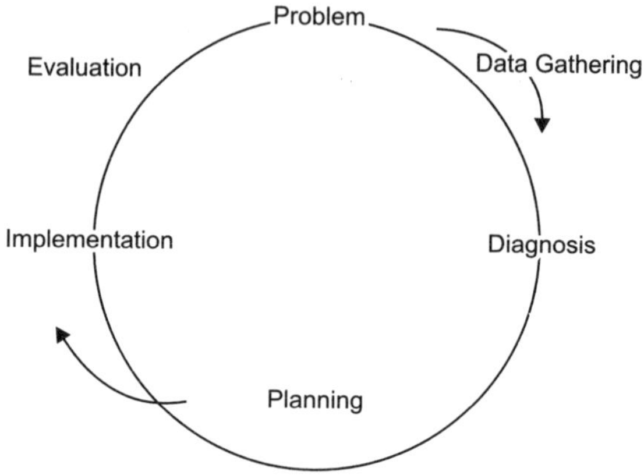

Team Building Cycle

the current problems such as inefficient procedures, ineffective policies and role ambiguities, etc. Members of the team building contribute information concerning their individual perceptions of issues, problems and task relationship having agreed on the key problems/difficulties. Assessments regarding the impact of these tactics are done in the final or concluding session.

Necessary Conditions for the Success of Team Building Programme

Before attempting to undertake the team building exercise the management has to ensure that:

(a) Basic interdependence among the members of the group exist (when task interdependencies do not exist, then team building is an inappropriate intervention).

(b) The group members understand the stated goals clearly.

(c) The group members unanimously agree with the objectives.

(d) The group is capable of taking corrective action on the problems identified or at least will be able to tackle some reasonable percentage of them.

Empirical Assessment

Research reveals that team building has resulted in many favourable outcomes such as (i) positive changes in employees participation and involvement, (ii) job satisfaction, (iii) organisational climate, and (iv) attitudes of employees. It is also revealed that team building fostered the group's decision-making and problem-solving skills and other aspects of group behaviour.

Evaluation

Team building as an OD activity has become more popular than sensitivity training in the recent past. It is because of certain inherent advantages.

(a) Team building improves the organisation's problem-solving ability and decision-making skills.

(b) It results in effective inter-personal relationships.

(c) It helps understand intergroup communication and remove the barriers, if any, in the organisational communication pattern.

(d) It provides a useful way for the group to examine inter-personal issues.

(e) It provides a useful platform for the employees to involve in their OD programmes.

(f) It increases the probability of occurrence of collaborative behaviour.

Inspite of these benefits, team building as an OD intervention is severely criticized on the following grounds:

(a) Team building focuses only on work groups. It fails to consider the other organisational variables such as technology and structure.

(b) Team building becomes a complicated exercise especially when new groups are formed. When new groups emerge:

- Confusion arises in the roles and relationships among the group members when new members join.
- The technical competence of the new members may be distinctly different and they (new members) may find it very difficult to get along with the existing members.

– New members may often pay more attention to the tasks of the team rather than to the relationships among the team members.

Conclusions

As against sensitivity training where the primary focus is on individuals, the fundamental emphasis of the team building is on the work groups. The basic building blocks of organisations are groups of people and therefore, the basic units of change are also groups, not simply individuals. Managers appreciate the logic that the focal point for improving the organisational effectiveness is to improve the effectiveness of the building blocks–work teams. The practicing managers and OD consultants consider team building as one of the powerful and well developed organisational change approaches.

3. Survey Feedback

A well organised and systematic approach with relatively a long history of good performance is the survey feedback intervention of OD. The survey feedback technique is derived from a long and sound tradition of attitude measurement and survey research. It is a very valuable information and efficient technique for fostering organisational effectiveness. As it does not involve a high degree of emotional and soul searching on the part of participants, this technique is devoid of the main limitations of the emotional instability or psychological damage of the participants.

Of OD interventions survey feedback has much appeal and application. This intervention, which enjoys a widespread use nowadays, includes a package of four distinct steps:

(a) Collection of Data. First of all, information is gathered through comprehensive questionnaire. The questionnaire consists of company related multiple choice items. The items contained in the questionnaire focus on such key organisational issues as employees' satisfaction, quality and styles of leadership and various facets of organisational climate like decision-making and coordination.

(b) Feedback the Information. Reporting the information and the key findings to employees is another crucial step in survey feedback. The survey feedback results are fed directly to the participants rather than to the top management. The information that is fed must be clear and accurate.

Survey generated results must be presented in a non-threatening but constructive manner to the employees. Usually, the data are fedback in group discussion and problem-solving sessions. The OD expert conducting the survey feedback programme summarizes the findings in the clear-cut manner and elicits employees' reaction to them. But in the recent years, emphasis was placed upon sending written summaries of the results of the participants. This way, this approach is devoid of emotional involvement of organisational members, making of more productive as OD technique.

(c) **Develop an Action Plan.** Survey feedback programme will be rendered incomplete and meaningless if it does not contain the provision of developing an action plan to deal with the problem. The management should develop an action plan that is both (i) straightforward and (ii) workable. In this stage, participants are asked about their recommendations as how to resolve the problems that are uncovered in the survey.

(d) **Follow-up.** Without continuous feedback and correction of the programmes this intervention (for that matter any interventions) will be short-lived. It will be at the most an interesting experience. Normally, several months after the survey is conducted a check should be made to determine whether the action plans are implemented or not.

Necessary Conditions for the Success of the Survey Feedback Approach

For survey feedback to be successful, management should ensure that:

(i) The questionnaire administered must be valid and reliable.

(ii) Employees must be willing to report their views and reactions honestly.

(iii) The OD consultant conducting the programme must be skilled at interpreting the survey data.

(iv) Top management must be willing to use the information it gathers.

(v) The sessions are conducted in a factual and task oriented environment.

(vi) Each group has enough discretion to consider and acts upon its findings and analysis.

(vii) Organisational members trust each other (it is because distrust leads to response bias).

(viii) Participants do not feel deceived, manipulated or mis-represented.

Empirical Assessment

Survey feedback is proved to be fruitful OD technique. A study evaluating the effects of change techniques in several organisations revealed that survey feedback was a more effective change strategy than many other types. Some other researchers have also noted that it is a cost effective means of implementing a comprehensive programme, making it highly desirable and better rated technique.

The Institute for Social Research of the Michigan University has conducted empirical investigation over the survey feedback method of OD intervention. After a detailed review of the literature and research on survey feedback, researchers conclude, *the available data seems to indicate that the survey feedback can be an effective approach towards meeting organisational goals and individual needs.*

Evaluation

Survey feedback, as OD technique, is appreciated on many grounds:

(i) It can yield a great amount of information and data efficiently and quickly.

(ii) Decision-making and problem-solving abilities of the organisation can be improved tremendously because this approach applies the competence and knowledge throughout the organisation to the organisationally related issues.

(iii) It emphasizes and promotes two-way communication in the organisation.

(iv) It can increase the influence of the lower level managers.

(v) It has a broad coverage and includes all the members of the organisation.

(vi) Information, it provides often serves as the basis for concrete plans to enhance organisational effectiveness.

(vii) It is flexible and can be applied to many different organisations and to many different problems.

4. Grid Training

One of the most publicised techniques of OD is the Grid Organisational Development. Grid training is based on the "Managerial Grid" developed by Blake and Mouton of the University of Texas. It is a comprehensive step-by-step approach and represents a breakthrough in organisational development. Grid training approach offers a complete plan for OD.

Grid identifies a range of management behaviours based on various ways in which task oriented and people oriented styles can interact with each other. Instead of de-colonising the two dimensions of leadership concern for production and concern for people, Blake and Mouton contend that managers should be concerned with both people and production oriented in order to achieve effective performance results.

Out of the five styles, 9,9 or team manager style is the most desirable one according to Blake and Mouton, i.e., high concern for both (i) production and (ii) people. They contend that in order to maximize organisational effectiveness, managers must be trained to develop this 9,9 style of leadership. Blake and Mouton's Grid Training focuses on this perspective. It helps the managers to see their current leadership style and educate them to develop the most desirable style, i.e., 9,9 style.

The specific objectives of a Grid Organisation Development programme are to:

(i) Study the organisation as an interacting system and apply techniques of analysis in diagnosing its problems.

(ii) Understand the importance and rationale of systematic change in contrast to change by evolution and revolution.

(iii) Evaluate the styles of leadership and techniques of participation most likely to produce high quality results.

Development of managers leadership skills through good programme involves two parts and six overlapping phases as shown below:

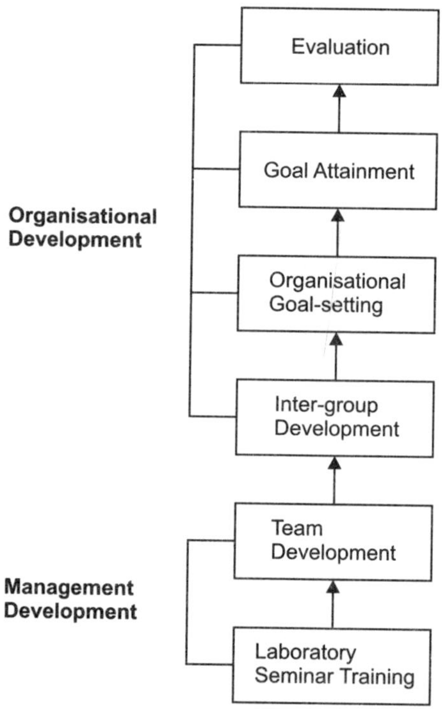

Part I: Management Development

Phase 1: Laboratory Seminar Training. First of all, grid concepts are introduced to the managers. At the outset of the grid seminar programme each participant's leadership style is assessed, evaluated and reviewed. After appropriate instructions, the key managers work to implement the grid programme throughout the organisation. The essence of this stage is that the managers are educated about the desirability of 9,9 style of leadership.

Phase 2: Team Development. Leaders learn here how to effectively function in group situations. They are made familiar with such concepts as team work, team culture, team conditions and alike. Managers here learn how to foster the team spirit.

An important objective of these first two phases is to build more effective relationships among groups, coworkers and between superiors and subordinates.

Part II: Organisational Development

Phase 3: Intergroup Development. The first two phases of Grid Training concentrates on individuals and single work-groups. The next four phases throw light on the overall organisation.

An important objective of the third phase is joint problem-solving. During this phase the emphasis is shifted to intergroup behavioural relations. Sources of intergroup conflict are carefully analysed and ways of fostering cooperation are considered here. The typical win-lose mentality in intergroup relations gets changed radically and the method of joint problem-solving is achieved in an atmosphere of problem, confrontation.

Phase 4: Organisational Goal-setting. During this phase, managers discuss and agree upon an ideal model for their organisation. Development of this blueprint involves developing convictions about ideal management practices, description of its major goals, structure, reward system and decision-making procedures. The model so developed by the top management is then reviewed by the lower level managers and commitment of the employees towards the major objectives is also attained.

Phase 5: Goal Attainment. It is the crucial phase where the managers attempt to accomplish the goals as set in the fourth phase. Participants seek to translate their thoughts about an organisational model into reality. Each sub-unit examines how their activities are to be carried out in order to achieve excellence and they proceed to take necessary and corrective action for any deviation.

Phase 6: Evaluation. Evaluating the pros and cons of grid training is the final fundamental phase. The current state of organisation is compared with this state prior to grid training during the phase. It helps in determining the areas of organisation that still need improvement or alterations. Also in this stage, efforts are made to stabilize positive and favourable changes and to identify the new areas of opportunity for the organisation. The underlying philosophy here is that, a consolidation is the capstone. It is also necessary to reinforce the new patterns of management learned from phase one to phase five.

Evaluation is an indispensable phase in grid training. It generally takes about one year (or more) after the first five phases are completed, so that weakness in the goals and plans are identified.

5. Process Consultation

No organisation operates perfectly. Managers often sense that their unit's performance can be improved, but they are unable to identify (i) what can be improved and (ii) how it can be improved. The purpose of 'process consultation' is for an outside consultant to assist a client, usually a manager, "to perceive, understand and act upon process events" with which he must deal.

Process consultation concentrates on certain specific area, such as, communication, functional roles of members, group problem-solving and decision-making, group norms and growth, leadership and authority and inter-group cooperation and competition.

The assumptions underlying the process consultation model are:

(i) Managers often need special diagnostic help in knowing what is wrong with the organisation.

(ii) Most managers have constant desire to increase organisational effectiveness, but they need help in deciding 'how' to achieve it.

(iii) Managers can be effective if they learn to diagnose their own strengths and weaknesses without exhaustive and time-consuming study of the organisation.

(iv) The outside consultant cannot learn enough about the culture of the organisation, to suggest reliable new courses of action. He should, therefore, work jointly with the members of the organisation.

(v) The client must learn to see the problem for himself, understand the problem and suggest a remedy. The consultant should provide new and challenging alternatives for the client to consider. However, the decision-making authority on these alternatives about organisational changes remains with the client.

(vi) It is essential that the process consultant is an expert in diagnosing and establishing effective helping relationships with the client. Effective process consultant involves passing those skills to the client.

Process Consultation–Steps

The process consultation normally proceeds along the following lines:

(a) **Initial Contact.** Here the client comes into contact with the consultant and specifies the problems that cannot be solved by normal organisational procedures or resources.

(b) **Define the Relationship.** After identifying the specific problem areas, the consultant and the client enter into a formal contract. The formal contract spells out the services, time and the fees of the consultant. Actually this is also a psychological contract because both parties are involved in the satisfaction of certain expectations.

(c) **Select the Method of Work.** It involves the clear-cut understanding of where and how the consultant will perform the job. Each individual employee in the organisation is made aware of who the consultant is so that he can help the consultant by furnishing the required information.

(d) **Collection of Data and Diagnosis.** The consultant invests a great deal of time in collecting the relevant information. Normally he gathers data through questionnaires, observations and personal interviews, etc., and then makes an indepth diagnosis of the problem.

(e) **Intervention.** Various interventions by the consultant such as agenda setting, feedback, coaching and structural suggestions are made in the process consultation approach. During this phase, the solutions designed by the consultant will be translated into action in the organisation.

(f) **Reducing Involvement and Termination.** When the goals of OD intervention have been successfully achieved, the consultant leaves the organisation by closing the formal contract with the client.

Empirical Assessment

Process consultation is designed to change attitudes, values, inter-personal skills, group norms and cohesiveness and other process variables. Evidence shows that it is often effective in facilitating these changes. As against this, there is also evidence stating that there is no correlation between the outcome variables such as task performance, and satisfaction of the employees and the process consultation. There is conspicuous absence of evidence that process consultation is seldom the role component of organisational change programme, it is generally combined with other OD interventions.

Evaluation

Process consultation is relatively speaking, a traditional approach to OD. One important advantage of this technique is that it focuses attention on the inter-personal and inter-group problem faced by the organisations in a direct way. The professional consultant assists the organisational members in facing the problems, squarely and resolve the conflicts in a dispassionate way. However, the success of this technique to a large extent, depends on the diagnostic skills of the consultant. If the consultant is lacking the requisite experience and skills the whole exercise may be self-defeating. Again, it is always not possible to ascertain how effectively the consultant works.

6. Management by Objectives

Management by objective (MBO) is an extremely popular tool of OD. In fact, it is one of the thirteen most popular management techniques used in the industry. As an OD technique it involves the following steps:

(i) People who are involved in the programme must be educated about the basic principles and procedures of MBO.

(ii) Employees and managers meet formally and agree upon clear-cut and quantifiable objectives.

(iii) Progress towards the chosen objectives is reviewed after some internal feedback is provided to employees.

(iv) An overall evaluation is made to assess the current progress for the next cycle of objective setting and planning.

MBO is a comprehensive overall managerial philosophy, the main emphasis being the joint goal setting. It tries to coordinate the efforts of individual employees with the organisational goals. Many firms have instituted programmes and practices based on MBO. MBO is increasingly used in a large number of modern organisations and one study reports that 83 per cent of business firms in United States are employing MBO.

Evaluation

Both forces of light and the forces of darkness have polarized the field of MBO. Forces of light have been characterised by certain benefits that MBO provides to an organisation, and forces of darkness have been represented by the criticism leveled against the practices of MBO.

Strengths

Advocates of MBO claim that it provides the following advantages:

Benefits for the Enterprise

- Focuses the manager's efforts on the right objectives.
- Improves the potential for achieving objectives such as profits, productivity and satisfaction.
- Provides the necessary data to reward managers 'objectively'.

- Helps in pinpointing the human development needs.
- Assists in identifying promotable managers.
- Facilitates the enterprises ability to change.
- Helps in bringing coordination of the efforts of the enterprise.

Benefits for Superiors

- Helps the superior in coaching the subordinates.
- Helps in eliminating the vague and rigid performance appraisal tools.
- Effectively motivates the subordinates to perform better.

Benefits for Employees and Lower-level Managers

- It lets individuals know what is expected of them.
- It makes individuals more aware of the organisation's goals.
- It increases employee job satisfaction.
- It also lets subordinates know how well they are doing in relation to the organisation's goals.
- It provides measurable objectives that the employees are expected to achieve.

MBO thus has many advantages to offer to the individual employees, superiors and also for the top management. Since all levels of organisations are involved in goal setting, the organisation will have the feeling of 'unity'; lower-level managers are more aware of the top management's expectations and in turn assist in establishing attainable objectives.

Weaknesses

But all is not a bed of roses in the case of MBO. MBO is fraught with a number of limitations, viz.:

(a) **Some Questions.** Critics have pounced upon the MBO with a number of questions such as:

- Whether joint goal setting among unequals is really possible?
- Can MBO be applied at lower levels in an organisation?

- Whether MBO aids in evaluating and rewarding the performance of the employees?
- Whether setting objectives as explicitly as possible is always functional?
- Can MBO be applied to dynamic and changing environment?

(b) Conflicting Goals. Goal setting is a major component of MBO. Another potential drawback of MBO is that the goals of organisation may be conflicting in nature. They may be sometimes inconsistent too.

> Organisations may wish to maximize productivity as well as to maintain good labour management relations. Also participation of the employees in goal setting may result in goal displacement. With participation individuals may optimize their own objectives at the cost of overall objectives.

(c) Excessive Paper Work. The programme requires excessive formality in filling out the processing forms and the managers are frequently caught up in report writing. Consequently an excessive amount of paper work and red-tape develops.

(d) Long Span. Another notable drawback of MBO is that its implementation requires a considerably long span ranging from two to five years. Many organisations are tempted to terminate this programme on this score alone.

Empirical Assessment

Although the assured benefits of MBO are not wholly scientifically validated, some research evidence is available in support of MBO as an OD technique:

(i) Some studies by Meyer et al. suggests that MBO is associated with improved planning and organisation of work. These researchers conclude that the experimental groups using MBO achieved the benefits more than the control group using the standard performance appraisal methods.

(ii) Another researcher is of the view that MBO improved planning and utilization of resources and interpersonal communication. He, however, contends that goal achievement is improved only when managers and superiors are strongly pro-MBO.

(iii) In one study by Fred Luthans about MBO in hospitals it was found that 41 per cent of the hospitals surveyed were using MBO and another 33 per cent were planning to start it in the near future. The great majority of respondents reported that MBO had improved the performance in some major areas like planning, coordination, control and communication.

ORGANISATIONAL DEVELOPMENT–BENEFITS

Individual employees, groups/teams and the organisations are benefited by the organisational development programmes. The benefits of OD include:

- Performance improvements.
- Job specification.
- Self-change.

– OD programmes contribute to the increase in the job performance of individual employees, groups and the organisation. Impact of OD can be measured by comparing the performance of the controlled group with that of the non-controlled group. Group performance will be enhanced much as OD emphasis on group activity.

– OD programmes encourage, (i) team work, (ii) communication skills, (iii) cooperation, (iv) interpersonal relations, (v) openness, etc. Employees with these changing behavioural dimensions feel happy and have a sense of satisfaction about the job and the organisation.

– OD programmes contribute to the change in behaviour, values, attitudes, perceptions, etc., by enabling the employees to understand about themselves and others in the group and the organisation. This results in self-change of the employees.

CASE STUDY

The High-priced OD Consultant

The middle managers of a large firm were told by corporate personnel office that a group of consultants would be calling on them later in the week. The purpose of the consultants visit would be to analyse intergroup relations throughout the firm. The consultants had been very effective in using an OD intervention called team building. Their particular approach used six steps. When their approach was explained to the managers, a great deal of tension was relieved. They had initially thought that team building was a lot of hocus pocus, like sensitivity training where people attack each other and let out their aggressions by heaping abuses on those they dislike. By the same token, these managers generally felt that perhaps the consultants were not needed. One of them put it this way: "Now that we understand what is involved in team building, we can go ahead and conduct the session ourselves. All we have to do is to choose a manager who is liked by everyone and put him in the role of the change agent/consultant. After all, you really don't need a high priced consultant to do this team building stuff, you just have to have a good feel for human nature." The other managers generally agreed. However, the corporate personnel director turned their suggestion down. He hired the OD consultants to do the team building.

DISCUSSION POINTS

1. What is a team building approach to organisation development? Do you think the managers had an accurate view of the technique?
2. Do you think the managers had an accurate view of the role of the external consultants? Do you agree or disagree with the corporate personnel director's decision to turn down their suggestions? Why?

QUESTIONS

- Define Organisational Development. What are its techniques? Do they really work?

- List a variety of methods for helping employees unfreeze their attitudes and behaviour. Why, or why not these are used often?
- Write notes on:
  - (a) OD movement.
  - (b) OD process.
- Differentiate between:
  - (a) Behavioural and non-behavioural interventions.
  - (b) Laboratory training and managerial grid training.
  - (c) Individual training and organisational development.
- "Traditional training helps employees learn something, but OD helps them learn how to learn something?" Discuss this statement suggested by a manager.
- Think of some organisations, where you have worked or of which you are a member. How can it benefit from OD? What specific OD interventions would you recommend and why?
- Indicate the correct response against the following multiple choice questions:
  - OD:
    - (a) is a simple process.
    - (b) is a clearly defined field of study.
    - (c) involves unplanned change.
    - (d) is based on knowledge of the behavioural sciences.
    - (e) utilizes an unsystematic change process.
  - A collateral organisation:
    - (a) is a temporary structure.
    - (b) maintains output maximization as its primary purpose.
    - (c) has a high division of labour.
    - (d) consists of many levels of authority.
    - (e) has rotational, flexible, job assignments.

PART V

Organisational Power and Politics

13

Learning Objectives

- Definition, Characteristics and Significance of Power
- Power Versus Authority
- Bases and Sources of Power in Organisations
- Power Dynamics
- Meaning of Organisational Politics
- Reasons of Political Behaviour/Universality of Political Behaviour
- Techniques of Political Behaviour/Types of Organisational Politics
- Managing Political Behaviour

POWER–DEFINED

Power is easy to feel and happy to exercise but difficult to define. It is a force that cannot be seen, but its impact (effects) can be felt. Power is extremely difficult to identify and measure objectively. Researchers exhibit an aversion to deal with matters of power because it defies precise definition and quantification. Much difficulty is due to the multi-dimensional nature of power.

Many definitions of power have been advanced, let us consider some of them:

> "*Power is the ability to get things done the way one wants them to be done.*"
>
> (G.R. Salancik and J. Pffifer)

"*Power is the potential ability of the person or group to influence another person or group.*"

(Ricky W. Griffin and Gregory Moorhead)

"*Power refers to a capacity that A has to influence the behaviour of B, so that B does something he or she would not otherwise do.*"

(Stephen P. Robbins)

"*The possibility of imposing one's will on the behaviour of others.*"

(John Keeneth Galbraith)

From the above definitions the following points emerge:

- Power represents the capacity, ability or potential to influence the behaviour of other people to achieve a certain goal.
- Power is based on the two tier concept of influencing others and being influenced.
- Power can be potential or enacted.
- Power is neither completely formal nor informal. It is rather a judicious mixture of the two.
- Leaders exercise power to accomplish goals of an organisation.
- Leaders have only as much power as others allow them to have.
- Sometimes appearing to be powerful is just as important as being powerful.
- Power is the difference between the two probabilities: (i) the probability of an event occurring by the given action of the power-holder, (ii) the probability of event occurring without the power-holder's action.

POWER–SIGNIFICANCE

In spite of all negative connotations, power is a vital and necessary part of organisations. It is essential because it is like fuel that provides energy to run organisational machinery. It is a necessity because managers without power are merely figureheads and cannot effectively function to deliver goods.

Unlike in the past, there is a growing interest in power currently. We can attribute this renewal of interest to change in organisational structure and the corresponding change in philosophy of management. Traditional structures emphasize rationality in organisational procedures; whereas, contemporary behaviour theories give tremendous weight to power and politics and in fact, the current systems theory has made a convenient berth to power sub-system. The contemporary social scholars considered power and influence and political factors as the major determinants of behaviour. The modern organisation structure is the outcome of a contest for power between coalitions in the organisation.

Researchers stress that organisational processes are political processes in which power-holders try to influence goals, directions and other major parameters of an organisation. Power has emerged as the most important part in modern organisations. Failure to understand power will dramatically reduce the ability to understand organisational behaviour.

POWER–CHARACTERISTICS

The following are the basic characteristics of power:

1. Dependency Relationships

The fundamental features of power is dependence. The higher the dependence of one person on another the higher is the amount of power he can exert on him.

> If 'P' is the power a person 'x' has on another person 'y'. It tantamounts to saying something as dependence 'D' of y on x. Symbolically Pxy = Dyx.

When an employee is not depending on the supervisor for receiving rewards then, truly speaking the supervisor has no power over such employee.

John P. Kotter asserts that "an effective manager quite often gains power by feeding others" believes that they are dependent on manager for help or not for being inflicted or hurt.

Dependence may be, in fact, actual or perceived. But whatever may be the dependence, it leads to the creation of power.

2. Power is Specific

Another associated feature of power is that it is specific. It is specific in the sense that it can be exercised by some people that too in some circumstances. Power cannot be exercised by all people all times. The domain of power, i.e., the extent to which one has power over wide range of issues, however, is different for different people. The range may be higher in some, lower in others.

3. Reciprocal Relationships

"Only supervisors or managers or top ranking officials have power" is a misconception. Power relationships in an organisation are essentially reciprocal in nature. Power exists only in a relationship between two or more persons. It is based on the two-way concept of influencing others and being influenced. True that the nature of power exercised by different people in organisations at different levels is somewhat basically different, but all can have power, including those in the lower rungs. Therefore, there is no specific power center in an organisation. Moreover, power is neither completely formal nor completely informal.

4. Power can Expand or Contract

Power is elastic. People who are habituated to exercise power, try to acquire more power and expand it. As people reach higher and higher positions the legitimate power attached to the positions also simultaneously increases. Sometimes due to change in position of a manager in an organisation, i.e. shift from the one department to another can cause contraction in power.

POWER *VS.* AUTHORITY

Power and authority should not be taken as same for there are some differences between these two concepts. The table given on the next page highlights the main differences.

	Power	Authority
1.	Ability	Right
	Power is the ability of an individual to affect and influence others.	Authority is the right to command and extract work from employees.
2.	Leadership	Managership
	Power is generally associated with leadership.	Authority is vested with managers.
3.	Broad	Narrow
	Power is a broader concept and includes authority also in some sense. Authority is nothing but institutionalized power.	Authority is a narrow concept a manager may have considerable authority but still may be powerless.
4.	Two faces	No distinctive faces
	Power has two faces. Negative and positive. Personal domination at the expense of other is negative; socialized power is its praiseworthy positive face.	We cannot make such markedly distinct faces of authority. Any such distinction becomes ridiculous with regard to authority.
5.	Personal	Positional
	Power is a personal quality.	Authority is mostly vested in the position. Legitimate power is similar to authority.

POWER–BASIS AND SOURCES

The most widely used and recognized analysis of the bases of power is the framework developed by French and Raven. They identified five general bases of power in organisational setting, viz.:

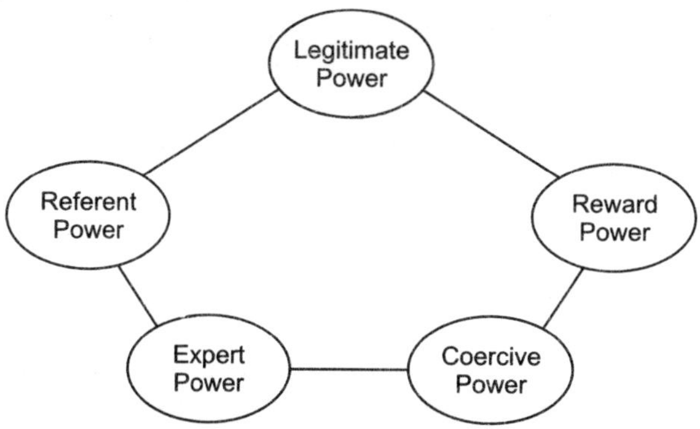

Bases of Organisational Power

1. Legitimate Power

Legitimate power is granted by virtue of one's position in the organisation. The organisation itself thus provides the power. A manager has legitimate power over his or her subordinates, as well as over their subordinates. Thus, legitimate power is essentially the same as authority. It can be created, granted, changed and withdrawn by the formal organisation. The organisation declares whether it is proper, or legitimate, for the designated individual to direct the activities of others. The quantum of legitimate power a manager exercises depends on the nature of his task, the organisation and the willingness of the manager to exercise power.

2. Reward Power

The ability to reward or punish is another base of power. Managers have power because they have a considerable say over the organisational rewards such as promotions, increase in pay or salary, desirable work assignments, etc. Managers who have control over the resources and who can distribute rewards to employees are perceived by the employees that the managers have power. Managers exercise this power by appreciating the employees performance and rewarding him suitably.

> In an organisation, the line managers who have a direct control over much of the resources have this kind of reward lower than those in the advisory roles.

Reward power can extend beyond extrinsic rewards. It may include such (i) subjective and (ii) intrinsic rewards as praise and recognition. If the subordinate is interested in acceptance and recognition of his contributions and the manager can provide such rewards, then this serves as an additional form of reward.

3. Coercive Power

On the other end of the reward power is the coercive power which is the ability to influence punishment. It reflects the extent to which a manager can deny desired rewards or administer punishment to control other people. The more sanctions a manager is able to bear upon others, the stronger is his coercive power. Some managers belittle the efforts of others in front of their peers and get away with it. To that degree, they possess the coercive power. The coercive power, which is the power to reprimand, demote or fire subordinates for unsatisfactory performance is seldom exercised because of the cost involved in the form of employee resentment and hostility.

4. Expert Power

It is more of a personal power, rather than organisational power and is the ability to control another person's behaviour through the possession of (i) knowledge and (ii) expertise that the other person needs and does not possess himself.

> A subordinate will obey the superior simply because the subordinate believes that the superior 'knows' what is to be done and how it is to be done.

> We generally follow our doctors or our accountants advice and instructions because we believe in their ability and knowledge in those specified areas.

5. Referent Power

It is also known as charismatic power. Some people have unusual flair and pleasing personality and attract others. Through attraction they influence others and this is called referent power.

> Advertisers take advantage of this type of power when they use celebrities, such as movie stars or sports figures, to do testimonial advertising.

The managers who have good inter-personal relations, who are good at public meetings and speeches, who maintain high moral standards command this kind of power. People try to emulate highly visible behaviours of their executives regardless of whether the managers later have the legitimacy to reward or punish.

SOURCES OF POWER

The sources of power tell us where the power-holder gets his/her power from, i.e., sources refer to how you come to control your base of power. There are two sources:

1. Position Power

Position power resides in the position, regardless of the person involved. Thus, legitimate, reward, and some aspects of coercive and expert power can all contribute to position power. Position power is thus parallel to authority.

In creating a position, the organisation creates a sphere of power for the incumbent. He or she will generally have the power to direct the activities of subordinates in the performance of their jobs, control some of the potential rewards and have a say in their punishment and discipline.

There are, however, limits to the manager's position power. The manager cannot order or control activities falling outside his or her sphere of power such as directing a subordinate to engage in illegal activities, perform personal services or undertake actions that are clearly beyond the boundaries of the subordinate's role.

2. Personal Power

Personal power resides in the person, regardless of his or her position in the organisation. Thus, the primary bases of personal power are referent and some traces of expert, coercive and reward power. Personal power is usually exercised through rational persuasion by the powerful person or through follower's identification with him or her.

DYNAMICS OF POWER

Power dynamics can be seen from four angles, viz.:

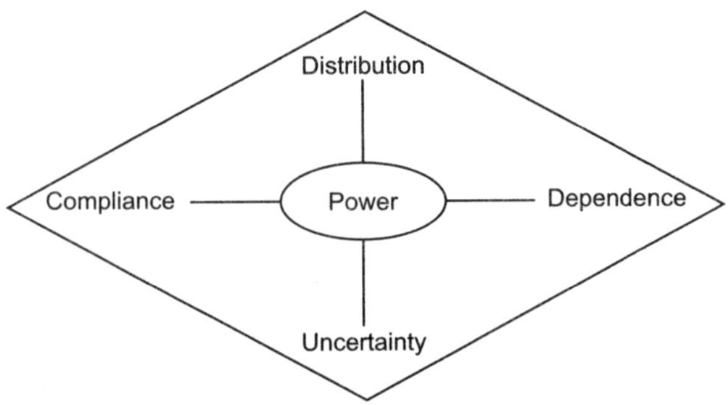

1. Distribution

The following points are worth noting about distribution in the dynamics of power.

(a) There is no rational and equal distribution of power among the organisational members.

(b) Those in power develop a tendency to resist change in power in the distribution of it among the members of the group. They rather become greedy of acquiring it further.

(c) No individual can have power at all (i) times and (ii) places. They might have to forego or sometimes get deprived of it. In such cases they try their best to retain it, in the event of a failure to retain the power they form a coalition.

2. Dependency

The dynamics of power can also be understood by considering the following points regarding 'dependency':

(a) Power one exercises largely depends on the dependency relationships. The greater the dependency of x on y, the greater the power of y on x.

(b) The greater the dependency of an organisation on some limited number of individuals, the greater the power these individual have.

(c) Sometimes, low ranking members who have expertise over high ranking members, have power. It is because high ranking officials may have to depend on rank and file.

(d) A person difficult to be replaced has a greater power than one who can be easily replaceable.

3. Uncertainty

The uncertainty element in the dynamics of power can be understood by considering the following points:

(a) Organisations seek to avoid uncertainty as far as possible. Those people who can absorb the organisations uncertainty are likely to have more power than others.

(b) Uncertainty dependents on the nature of the organisation.

> In a marketing firm, sales executives confront uncertainty and have more power.

> In a factory where production takes place, labourers are more powerful; engineers are powerful in managing and dealing with machines and technologies.

4. Compliance

The dynamics of power with regard to compliance can be understood by considering the following:

(a) People comply with legitimate power most often, of the five bases of power (legitimate, reward, coercive, expert, referent). People, also, emulate referent power and comply with expert power.

(b) People perceive reward and coercive power as weak for complying with manager's requests. Research on college teachers and marketing people, both demonstrated this conclusion.

POLITICS–DEFINED

A concept closely related to power in organisational setting is politics, or political behaviour. Jeffrey Pfeffer has defined 'organisational politics' as, "*activities carried out by people to acquire, enhance and use power and other resources to obtain their preferred outcomes in a situation where there is uncertainty or disagreement.*"

Thus, political behaviour is the general means by which people attempt to use power. The goal of such behaviour is to get one's own way about things. The following points are worth noting in this connection:

- Power characterises political action.
- Political action take place when an actor recognises that achievement of his goals is influenced by the behaviour of others.

- Politicking involves the elimination of adversaries by the influential maneuvers of a member of the organisation.
- Politics also involve the management of influence to obtain ends not sanctioned by the formal organisation.
- Any behaviour by organisational member that is self-serving may be termed 'political'.
- Organisational politics exist wherever people work together.
- Behaviour referred to as politics takes place in varying degrees in all organisations.
- Not all behaviour can be categorised as 'political'.

> An employee asking for a rise in pay is not political behaviour, but the use of threat to unionise to obtain a raise would be a political act.

Politics is, thus intentional act of influencing others through the acquired power to enhance self-interest and advancement.

POLITICAL BEHAVIOUR–REASONS/UNIVERSALITY OF POLITICAL BEHAVIOUR

Robert Miles identified five major reasons that have strong influences on political orientation of organisation. These are mentioned hereunder:

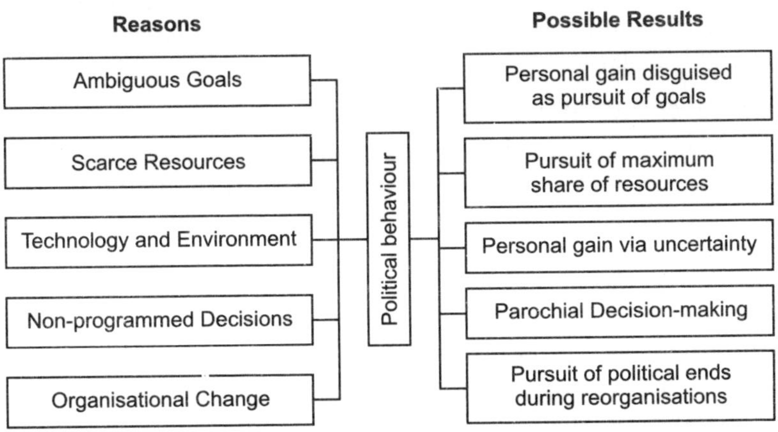

1. Ambiguous Goals

When the goals of an organisation are clearly defined and each member of the organisation is aware of these and is also aware of his role in contributing towards achievements of such goals then there are limited grounds for political influence. However, when the goals of a department or the entire organisation are ambiguous then more room is available for playing politics.

2. Scarce Resource

Whenever resources are scarce, some people will not get everything they believe they deserve or need. Thus, they are likely to engage in political behaviour as a strategy to maximize their share of resources.

> A manager seeking a larger budget might present accurate but misleading or incomplete statistics to inflate the perceived importance of her department. Because no organisation has unlimited resources, incentives for this kind of political behaviour are always present.

3. Technology and Environment

Organisational effectiveness is largely a function of the organisation's ability to appropriately respond to external environment which is highly dynamic and generally unpredictable as well as adequately adopt to complex technological developments. Thus, political behaviour is increased when the internal technology is complex and when external environment is highly volatile.

4. Non-programmed Decisions

Non-programmed decisions involve unique problems which cannot be solved by known and structure methods and procedures. These unique problems involve many factors and variables that are ambiguous in nature leaving room for political maneuvering by those who have the knowledge and techniques to successfully confront and solve such complex problems. Such non-programmed decisions are likely to be made in the areas of strategic planning, mergers and acquisitions, policy change, etc.

5. Organisational Change

Changes in organisations occur regularly and can take different (i) shapes and (ii) forms. Each such change introduces some (i) uncertainty and (ii) ambiguity into the organisational system, at least it has been completely institutionalized. This period usually affords ample opportunity for political activity.

> A manager worried about the consequences of a reorganisation may resort to politics to protect the scope of her authority.

POLITICAL BEHAVIOUR–TECHNIQUES/TYPES OF ORGANISATIONAL POLITICS

Several techniques are used in the practice of political behaviour. Unfortunately, these have not been systematically studied. This problem is further complicated because the participants themselves are not aware that they are using particular techniques. The most frequently used techniques are summarized hereunder:

1. Control Communication Channels

People who may be in low level hierarchical position but have some control over lines of communication can yield considerable political power.

> Secretaries frequently control access to their bosses. The secretary may have considerable power in deciding who see the boss and who does not at a given time. She may use this power in favouring those whom she likes and frustrating those against whom she may have a grudge.

2. Controlling Information

One technique of political behaviour is to control the dissemination of critical information to others. Releasing good or bad news when it is likely to have its fullest impact can promote someone's self-interest and may thwart the hopes of others. The more critical the information and fewer the people who have it the stronger, the power base of those who possess such information.

> If a manager comes to know that a subordinate would be reprimanded for some actions and if he informs the subordinate so that the subordinate can prepare an adequate and timely defense, then the manager has gained some power over the subordinate for future use.

3. Image Building

Image building is a subtle form of behaviour and a positive impression on others by personality, appearance and style. Some of the factors that enhance a preferred image consist of being well dressed, having a pleasant smile, being attentive, honest, sociable and loyal to the organisational interests. In addition, always project an image of competence and self-assurance. Be on top of everything and work hard and be associated with successful projects.

4. Game Playing

A complex technique that may take many different forms is game playing. When playing games, the manager simply works within the rules of the organisation to increase the probability that his preferred outcomes will come about.

> A manager making recommendations about pay raises might tell, each subordinate, in strictest confidence, that he has recommended him for the largest pay rise in the department, when in truth everyone will be getting exactly the same increase. However, the manager is using his control over information to play games with his subordinates.

5. Cultivate the Right Allies

There is strength in numbers and more people you have on your side, the more political power you will have. It is necessary, however, to have the alliances with the right people. Alliances with people who are rising up the corporate ladder is much more advantageous than alliance with those whose careers are on the decline. It is necessary and useful to be friends with upper level management and it may also be obviously advantageous to form alliances with the boss's secretary or someone who is close to the powerful person.

In academic institutions where promotions and reappointments are primarily at the discretion of the divisional chairperson, a favourable association with the chairperson is highly beneficial.

6. Controlling Decision Parameters

This technique can be used only in certain situations and requires a high degree of subtlety. Instead of trying to control the actual decision, the manager backs up one step and tries to control the parameters by which the decision is made. This allows him to take less active role in the actual decision but still achieve his preferred outcome.

A district manager wants a proposed new factory to be constructed on a site in his region. If he tries to influence the decision directly, his arguments will be seen as biased and self-serving. Instead he may take a very active role in defining the criteria on which the decision will be based, such as target population, access to rail transportation, tax rates, etc. If he is a skilful negotiator, he may be able to influence the decision parameters in such a way that his desired location subsequently appears to be the ideal site. Hence, he brings about his desired outcome without playing a prominent role in the actual decision.

7. Try to be Positively Popular

Most people like to be appreciated and complemented. When you appreciate other people they will think very positively towards you. Do not talk ill of any person. Always talk good of others especially when they are not present. This will create extensive goodwill about you and this will always be useful whenever you would need their support.

MANAGING POLITICAL BEHAVIOUR

Though it is virtually impossible to eliminate political behaviour in organisations, it is, however, possible to contain it in such a manner as to limit its dysfunctional consequences. Some of the steps that can be taken for purposes of constraining political activity are summarized as under:

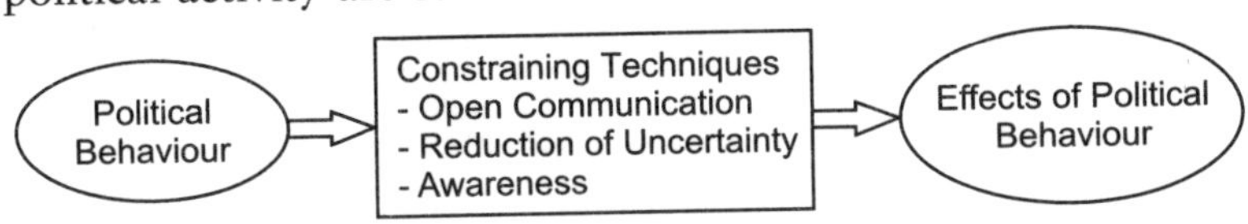

Open Communication

Since political behaviour is a function of control over (i) resources, (ii) information, and (iii) lines of communication, open and honest communication is an effective technique in constraining the effects of political behaviour. If the lines of communication are open to all and the necessary information is available to all including the information regarding the availability and allocation of scarce resources, then it would not be necessary to engage in political behaviour in order to acquire or control these resources.

Reduction of Uncertainty

Politics seems to be more prevalent when overall purposes and organisational goals are ambiguous and when expectations of subordinates are not clear and when organisational changes are not made known to all. These elements of uncertainty can provide grounds for political play. Thus political behaviour can be limited if such uncertainty can be reduced or eliminated. This can be done by giving well defined assignments to all employees making it clear to them as to what the management's expectations of the employees are relative to achievement of clearly defined organisational goals.

Thus, participative decision-making and making all relevant information known to all members of the organisation at the appropriate time and helping them integrate their personal objectives with organisational objectives will reduce the necessity of political behaviour.

Awareness

It is important that top management be aware of the (i) psychology and (ii) philosophy of political behaviour. Simply being aware of the (i) causes and (ii) techniques of political behaviour can minimize their effects. This knowledge could prepare the top management not only in combating political behaviour when it occurs but also in anticipating it and taking appropriate steps to avoid it from accruing.

> An organisational change may be expected to result in formation of a coaliation of certain members who would oppose such a change. By being aware of such possibility, the management can take steps to stop such a coalition from forming or take appropriate measures to successfully confront such a coaliation, should it form.

CASE STUDY

Throwing Away a Golden Opportunity

Roger Allen was a man on the move. Everyone in the firm felt that someday he would be company President. To listen to his boss, Harry Walden, it was only a matter of time before Roger would be at the helm of affairs.

The current President of the firm was a marketing person. She had worked her way up from field salesperson to President by selling both the product and herself to customers and the company alike. In a manner of speaking, the department was the 'well-oiled' road to the top. Roger was the number one salesperson and, according to the grapevine, was due to get Harry Walden's job when the latter retired in two years. However, Roger was not sure that he wanted to be Vice President of marketing. Another slot was opening up in foreign sales. Roger knew nothing about selling to Europe, but this was the firm's first venture outside the United States, and he thought he might like to give it a try. He talked to Harry about it, but the Vice President tried to discourage him. In fact, Harry seemed to think that Roger was crazy to consider the job at all. 'Kid', he said, "that is no place for you. Things are soft and cozy back here. You do not have to prove yourself to anyone. You are the number 1 boy around here. Just sit tight and you will be President. Do not go out and make some end runs. Just keeping barreling up the middle for 4 yards on each carry, and you will score the bit touchdown." Roger was not convinced. He thought perhaps it would be wise to discuss the matter with the President herself. This he did. The President was very interested in Roger's ideas about international marketing. "If you really think you'd like to head up this office for us, I will recommend you for the job."

After thinking over the matter carefully, Roger decided that he would much rather go to Europe and try to help establish a foothold over there than sit back and wait for the stateside opening. He told his decision to Harry. "Harry, I have talked to the President, and she tells me that this new opening in foreign sales is really going to get a big push from the company. It is where the action is. I realize that I could sit back and take it easy for the next couple of years, but I did rather have the international job." Harry again told Roger that he was making a mistake. "You are throwing away a golden opportunity. However, if you want it, I will support you."

A week later, when the company selected somebody else from sales to head the international division, Roger was crushed. The President explained the situation to him in this way: "I thought you wanted the job and I pushed for you. However, the other members of the selection committee voted against me. I can tell you that you certainly did not sell Harry very strongly on your idea. He led the committee to believe that you were really undecided about the entire matter. In fact, I felt rather foolish telling them how excited you were about the whole thing. Only to have Harry say he'd talked to you since that time and you were not that sure at all. Harry got done, the committee figured you had changed your mind after talking to me, and they went on to discuss other likely candidates."

DISCUSSION POINTS

1. Who had power in this organisation? What type of power did Harry Walden have?
2. Do you think Roger played company politics well? If so, why didn't he get the international sales job?
3. At this point, what would you do if you were Roger? What political strategies could you use?

QUESTIONS

- What is power? Discuss various sources of power.
- How do you measure power? What are the positive and negative consequences of power?
- How power and politics influence behaviour? Explain the ethical issues involved in power and politics.

- Explain in detail some methodologies for managing political behaviour.
- Differentiate between:
  - (a) Positional power and personal power.
  - (b) Structural sources of power and situational sources of power.
  - (c) Power and authority.
- "Several techniques used in the practice of political behaviour have not been systematically studied. This problem is further complicated because the participants themselves are not aware that they are using a particular problem." In the light of this statement summarise the various techniques of organisational politics.
- What mistakes can you make to fall from political grace? Give historical examples to support your answer.
- Indicate the correct response against the following multiple choice questions:
  - One reason that political behaviour occurs so often in an organisation is:
    - (a) Organisational change.
    - (b) Abundant resources.
    - (c) Clear goals.
    - (d) Programmed decisions.
    - (e) Routine techniques.
  - Individuals that often have expert power on the organisation are:
    - (a) Upper level managers.
    - (b) Lower level employees.
    - (c) Middle level managers.
    - (d) CEOs.
    - (e) All of the above.

Organisational Culture and Climate

14

Learning Objectives

- Definition and Characteristics of Organisational Culture
- Types of Organisational Culture
- Cultural Concepts
- Functions and Dysfunctions of Culture
- Maintaining Cultures Through Steps of Socialisation
- How Employees Learn Cultures?
- Organisational Climate Defined
- Factors Affecting Organisational Climate
- Emerging Issues of Organisational Climate
- Meaning and Nature of Organisational Effectiveness

ORGANISATIONAL CULTURE–DEFINED

Culture is an anthropological term that is applicable to organisations too. It represents a pattern of beliefs and behaviours that have been learned from other members of the society. It is, in its broadest sense, the cultivated behaviour i.e., the totality of man's learned experience which is socially transmitted. It is most frequently described as custom and includes both actions, man-made objects called artifacts and also ideas. Organisational culture plays a significant role in the area of motivation and the level of economic rewards. Organisational culture also influences the level of commitment to work on the part of the members. Individuals with altogether different backgrounds or at different levels in the organisation have a tendency to describe the organisational culture in most similar terms. Actually, organisational culture is a descriptive term. Different researchers defined it differently. Let us consider some of them.

> "*A system of shared meaning held by members that distinguishes the organisation from other organisations.*"
>
> (Stephen P. Robbins)

> "*Organisational culture is concerned with how employees perceive the six basic characteristics (i) individual, (ii) autonomy, (iii) structure, (iv) reward, (v) consideration, and (vi) conflict.*"
>
> (John P. Compbell)

> "*The cultural characteristics of an organisation are relatively enduring over time and relatively static in their propensity to change.*"
>
> (Garlic A. Forehand and Haller Glimer)

Organisational culture is very important to study because it conveys some important assumptions and norms governing values, attitudes and goals of organisational members. It also tells employees how to do things, and in what fashion. It also allows members to know what is important and what is not. It, thus, specifies what are acceptable behaviours and what are not.

It is suggested that organisation culture can exist on several levels which may vary in terms of (i) visibility and (ii) resistance to change.

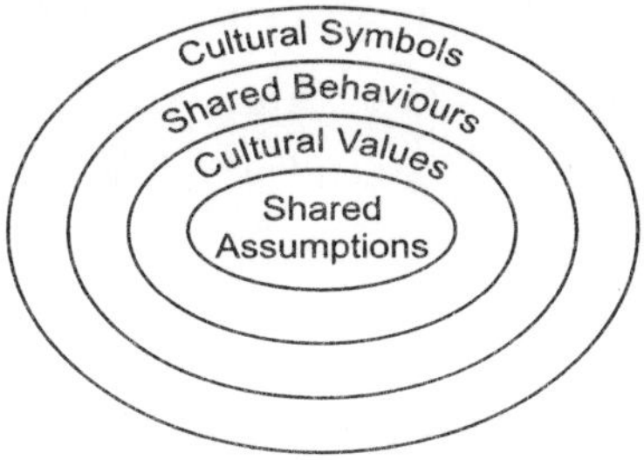

Levels of Organisational Culture

Source: Adapted from Cummings, T.G. and Worley, C.G. *Organisation Development and Change*, 6th ed., Cincinnati South Western, 1997.

As illustrated in the above figure, the various levels of organisation culture are:

Shared Assumptions

These are the deepest level of organisational culture representing beliefs about human nature and reality which are taken for granted.

Cultural Values

The next level of culture is that of cultural values, which represents (i) collective beliefs, (ii) assumption, and (iii) feelings about what things are good, normal, rational, valuable and so on. Cultural values might be very different in different organisations, in some, employees may care deeply about money, but in others, they may care more about technological innovation or employee well-being. These values tend to persist over time even when organisational membership changes.

Shared Behaviours

These refer to those norms which are more visible and easier to change as compared to values.

Cultural Symbols

This is the most superficial level of organisational culture which may consist of symbols–words, gestures, pictures or other physical objects which convey a particular meaning within a culture.

ORGANISATIONAL CULTURE–CHARACTERISTICS

Recent research suggests that there are ten primary characteristics that, in aggregate, capture the essence of an organisation's culture.

1. Member Identity

The degree to which employees identify with the organisation as a whole rather than with their type of job or field of professional expertise.

2. Group Emphasis

The degree to which work activities are organised around groups, rather than individuals.

3. People Focus

The degree to which management decisions take into consideration the effect of outcomes on people within the organisation.

4. Unit Integration

The degree to which units within the organisation are encouraged to operate in a (i) coordinated or (ii) interdependent manner.

5. Control

The degree to which (i) rules, (ii) regulations, and (iii) direct supervision are used to oversee and control employee behaviour.

6. Risk Tolerance

The degree to which employees are encouraged to be aggressive, innovative and risk seeking.

7. Reward Criteria

The degree to which rewards such as (i) salary increases and (ii) promotions are allocated according to employee performance rather than seniority, favouritism, or other non-performance factors.

8. Conflict Tolerance

The degree to which employees are encouraged to air conflicts and criticisms openly.

9. Means-ends Orientation

The degree to which management focuses on (i) results or (ii) outcomes rather than on the techniques and processes used to achieve those outcomes.

10. Open System Focus

The degree to which the organisation (i) monitors and (ii) responds to changes in the external environment.

Job	1. Member Identity	Organisation
Individual	2. Group Emphasis	Group
Task	3. People Focus	People
Independent	4. Unit Integration	Interdependent

Loose	5. Control	Tight
Low	6. Risk Tolerance	High
Performance	7. Reward Criteria	Others
Low	8. Conflict Tolerance	High
Means	9. Means-ends Orientation	Ends
Internal	10. Open-system Focus	External

As shown in the figure, each of these characteristics exists on a continuum. Appraising the organisation on these ten characteristics gives a composite picture of the organisation's culture. This picture becomes the basis for feeling of shared understanding that members have about the organisation, how things are done in it, and the way members are supposed to behave. This figure demonstrates how these characteristics can be mixed to create highly diverse organisations.

CULTURAL TYPOLOGIES

Jeffrey Sonnenfeld of Emory University has developed a labeling scheme that can help us note the differences between organisational cultures and the importance of properly matching people to cultures. From his study of organisations, he has identified four cultural "types", viz.:

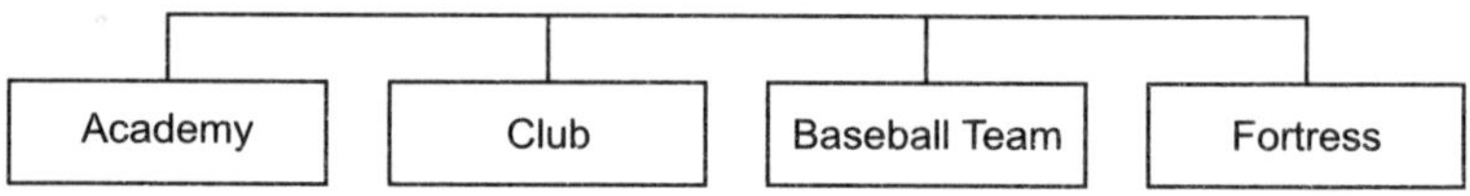

1. Academy

An academy is the place for steady climbers who want to thoroughly master each new job they hold. These companies like to recruit young college graduates, provide them with much special training and then carefully steer them through a myriad of specialized jobs within a particular function.

> (i) Coca-cola, (ii) Proctor and Gamble, (iii) IBM, and (iv) General Motors are classic academy.

2. Club

Clubs place a high value on "fitting in" on (i) loyalty and (ii) commitment. Seniority is the key at clubs, age and experience count. In contrast to an academy, the club grooms managers as generalists.

> Examples of clubs are (i) Delta Airlines, (ii) Government agencies, (iii) Military, (iv) United Parcel Service.

3. Baseball Team

These organisations are entrepreneurally oriented havens for (i) risk takers and (ii) innovators. Baseball teams seek out talented people of all ages and experiences, then reward them for what they produce. Because they offer huge financial incentives and great freedom to their star performers. Job hopping among these organisations is commonplace. Organisations that fit the baseball team description are common in (i) accounting, (ii) law, (iii) investment banking, (iv) consulting firms, (v) advertising agencies, (vi) software developers, and (vii) bio-research concerns.

4. Fortress

While baseball teams prize inventiveness, fortresses are preoccupied with survival. Many were once academics, clubs or baseball teams, but fell on hard times and are now seeking to reverse their sagging fortunes. Fortresses offer little job security, yet they can be exciting places to work for those who like the challenge of a turnaround.

> Fortress organisations include (i) large retailers, (ii) hotels, (iii) forest product companies, and (iv) oil and gas exploration firms.

Sonnenfeld found that many organisations cannot be neatly categorized into one of the four categories either because they have a blend of cultures or because they are in transition.

Sonnenfeld found that each of the four cultural types tends to attract certain personalities and the personality organisational cultures match affects how far and how easily a person will move up the management ranks.

> A risk taker will thrive at a baseball team, but fall flat on his or her face at an academy.

CULTURAL CONCEPTS

Do Organisations have Uniform Cultures?

A common misconception is that an organisation has a uniform culture. However, at least as anthropology uses the concept, it is probably more accurate to treat organisation "as if" they had a uniform culture. All organisations 'have' culture in the sense that they are embedded in specific societal cultures and are part of them. According to this view, an organisational culture is a common perception held by the organisations' members. Everyone in the organisation would have to share this perception. However, realistically, all may not do so to the same degree. As a result, there can be a (i) dominant culture and (ii) sub-culture.

Dominant Culture

A dominant culture is a set of core values shared by a majority of the organisation's members.

> Most employees at Delta Arilines seem to subscribe to such values as (i) hard work, (ii) company loyalty, and (iii) the need for customer service.

> At Hewelett, Packard, most of the employees seem to share a concern for (i) product innovativeness, (ii) product quality, and (iii) responsiveness to customer needs.

These values create a dominant culture in these organisations that helps guide the day-to-day behaviour of employees.

Sub-cultures

Important, but often overlooked, are the sub-cultures in an organisation. A sub-culture is a set of values shared by a minority, usually a small minority, of the organisation's members. Sub-cultures typically are a result of (i) problems or (ii) experience that are shared by members of a department or unit.

Sub-cultures can weaken and undermine an organisation if they are in conflict with the dominant culture and/or the overall objectives. Successful firms, however, find that this is not always the case. Most sub-cultures are formed to help the members of a particular group, deal with the specific day-to-day problems with which they are confronted. The members may also support many, if not all, of the core values of the dominant culture.

Strong Versus Weak Cultures

Some organisational cultures could be labeled "strong" others "weak". Strong organisational cultures are often shaped by strong leaders. However, besides this leadership factor, there seems to be two major factors that determine the strength of an organisational culture.

Sharedness

Sharedness refers to the degree to which the organisational members have the same core values.

Intensity

Intensity is the degree of commitment of the organisational members to the core value.

The degree of sharedness is affected by two major factors, viz.:

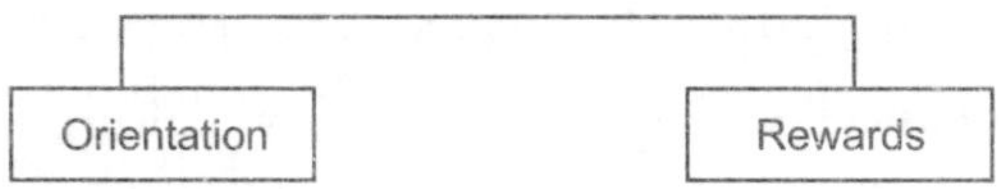

In order for people to share the same cultural values, they must know what these values are. Many organisations begin this process with an orientation programme. New employees are told about the organisation's (i) philosophy and (ii) method of operating. This orientation continues on the job where their (i) boss and (ii) coworkers share these values through both word of mouth and day-to-day work habits and example. Sharedness is also affected by rewards. When organisations give (i) promotions, (ii) raises, (iii) recognition, and (iv) other forms of reward to those who adhere to the core values, these actions help others better understand these values. Some organisations have been labeled "the best to work for" because the rewards they give to their people are exemplary and help reinforce commitment to core values.

> A majority of companies recently surveyed offered "perks" such as (i) company care, (ii) country club membership, (iii) first class air travel, and (iv) personal financial counseling to their upper level management.

The degree of intensity is a result of the reward structure. When employees realize that they will be rewarded for doing things "the organisation's way" their desire to do so increases. Conversely, when they are not rewarded or they feel there is more to be gained by not doing things the organisation's way, commitment to core values diminishes. Although recognition and other non-financial rewards are important, money still plays an important role.

CULTURE–FUNCTIONS AND DYSFUNCTIONS

Culture performs a number of functions within an organisation, viz.:

1. It has a boundary defining role, i.e. it creates distinctions between one organisation and others.
2. It conveys a sense of identity for organisational members.
3. Culture facilitates the generation of commitment to something larger than one's individual self-interest.
4. It enhances social system stability, culture is the social glue that helps hold the organisation together by providing appropriate standards for what employees should say and so.
5. Culture serves as a sense-making and control mechanism that guides and shapes the (i) attitudes and (ii) behaviour of employees.

It is this last function that is of particular interest to us. As the following quote makes clear, culture defines the rules of the game as:

Culture by definition is (i) elusive, (ii) intangible, (iii) implicit, and (iv) taken for granted. But every organisation develops a core set of (i) assumptions, (ii) understandings and (iii) implicit rules that govern day-to-day behaviour in the work place. Until newcomers learn the rules, they are not accepted as full-fledged members of the organisation. Transgressions of the rules on the part of high level executives or front line employees result in universal disapproval and powerful penalties. Conformity to the rules become the primary basis for reward and upward mobility.

(T.T. Deal and A.A. Kennedy)

Culture as a Liability

We are treating culture in a non-judgemental manner. We have not said that it is good or bad, only that it exists. Many of its functions, mentioned above, are valuable for both, the organisation and the employee. Culture enhances organisational commitment and increases the consistency of employee behaviour. These are clearly benefits to an organisation. From an employee's viewpoint, culture is valuable because it reduces ambiguity. It tells employees how things are done and what is important. But we should not ignore the potentially dysfunctional aspects of culture, especially a strong one, on an organisation's effectiveness.

Culture is a liability where the shared values are not in agreement with those that will further the organisation's effectiveness. This is most likely to occur when the organisation's environment is dynamic. When the environment is undergoing rapid change, the organisation's entrenched culture may no longer be appropriate. So consistency of behaviour is an asset to an organisation when it faces a stable environment. It may, however, burden the organisation and make it difficult to respond to changes in the environment.

MAINTAINING CULTURES THROUGH STEPS OF SOCIALISATION

Once an organisational culture is started and begins to develop, there are a number of practices that can help solidify the acceptance of core values and ensure that the culture maintains itself. These practices can be described in terms of several socialisation steps. The figure hereunder illustrates the sequence of these steps.

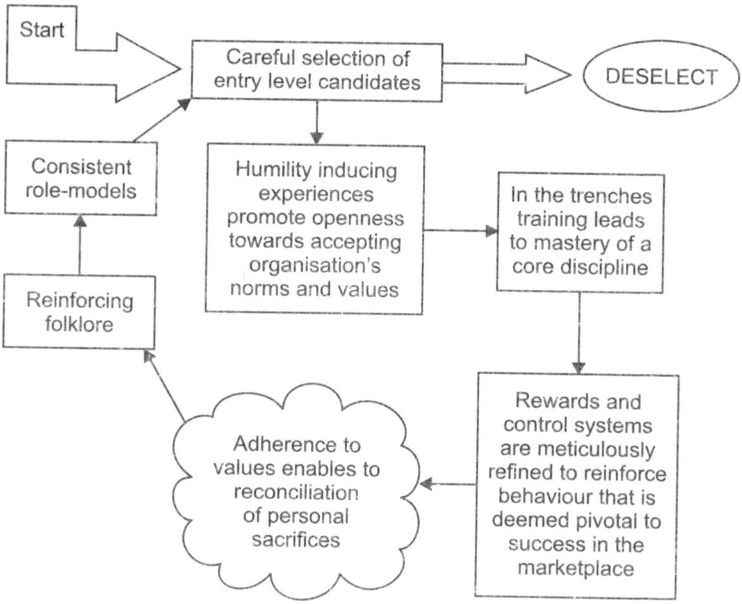

Selection of Entry-level Personnel

The first step is the careful selection of entry-level candidates. Using standardised procedures and seeking specific traits that tie to effective performance, trained recruiters interview candidates and attempt to screen out those whose personal styles and values do not make a "fit" with the organisation's culture. There is accumulating evidence that those who have a realistic preview (called realistic job preview or RJP) of the culture will turnout better.

Placement on the Job

The second step occurs on the job itself, after the person with a fit is hired. New personnel are subjected to a carefully orchestrated series of different experiences whose purpose is to cause them to question the organisation's (i) norms and (ii) values, and to decide whether or not they can accept them.

> Many organisations with strong cultures make it a point to give newly hired personnel more work than they can handle. Sometimes these assignments are beneath the individual's abilities.

> At Proctor and Gamble, new personnel may be required to colour in a sales territory map. The experience is designed to convey the message, "while you are smart in some ways, you are in kindergarten as far as what you know about this organisation."

The objective is also to teach the new entrant into the culture the importance of humility. The experiences are designed to make newly hired personnel vulnerable and to cause them to move closer emotionally to their colleagues, the intensifying group cohesiveness.

Job Mastery

Once the initial "cultural shock" is over, the next step is mastery of one's job. This is typically done via (i) extensive and (ii) carefully reinforced field experience.

> Many companies put their new employees through a programme that often takes as long as six years to produce an experienced marketing representative and twelve years to turnout a full-fledged controller. As personnel move along their career path, the performance is evaluated and additional responsibilities are assigned on the basis of progress.

Quite often companies establish a step-by-step approach to this career plan, which helps reduce efforts by the personal to use political power or to take short cuts in order to get ahead at a faster pace.

Measuring and Rewarding Performance

The next step of the socialisation process consists of meticulous attention to measuring operational results and to rewarding individual performance. These systems are (i) comprehensive, (ii) consistent, and (iii) focus on those aspects of the business that are most crucial to competitive success and to corporate values.

> At Proctor and Gamble there are three factors that are considered most important: (i) building volume, (ii) building profits, and (iii) making changes that increases effectiveness or add satisfaction to the job.

Operational measures are used to track these three factors, and performance appraisal are tied to milestones. Importantly, promotions and merit pay are determined by success in each of these critical areas.

Adherence to Important Values

The next step involves careful adherence to the firm's most important values. Identification with these values helps employees reconcile personal sacrifices brought about by their membership in the organisation. They learn to accept these values and to trust the organisation not to do anything that would hurt them. As Pascale observes:

> Placing one's self "at the mercy" of an organisation imposes real costs. There are long hours of work, missed weekends, criticism that seems unfair, job assignments and rotations that are inconvenient or undesirable.

However, the organisation attempts to overcome these costs by connecting the sacrifices to higher human values such as serving society with better products and/or services.

Reinforcing the Stories and Folklore

The next step involves reinforcing organisational folklore. This entails keeping alive stories that validate the organisation's culture and way of doing things. The folklore helps explain why the organisation does things in a particular way. One of the most common forms of folklore is stories with morals the enterprise wants to reinforce.

> At Proctor and Gamble there is a story about the outstanding brand manager who was fired for overstating the features of a product. The moral of the story is that ethical claims are more important than making money.

Recognition and Promotion

The final step is the recognition and promotion of individuals who have done their jobs well and who can serve as role models to new people in the organisation. By pointing out these people as winners, the organisation encourages others to follow their example. Role models in strong culture firms are regarded as the most powerful ongoing training programme of all.

> Proctor and Gamble looks for people who exhibit extraordinary consistency in such areas as (i) tough-mindedness, (ii) motivational skills, (iii) energy, and (iv) ability to get things done through others.

HOW EMPLOYEES LEARN CULTURE

Culture is transmitted to employees in a number of forms, the most potent being:

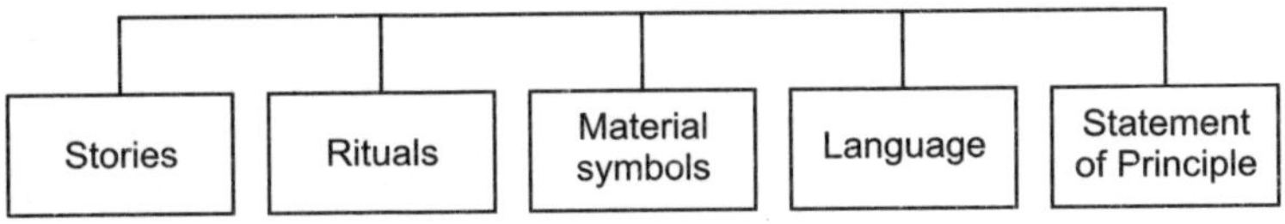

Stories

Lavinson and Rosenthal suggest that, "*Stories and myths about organisation's heroes are powerful tools to reinforce cultural values throughout the organisation and specially in orienting new employees. These stories and myths are often filtered through "cultural network" and remind employees as to 'why, we do things in a certain way'.*"

> The Japanse car Lexus has enjoyed a reputation for quality and customer service by such stories as the company flying in repairmen to help customers who had problems with their Lexus cars and could not find local repairmen because of the complexity and sophistication of the automobile.

Rituals

Ceremonies and rites reflect such activities that are enacted repeatedly on important occasions. Members of the organisation who have achieved success are recognised and rewarded on such occasions. Graduation ceremonies at colleges and universities where diplomas and other symbols of recognition such as special awards are given to students are reflections of culture in educational institutions.

These ceremonies bond organisation members together, such ceremonies are company picnics, retirement dinners, annual conventions and so on, encourage inter-personal communication and togetherness and thus bring about a common culture bondage.

Material Symbols

Symbols communicate organisational culture by unspoken messages. Certain code of dress or a company logo can reflect its values and orientations.

> Many people wear buttons on their jacket labels suggesting that they are members of a Rotary Club or International Lions Club, thus reflecting a sense of values about these people.

Some of the material artifacts created by an organisation also speak of its cultural orientation and make a statement about the company. These material benefits may range from assigned parking space and larger offices to luxury automobiles given to senior or successful members of the organisation.

> At Mary Kay Cosmetics, a highly successful cosmetics company in America, top sales performers are awarded a diamond "bumblebee" which has come to be known as a meaningful symbol of culture associated with success.

Language

Many organisations and units within organisations use language as a way to identify members of a culture or sub-culture. By learning this language, members attest to their acceptance of the culture and, in so doing, help to preserve it.

Organisations, over time, often develop unique terms to describe equipment, offices, key personnel, suppliers, customers, or products that relate to its business. New employees are frequently overwhelmed with acronyms and jargon that, after six months on the job, have become fully part of their language. Once assimilated, this terminology acts as a common denominator that unites members of a given culture or sub-culture.

Statement of Principle

The last way in which culture is transmitted is through the direct statements of principle. Some organisations have explicitly written their principles for all to see. Some other companies make explicit the moral aspects of their culture by publishing codes of ethics, specific statements of a company's ethical values. Statements of the type enables the newly hired employees to understand the culture of their organisation.

HOW ORGANISATIONAL CULTURE IMPACTS PERFORMANCE AND SATISFACTION

The figure hereunder depicts organisational culture as an intervening variable. Employees form an overall subjective perception of the organisation based on such factors as degree of group emphasis, support of people, risk tolerance and management's willingness to tolerate conflict. This overall perception becomes in effect, the organisation's culture or personality. These (i) favourable or (ii) unfavourable perceptions then affect employee performance and satisfaction, with the impact being greater for stronger cultures.

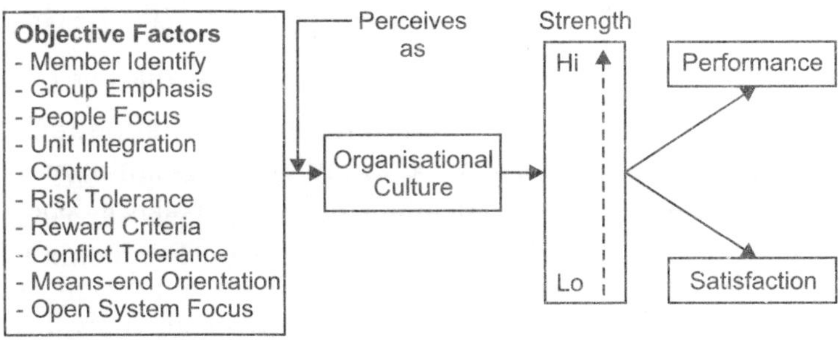

Does culture have an equal impact on both employee (i) performance and (ii) satisfaction? The evidence says, "No". There is a relatively strong relationship between culture and satisfaction, but this is moderated by individual differences. In general, it can be said that satisfaction will be highest when there is congruence between individual needs and culture.

> An organisation whose culture would be described as emphasizing individual tasks, having loose supervision, and rewarding people for high achievement is likely to have more satisfied employees if those employees have a high achievement need and prefer autonomy.

It means, therefore, that job satisfaction often varies according to the employee's perception of the organisation's culture.

The relationship between culture and performance is less clear, although a number of studies find the two related. But the relationship is moderated by the organisation's technology. Performance will be higher when the culture suits the technology. If the culture is informal, creative, and supports risk taking and conflict, performance will be higher if the technology is non-routine. The more formally structured organisations that risk oversize, seek to eliminate conflict, and prone to more task, oriented leadership will achieve higher performance when routine technology is utilized.

It has been noted that organisations have "absence cultures" that represent shared understandings about absence legitimacy and that define appropriate absence behaviour. Once a new employee has been socialised into an organisation, he learns whether, for example, it is acceptable to take three day weekends in the summer, uses sick leave days at the end of the year, etc.

We should also not overlook the influence socialisation has on employee performance. An employee's performance depends to a considerable degree on knowing what he should or should not do. Understanding the right way to do a job indicates proper socialisation. Further, the appraisal of an individual's performance includes how well the person fits into the organisation. Can he get along with co-workers? Has he accepted the work habits and demonstrate the right attitude? These qualities differ between jobs and organisations.

> On some jobs, employee will be evaluated more favourably if they are aggressive and outwardly indicate that they are ambitious. On another job, or on the same job in another organisation, such an approach may be evaluated negatively.

As a result, proper socialisation becomes a significant factor in influencing both actual job performance and how it is perceived by others.

ORGANISATIONAL CLIMATE–DEFINED

Although intangible, organisational climate is a real phenomenon, while a precise definition of climate may be lacking, this does not preclude its existence. In the literature of organisational behaviour several different definitions have been advanced and almost all have a greater degree of commonality. Organisational climate, however is:

> "*A relatively enduring quality of the internal environment that is experienced by its members, influences their behaviour, and can be described in terms of the values of a particular set of characteristics of the organisation.*"
>
> (Renote Tagiuri)

> "*A set of characteristics that describe an organisation and that (a) distinguish one organisation from another, (b) are relatively enduring over a period of time, and (c) influence the behaviour of people in the organisations.*"
>
> (G.A. Forehand and B.H. Gilmer)

Organisational climate is, thus, the manifestation of the attitudes of organisational members towards the organisation itself. An organisation tends to attract and keep people who fit its climate, so that its patterns are perpetuated at least to some extent. Organisational climate should be viewed from total system viewpoint. Some theorist opine, "*There are as many climates as there are people in organisation.*"

There may exist different climates within different departments in the organisation, and these sub-climates will be integrated in the similar fashion of integrating attitudes of employees, so as to form the organisational climate.

In organisations, there may be differences in climates in different work units, as we commonly observe. It is because one type of climate may be suitable to one particular unit and the same may be unsuitable for another unit.

ORGANISATIONAL CLIMATE–AFFECTING FACTORS

In every organisation there exist certain elements that exert profound influence on the existing climate. Lawrance James and Allan Jones have tried to identify the factors influencing climate and they grouped these factors under five heads:

1. Organisational Context

The first and foremost influential factor that affects the climate is the management philosophy. If the company is wedded to such a policy that it effectively utilizes its resources both human and non-human, then it can be concluded that the climate is good. The manpower philosophy is generally expressed by rules, regulations and politics, etc. The point here is that the reactions of the employees and the degree to which they welcome and accept the managerial philosophy is very crucial to the development of sound and favourable organisational climate. The climate is said to be highly favourable when the existing management techniques are such that employees' goals are perfectly matched to the ideals of organisation.

2. Structure

Structure of the organisation represents another variable that affects climate. It needs no reiteration that structure is a framework that establishes formal relationship and delineate authority and functional responsibility. Further, the actual arrangement of hierarchy is also to be considered, for it affects climate. Highly decentralised structure results in sound climate when the management feels the necessity of high degree of sound climate when the management feels the necessity of high degree of employee input in the total output. In other words, management has a strong belief that participative decision-making will promote decentralisation. In a sharp contrast, if the management feels the necessity of maintaining greater degree of consistency in operations regarding decision-making, it will be wedded to centralised structure. Thus, structure also affects the climate of organisations.

3. Processes

In every organisation certain processes are vital so that it runs (i) communication, (ii) decision-making, (iii) motivation, and (iv) leadership. These are some of the very important processes through which the management carries out its objectives. In all these processes, the relationship between superior and subordinate is visible and, therefore, the supervisor cannot afford to ignore this visible interface.

> If we consider leader-follower relationship in leadership process, it is the leader's choice whether to allow subordinates in decision-making. A leader has to be aware of the possible influences of his actions on the climate when deciding about the most appropriate supervisory technique for a given situation.

It should be noted that failure to give consideration to the affect, a climate would be a monumental error that could be reflected adversely on the performance of employees. When a leader mismatches his style to the situation, it might abort any hope of attaining organisational objectives.

4. Physical Environment

The external conditions of environment, the size and location of the building in which an employee works, the size of the city, weather or the place all affect the organisational climate. An employee performing his job in a relatively clean, quite and safe environment will undoubtedly have a favourable perception of the organisational climate. Office décor, size and space, a person has in doing the work are the important factors to be borne in mind, for these affect the climate. Noise has also been considered instrumental in influencing the climate of organisations. High levels of noise bring a bad feeling and lead to frustration, nervousness and aggression and will have a negative effect upon organisational climate. Loud and intermittent noise converts an organisation into a marketplace.

5. System Values and Norms

Every organisation has discernible and fairly evident formal value system where certain kinds of behaviours are rewarded and encouraged; where certain kinds of behaviours force an individual to formal sanctions. The formal value system is communicated to employees through rules, regulations and policies. Although in every organisation informal organisation also exists, the value system of informal organisations is very difficult to ascertain. But from the organisational climate viewpoint, both formal and informal groups are very powerful in exerting influence on climate.

> The organisation that treats employees with respect to understanding will have certainly a different climate than one which is very cold and impersonal.

ORGANISATIONAL CULTURE–EMERGING ISSUES

As we know cultures change gradually, picking up new ideas and dropping old ones. Therefore, new issues emerge in cultures, viz.:

Innovation

According to *Fortune Magazine*, most innovative organisations, which pick up new values continuously are the most admired organisations. Innovation is the process of creating and doing new things that are introduced into the marketplace as products, processes or services. Types of innovations include:

- Radical innovation is a major breakthrough that changes or creates whole industries e.g., information technology.
- System innovation creates a new functionality by assembling parts in new ways. Combing information technology and process technology and formation of new business process (supply chain management) is an example for system innovation.
- Incremental innovation–it continues technical improvement and extends the application of radical systems innovation.

Entrepreneurship

Entrepreneur is the one who creates the total venture.

Intrapreneurship

Intrapreneurship is an entrepreneurial activity that takes place within the context of a large organisation.

Empowerment

Empowerment is the process of enabling workers to set their own work goals, make decisions and solve problems within their sphere of responsibility and authority.

Information Technology

Information technology brought significant changes in the organisational culture through adding value like team work, charging for the customer the most, downsizing, delaying, de-jobbing, autonomous work-groups and deleting culture values like bureaucracy, authoritarian styles, treating efficient and inefficient differently and the like.

ORGANISATIONAL EFFECTIVENESS–MEANING

Though we use the term "organisational effectiveness" more often, it is rather difficult to define the term precisely. This is because, the finance manager equates effectiveness with return on investment or market capitalisation, while as the marketing manager equates effectiveness with increase in sales. The human resource manager prefers to mean effectiveness with employee satisfaction while Research and Development Managers' mean effectiveness to innovations. However, there are certain comprehensive definitions on effectiveness. Let us consider some of them:

> Amitai Etizioni is of the opinion, "*Effectiveness is the degree to which organisation realises its goals.*"
>
> Paul E. Mott opine effectiveness as, "*The ability of an organisation to mobilize its centers of power for action production and adaptation.*"
>
> Basil Georgopolous and Arnold S. Tannenbaum define O.E. as, "*The extent to which an organisation, given certain resources and means, achieves its objectives without placing undue strain on its members.*"

Thus, the essence of above definitions is that:

- Effectiveness is not one dimensional concept that can be precisely measured by a single, clear cut criterion.

- Effectiveness is a matter of degree. No organisation is effective as it could be. Effectiveness is a label to which an organisation has performed according to its capacities, potentials and general goals.

ORGANISATIONAL EFFECTIVENESS–NATURE

Different approaches to organisational effectiveness indicate that the achievement of organisational objectives efficiently is the outcome of organisational effectiveness. Actually three levels of effectiveness can be identified as shown in the figure below:

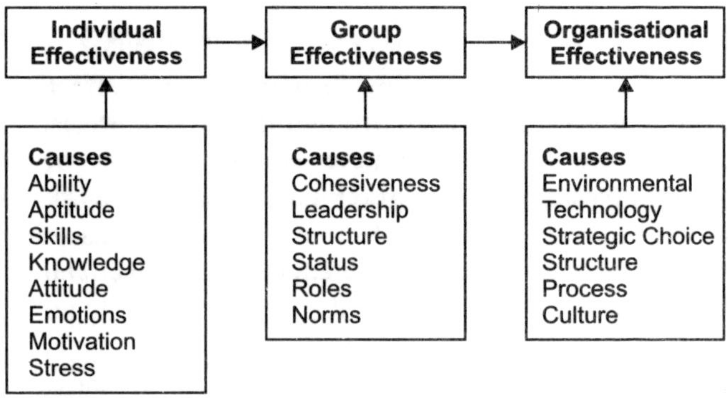

The Three Levels of Effectiveness

Source: Modified version from James L. Gibson, et al. *Organisation*, p. 28.

As we see at the basic level of individual effectiveness, which emphasizes the task performance of specific employees or members of the organisation, the tasks to be performed are contained in job descriptions. Managers assess effectiveness of individuals through performance appraisal.

Individuals seldom work alone. They usually work in groups, necessitating another level, viz., group effectiveness. In some instances, group effectiveness is simply the sum of the combinations of all its members.

> A group of scientists working on unrelated projects would be effective to the extent that each individual is effective.

In other instances, group effectiveness is more than the sum of the individual contributions.

> An assembly line that produces a finished product is the result of the contributions of each individual.

The third phase is that of organisational effectiveness. Organisations consist of individuals and groups. Therefore, organisational effectiveness consists of individual and group effectiveness. However, organisational effectiveness is more than the sum of individual and group effectiveness. Through synergetic effects, organisations are able to achieve higher level of performance than the sum of their parts. In fact, the rationale for organisations as means for doing the work of society is that they can do more work than is possible through individual effort. The effectiveness of business organisations is important for society.

We observe in the figure given above that there is close relationship among the three levels of effectiveness. The connecting arrows in above Figure imply that group effectiveness depends on individual effectiveness and that organisational effectiveness depends on group effectiveness. The exact relationships among the three views vary depending on factors as the type of organisation, the work it does and the technology used in doing that work. The figure also recognizes the synergetic effects of the three perspectives. Thus, group effectiveness is larger than the sum of individual effectiveness because of the synergies realized through joint efforts.

CASE STUDY

Out with the Old, In with the New

The Anderson Corporation was started in 1962 as a small consumer products company. During the first twenty years the company's Research and Development (R&D) staff developed a series of new products that proved to be very popular in the marketplace. Things went so well that the company had to add a second production shift just to keep up with the demand. During this time period the firm expanded its plant on three different occasions. During an interview with the national magazine, the firm's founder, Paul Anderson, said, "We do not sell our products, we allocate them." This comment was in reference to the fact that the firm had only twenty four salespeople and was able to garner annual revenue in excess of $62 million.

Three years ago Anderson suffered its first financial setback. The company had a net operating loss of $1.2 million. Two years ago the loss was $2.8 million, and last year it was $4.7 million. The accountant estimates that this year the firm will lose approximately $10 million.

Alarmed by this information, the Citizen's Bank, the company's largest creditor, insisted that the firm make some changes and start turning things around. In response to this request, Paul Anderson agreed to step aside. The board of directors replaced him with Bill Hartmann, head of the marketing division of one of the country's largest consumer products firms.

After making an analysis of the situation, Bill has come to the conclusion that there are a number of changes that must be made if the firm is to be turned around. The three most important are:

1. More attention must be given to the marketing side of the business. The most vital factor for success in the sale of consumer goods produced by Anderson is an effective sales force.
2. There must be an improvement in product quality. Two per cent of Anderson's output is defective as against ½ of 1 per cent for the average firm in the industry. In the past the demand for Anderson's output was so great that quality was not an important factor. Now it is proving to be a very costly area.
3. There must be reduction in the number of people in the operation. Anderson can get by with 2/3 of its current production personnel and only half of its administrative staff.

Bill has not shared these ideas with the board of directors, but he intends to do so. For the moment he is considering the steps that will have to be taken in making these changes and the effect that all of his might have on the employees and the overall operations.

DISCUSSION POINTS

1. What is wrong with the old organisational culture? What needs to be done to change it?
2. Why might it be difficult for Bill to change the existing culture?
3. What specific steps does Bill need to take in changing the culture? Identify and describe at least two.

QUESTIONS

- Define organisational culture. What are its functional and dysfunctional consequences?
- Discuss various organisational cultural concepts. What are the emerging issues in organisational culture?
- How does?
  (a) Organisational climate differ from organisational culture.
  (b) Organisational efficiency differ from organisational effectiveness.
- Write short notes on:
  (a) Organisational cultural values.
  (b) Organisational cultural concepts.
  (c) Organisational cultural symbols.
- "Organisational culture generally reflects the benefits and ideologies of the founders of such organisations." Do you agree with this assumption? Give reasons.
- How will you create and maintain organisational culture? What steps will you indicate to enable employees learn organisational culture?

- What steps can the management take to maintain the cultural values within the organisations in the face of dynamics of external environment? Do you think it is necessary to maintain such cultural values? Defend your position with the support of arguments.
- An organisation which values formal rules, standard operating procedures and hierarchical coordination is said to have:
  (a) Bureaucratic culture.
  (b) Clean culture.
  (c) Entrepreneurial culture.
  (d) Market culture.
  (e) None of the above.
- The team building effort must start with:
  (a) Identification of the problem.
  (b) Brainstorming.
  (c) Data gathering.
  (d) Establishing team building goals.
  (e) Planning.

Organisational Structure

15

Learning Objectives

- Meaning of Organisational Structure
- Steps in Organisational Structure
- Elements in Designing an Organisational Structure
- Dimensions of Organisational Structure
- Determinants of Organisational Structure

ORGANISATIONAL STRUCTURE–INTRODUCTION

Organisational structure involves arrangement of activities and assignments of personnel to these activities in order to achieve the organisational goals. It is a way by which various parts of an organisation are tied together in a coordinated manner and it illustrates relationships among various levels of the hierarchy within the organisation as well as horizontal relationships among various aspects of the organisational operations. A well planned organisation structure results in the better use of resources.

Sheldon Oliver opines,

"*Organisation is the process of combining the work, which (i) individuals, (ii) groups have to perform with the facilities necessary for its execution, that the duties so performed provide the best channels for the efficient, systematic, positive and coordinated application of the available effort.*"

A good organisational structure is needed so that:

(a) The individuals in the organisation are assigned a role, responsibility and necessary authority. Each person who is assigned an activity must know his (i) position, (ii) role, and (iii) relationship with others. He is also responsible for efficient execution of his (i) roles and (ii) duties and is given the authority to do so.

(b) The activities of all individuals are (i) coordinated and (ii) integrated into a common pattern in order to achieve the organisational objectives. Organisation is needed for the purpose of integration of diverse activities in a cohesive manner.

(c) The optimum use of human (i) skills and (ii) efforts is achieved. Half of the work is completed when you know what you have to do and how you have to do it. A good organisation does that. It helps in smooth operations and flow, thus avoiding (i) bottlenecks, (ii) idle time, and (iii) idle machines. A good organisation requires the right person for the right job and this avoids misapplication of human resources thus resulting in optimal utilization of employee efforts. This would ensure efficiency in the functioning of the enterprise.

ORGANISATIONAL STRUCTURE–STEPS

The following are the main steps in organisational structure, viz.:

1. Determination, Identification and Enumeration of Activities

Once the goals and objectives of the organisation have been established, the activities required to achieve these objectives are identified. The activities are broken down into sub-activities as far down the hierarchy as possible so that each individual knows as to what part of the activity he/she is responsible for. Care must be taken so that all necessary activities are taken into account and any activity that is unnecessary is taken out. The process applies to both managerial and operational activities.

2. Grouping and Assigning of Activities

All similar activities are grouped together and assigned on the basis of divisions and departments. These sets of activities may further be sub-divided into sections or units. These groupings may be done on the basis of primary functions such as (i) production, (ii) finance, (iii) sales, (iv) personnel and so on, or these may be done on derivative basis such as (i) types of customers, (ii) geographical areas and so on. These activities are then assigned to personnel as head of the departments, such as (i) production managers, (ii) marketing managers, (iii) personnel directors and so on. They in turn delegate and distribute jobs to their subordinates down the line. Care should be taken that the personnel and their jobs are well matched.

3. Delegation of Authority

Since the persons who are assigned particular activities are responsible for performing these duties to the best of their ability, they must be given corresponding authority to discharge their obligations. Responsibility and authority are tied together. Responsibility is really the accountability of authority. Authority without responsibility is a dangerous element.

> If a marketing manager has the responsibility to increase sales, but does not have the authority to hire and maintain a competent sales force, then the responsibility in itself has little meaning.

ORGANISATIONAL STRUCTURE–ELEMENTS

There are four elements of organisation structure, viz.:

1. Division of Labour

Division of labour concerns the extent to which jobs are specialized. Managers divide the total task of the organisation into specific jobs having specified activities. The activities define what the person performing a particular job is to do and to get done.

Thus, job can be specialised both by method and by application of the method.

> The activities of the job "accounting clerk" can be defined in terms of the methods and procedures required to process a certain quantity of transactions during a specified period of time. Various accounting clerks could use the same methods and procedures to process different types of transactions. One accounting clerk could be processing accounts receivables, the other could be processing accounts payables.

The economic advantage of dividing work into specialized jobs are the principal historical reasons for the creation of organisation. As societies became more and more (i) industrialised and (ii) urbanised, craft production gave a way to mass production. Mass production depends on the ability to obtain the economic benefits of specialised labour, and organisations are the most effective means for employing specialised work force. Although managers are concerned with more than the economic implications of jobs, they seldom lose sight of specialisation as the rationale for dividing work among jobs.

Organisations make use of division of labour in two ways:

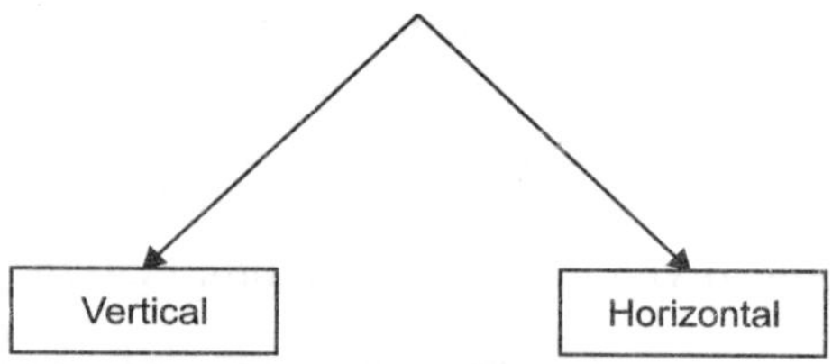

1. Vertical

The vertical component exists in the form of chain of command which supplies critically to hierarchy of relationship. Chain of command is essential for job distinction and job execution. One can distinguish one job from another on the basis of assigned authority which has the vertical dimension of organisational structure. The vertical dimension relates to delegation of authority.

2. Horizontal

The horizontal dimension relates to:

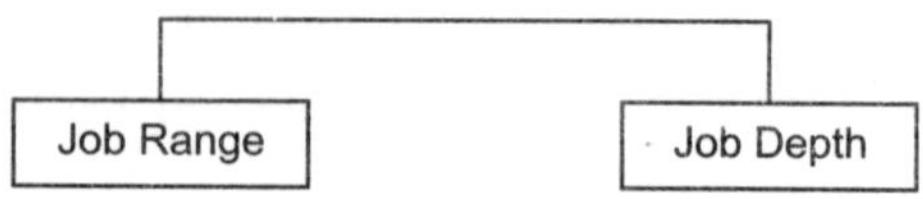

(i) **Job Range.** Job range implies the spectrum of tasks supposed to be performed by the individual in relation to performing his job.

> What is spectrum of job task to be performed by a teacher in the university or a lawyer in the law court or a worker at the shop floor level?

(ii) **Job Depth.** Job depth refers to the discretion which the individual may exercise in selecting the means to perform the tasks and the sequence in which the task could be performed. However, a balance between the depth and range could be struck by management.

2. Delegation of Authority

Managers decide how much authority is to be delegated to each job and each job-holder. As mentioned, authority refers to the right of individuals to make decisions without approval by higher management and to exact obedience from others.

> A sales manager can be delegated the right to hire salespersons (a decision) and the right to assign them to specific territories (obedience). Another sales manager may not have the right to hire but may have the right to assign territories.

Thus, the degree of delegated authority can be relatively (i) high or (ii) low with respect to both aspects of authority. And for any particular job, there is a range of alternative configurations of authority delegation. Managers must balance the relative (i) gains and (ii) losses of alternatives. Let us evaluate some of these.

- First relatively high delegation of authority encourages the development of professional managers. As decision-making authority is pushed down (delegated) in the organisation, managers have opportunities to make significant decisions and to gain skills that enable them to cope with problems of higher management and to advance in the company. The advancement of managers on the basis of demonstrated performance can eliminate favouritism and result in improved promotion decisions.

- Second, high delegation of authority can lead to a competitive climate within the organisation. Managers are motivated to contribute in this competitive atmosphere, since they are compared with their peers on various performance measures. A competitive environment in which managers compete on how well they achieve sales, cost reduction, and employee development targets can be a positive factor in overall organisational performance.
- Finally, high delegation of authority enables managers to exercise more autonomy, and thus satisfy their desires to participate in problem-solving. This autonomy can lead to managerial creativity and ingenuity that contribute to the adaptiveness and development of the organisation and managers.

These are only three of the benefits associated with delegated authority. As is usually the case, benefits are not totally free of costs. Costs of delegated authority include the expense associated with training managers to make the decisions that go along with their authority, and the fact that many managers become accustomed to making decisions and consequently resist delegating authority to subordinates. There are, of course, other costs, like mostly managerial decisions, whether authority should be delegated in high or low degrees is not necessarily a simple issue to resolve.

3. Departmentalisation

After designing individual jobs, each job is carefully analysed and the job specification are laid down to ascertain if the specified task has been performed in accordance with the prescribed norms and specifications of jobs. Thereafter, the jobs are grouped together so that the whole group of job is assigned to a single supervisor. The departmentalisation is usually done on the basis of:

Functional Departmentalisation. Managers can combine jobs according to the functions of the organisation. Every organisation must undertake certain activities in order to do its work. The necessary activities are the organisation's functions.

The functions of a hospital include (i) surgery, (ii) psychiatry (iii) housekeeping, (iv) pharmacy and (v) personnel.

The principal advantage of functional departmentalisation is its efficiency. It seems logical to have department that consists of experts in a particular field such as production or accounting. By having departments of specialists, management creates highly efficient units. An accountant generally is more efficient when working with accountants and other individuals who have similar backgrounds and interests. They can share expertise to get the work done.

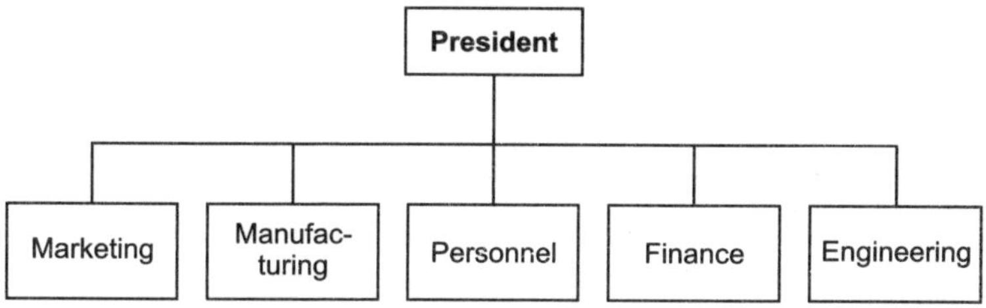

Departmentalisation Business Function. A major disadvantage of this departmental basis, however is that because specialists are working with and encouraging one another in their area of expertise and interest, the organisational goals may be scarified in favour of departmental goals. Accountants may see only their problems and not those of (i) production, (ii) marketing, or (iii) the total organisation. In other words, identification with the department and its culture often is stronger than identification with the organisation and its culture.

Territorial Departmentalisation. Territorial departmentalisation seeks to assign jobs according to location, sometimes the territorial managers are required to coordinate the tasks because the managers at the headquarters will find it difficult to do so because of distance and effective supervision and control.

Territorial departmentalisation provides a training ground for managerial personnel. The company is able to place managers in territories, then assess their progress in that geographical region. The experience that managers acquire in a territory away from headquarters provides valuable insights about how products and services are accepted in the field.

Product Departmentalisation. Managers of many large, diversified companies group jobs on the basis of products. All of the jobs associated with producing and selling a product or product line are placed under the direction of one manager. Product becomes the preferred basis as a firm grows by increasing the number of products it markets. As a firm grows, it becomes difficult to coordinate the various functional departments and establishing product units becomes advantageous. This form of organisation allows personnel to develop total expertise in researching, manufacturing and distributing a product line. Concentration of the authority, responsibility and accountability in a specific product department allows top management to coordinate actions.

Customer Departmentalisation. Departmentalisation according to customer seeks to structure jobs which focus on the needs of specific customers in the same department.

> The Education Department of the Government of India may focus separately on the needs of (i) school, (iii) college, (iii) university, (iv) professional, and (v) technical education.

Another form of customer departmentalisation is the credit department in a commercial bank. Loan officers often are associated with industrial, commercial or agricultural loans. The customer will be served by one of these three loan officers.

Project Departmentalisation. Project departmentalisation is followed by such organisations which produce "large and unique" products such as aircraft, spacecraft or naval ships. If an organisation is assigned with a project of developing a new spacecraft, the responsibility is entrusted to the project manager. The project manager will accordingly be provided with the services of technical experts, engineers and scientists to execute the project. After the completion of the project, all of them will go back to their original positions, i.e., permanent assignments. It is like product departmentalisation except for the difference that the assignments of people in the project are temporary.

4. Span of Control

Span of control is also referred to as span of management. Span of control is the number of people reporting to a manager, thus it defines the size of the organisation's work-groups. When a manager has a small span of control, he can maintain close control over the workers and stay in contact with daily operations. If the span of control is large, close control is not possible. Examples of (i) small and (ii) large span of control are illustrated hereunder:

(a) Large Span of Control

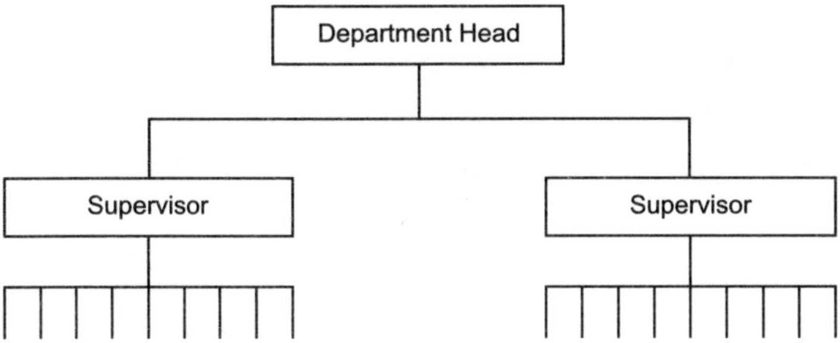

Span of control = 16
Number of levels in the hierarchy = 2

(b) Small Span of Control

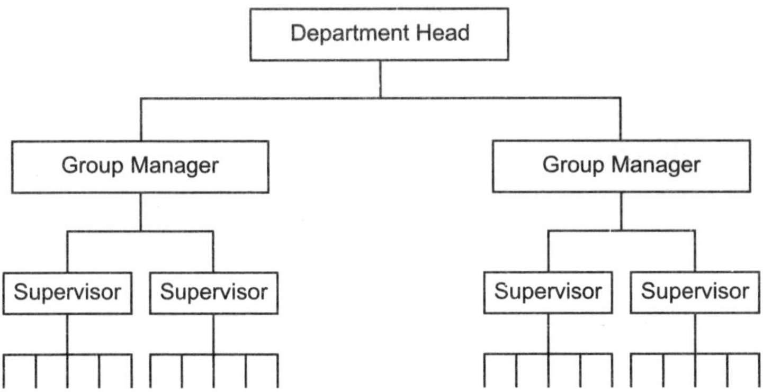

Span of control = 8
Number of levels in the hierarchy = 3

A number of formulae and rules have been offered for determining the optimal span of control in an organisation. However, research on the topic does not conclusively or specifically indicate the span of control that will optimize organisational performance. Henry Mintzberg has concluded that the optimal unit size depends on the coordination requirement within the unit, including such things as the degree of specialisation of information available or needed by (i) unit members, (ii) differences in the members need for autonomy, and (iii) the members need to have direct access to the supervisor. Because results so far are inclusive, research on span of control continues.

ORGANISATIONAL STRUCTURE–DIMENSIONS

The four design decisions (division of labour, delegation of authority, departmentalisation, and span of control) result in a structure of organisations. Researchers and Practitioners of management have attempted to develop their understanding of relationships between (i) structure and (ii) performance and other variables thought to be important. The development of understanding has been hampered not only by the complexity of the relationships themselves, but also by the difficulty of defining and measuring the concept of organisational structure.

Although universal agreement on a common set of dimensions that measure differences in structure is neither possible nor desirable, some suggestions can be made. At present, three dimensions often are used in research and practice to describe structure. They are:

1. Formalisation

The dimension of formalisation refers to the extent to which expectations regarding the means and ends of work are specified and written. An organisational structure that is described as highly formalised is one in which (i) rules and (ii) procedures are available to prescribe what each individual should be doing. Organisations with such structures would have written standards operating procedures, specified directives and explicit policies. In terms of the four design decisions, formalisation is the result of high specialisation of labour, high delegation of authority, the use of functional departments, and wide span of control.

Although formalisation is defined in terms of the existence of written rules and procedures, it is important to understand how these are viewed by the employees. In organisations with all the appearances of formalisation, complete with thick manuals of rules, procedures and policies–employees may not perceive the manuals as affecting their behaviour. Thus, even though rules and procedures exist, they must be enforced if they are to affect behaviour.

2. Centralisation

Centralisation refers to the location of decision-making authority in the hierarchy of the organisation. More specifically, the concept refers to the delegation of authority among the jobs in the organisation. Typically, researchers and practitioners think of centralisation in terms of decision-making and control. Despite the apparent simplicity of the concept, it can be complex.

The complexity of centralisation derives from three sources:

- People at the same level can have different decision-making authority.
- Not all decisions are of equal importance in organisations.

> A typical management practice is to delegate authority to make routine operating decisions (i.e., decentralisation) but to retain authority to make strategic decisions (i.e., centralisation).

- Individuals may not perceive that they really have authority, even though their job description includes it. Thus, objectively they have authority, but subjectively they do not have it.

3. Complexity

Complexity is the direct outgrowth of dividing work and creating departments specifically. The concept refers to the number of distinctly different job titles, or occupational groupings and the number of distinctly different units, or departments.

The fundamental idea is that organisations with a great many different kinds and types of jobs and units create more complicated managerial and organisational problems than do those with fewer jobs and departments.

Complexity, then, relates to differences among jobs and units. It is not surprising, therefore, that differentiation is often used synonymously with complexity. Moreover, it has become a standard practice to use the term.

- Horizontal differentiation refers to the number of different units at the same level.
- Vertical differentiation refers to the number of levels in the organisation.

ORGANISATIONAL STRUCTURE–DETERMINANTS

Since organisations have different characteristics and requirements it would not be possible to identify an ideal structure that would fulfil all these diversified needs. Accordingly, each organisational structure must suit the situation and be optimally useful in meeting the organisational objectives. Good organisational design is a function of a number of factors including (i) environment, (ii) technology, and (iii) size of the company. These three factors would determine the philosophy and strategy of control management which forms the foundation for the organisational structure.

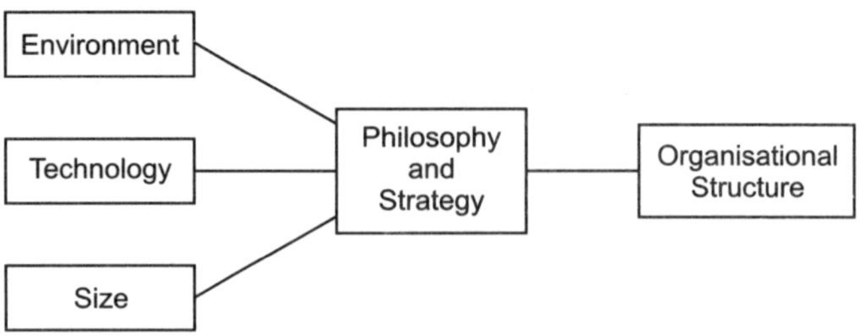

1. Environment

Organisations are open systems which continuously interact without side environment. The macro environment of business today has considerable impact on the internal operations of the organisations, specially if the organisation is a large one. These external factors include the customers, cultural and economic conditions as well as international environment. The organisational structure would depend upon whether such external environment is stable or whether there are dynamic and rapid changes in it.

Researchers have found that successful organisational structures vary with the environment. A more uncertain environment will have fewer predictable elements requiring the use of more specialised experts who are trained to deal with the problems created by an ever changing situation. A stable environment can go for a more mechanistic structure.

2. Technology

Technology is a combination of tools, techniques and know-how and has a major influence on organisational structure, which would depend upon whether the technology is simple and routine requiring few repetitive tasks, in which case a mechanistic structure would be more desirable. However, when the technology is advanced and intensive and complex requiring high interdependence among members of the workforce, then the organic structure would be operationally more effective.

Joan Woodword studied the relationship between technology and organisational structure in the early 1960s among some English manufacturing firms. She observed and calculated that technology is a major influence on organisational structure. She concluded that wherever the items are mass produced and where the work units depend upon each other in a sequential manner and wherever the production system is automated with use of robotics and cybernetics, the organic organisational structure brings out the optimal results.

3. Size

The size of the organisation, as measured by the number of people working in the organisation would determine as to which type of structure would be more effective. As the organisation grows in size, it increases the number of functional departments, the number of managerial levels, extent of specialisation, number of employees with diversified responsibilities, resulting in increase in the degree of coordination required among members of the organisation and this further results in increase in related problems. This requires a high degree of discipline and formally structured chain of command giving rise to classical and mechanistic structure.

4. Philosophy and Strategy

Strategy is typically defined as the, "determination of the basic long-term goals and objectives of an enterprise, and the adoption of courses of action and the allocation of resources necessary for carrying out these goals".

In his research, Alfred Chandler found a definite link between organisational philosophy and structure. In small and simple organisations, the structure is typically high on centralisation. However, as organisations grow and develop, such simple structures become increasingly ineffective and inefficient and the organisations change their strategies and thus change their structures.

There are primarily two strategies, namely, (i) stability strategy and (ii) growth strategy. The growth strategy involves expansion, thus introducing the element of complexity and uncertainty. In such type of environment, growth strategies will be more successful when supported by organic structures.

CASE STUDY

The Outdated Structure

Jake Harvey has a position on the corporate planning staff of a large company in a high technology industry. Although he has spent most of his time on long range, strategic planning for the company, he has been appointed to a task force to reorganise the company. The President and Board of Directors are concerned that they are losing their competitive position in the industry because of an outdated organisation structure. Being a planning expert, Jake convinced the task force that they should proceed by first determining exactly what type of structure they have now, then determining what type of environment the company faces now and in the future, and then designing the organisation structure accordingly. In the first phase they discovered that the organisation is currently structured along classical bureaucratic lines. In the second phase they found that they are competing in a highly dynamic, rapidly growing and uncertain environment that requires a great deal of flexibility and response to change.

DISCUSSION POINTS

1. What type or types of organisation design do you feel this task force should recommend in the third and final phase of the approach to their assignment?
2. Explain how the systems, information processing, contingency and ecological theories of organisation can each contribute to the analysis of this case.
3. Do you think Jake was correct in his suggestions of how the task force should proceed? What types of problems might develop as by-products of the recommendation you make in question 1?

QUESTIONS

- Define organisational structure. Discuss various steps of organisational structure.
- Distinguish between with respective merits and demerits:
  (a) Tall and flat organisational structure.
  (b) Mechanistic and organic pattern of organisation.
- What are some of the jobs caused origins of employee alienation? Discuss some of the ways in which effective organisational behaviour can reduce these causes.
- "The various types of organisation structure designs described for profit earning organisations are equally appropriate for non-profit organisations." Explain with illustrations.
- Do you experience:
  (a) Any red tape in your registration in the university?
  (b) The flow of work to and from the job organised and probable effects in this work system?

(c) Knowledge society may effect jobs in the next (a) decade and (b) quarter century.

- Assume that you lose your job due to technological change five years from now. Describe your probable feelings. How would your feelings differ if the same thing happened against just five years before you reached retirement age? Discuss.
- A variety of skills as a manager you need to effectively work in a matrix type organisation. Do you agree. If so, why?
- The purpose of organisation structure is to order and coordinate the actions of employees so as to:
  (a) Clarify reporting relationships.
  (b) Identify authority relationships.
  (c) Achieve organisational goals.
  (d) Establish an organisational chart.
  (e) Establish work groups.
- If the span of control is large:
  (a) Production workers are closely supervised.
  (b) There are more administrative levels.
  (c) It should be reduced.
  (d) Production workers are not closely supervised.
  (e) None of the above.

References

Albers, H. (1984), *Principles of Management: A Modern Approach*, John Wiley Publishers, New York.

Anselm, M. (1985), *Organisational Behaviour*, Himalaya Publishing House, New Delhi.

Arora, S.P. (1982), *Office Organisation and Management*, Vikas Publishing House Pvt. Ltd., New Delhi.

Banerjee, S. (1986), *Principles and Practice of Management*, Oxford and IBA Publishing Co. Pvt. Ltd., New Delhi.

Bhusan, V.K. (1987), *Principles of Management*, Sultan Chand and Sons, New Delhi.

Blanchard, K. and Peale, N.R. (1988), *The Power of Ethical Management*, William Morrow and Co. Inc., New York.

Bobbit, H.R., Breinholt, R.H., Doktor, R.H. and McNaul, J.P. (1978), *Organisational Behaviour*, Prentice Hall International Inc., London.

Byars, L. and Rve, L.W. (1986), *Management Theory and Practice*, Richard D. Irwin, New York.

Chandan, J.S. (1994), *Organisational Behaviour*, Vikas Publishing House Pvt. Ltd., New Delhi.

Chatterjee, S.S. (1993), *An Introduction to Management*, The World Press Pvt. Ltd., Calcutta.

Clough, D.J. (1980), *Concepts of Management Science*, Prentice Hall of India Pvt. Ltd., New Delhi.

Feldman, D.C. and Arnold, H.J. (1986), *Organisational Behaviour*, McGraw International ed., Management Series.

French, W.L., Kast, F.E. and Rosenzweig, J.E. (1985), *Understanding Human Behaviour in Organisations*, Harper and Row Publishers, New York.

Griffin, R.W. and Moorhead, G. (1986), *Organisational Behaviour*, Houghton Mifflin Company, Boston.

Gulett, C.R. and Hicks, H.G. (1986), *Organisational Theory and Behaviour*, McGraw Hill Kagakusha Ltd., Japan.

Gupta, N.S. (1986), *Management*, Atlantic Publishers and Distributors (P) Ltd., New Delhi.

Hall, R.H. *Management*, Prentice Hall of India Pvt. Ltd., New Delhi.

Hersey, P. and Balanchard, K. (1982), *Organizational Behaviour*, Prentice Hall of India Pvt. Ltd., New Delhi.

Hicks, H.G. and Gullet, C.R. (1980), *Modern Business Management*, McGraw Hill Kogakusha Ltd., Japan.

Ivancevich, J.M. and Metteson, M.T. (1987), *Organisational Behaviour and Management*, Business Publication Inc. Plano, Texas.

Johns, G. (1983), *Organisational Behaviour*, Scott Foreman and Company, Glenniev, III, London.

Kanugo, R.N. and MenDonch, M. (1994), *Work Motivation*, Sage Publications India Pvt. Ltd., New Delhi.

Kelly, J. (1987), *Management*, Surjeet Publications, New Delhi.

Koontz, H. and Weihrich, H. (1990), *Essentials of Management*, Prentice Hall Publishing Company, New Delhi.

Kossen, S. (1978), *The Human Side of Organisations*, Harper and Row Publishers Inc., New York.

Luthans, F. (1992), *Organisational Behaviour*, McGraw Hill International ed., Management Series.

Massie, J.L. (1979), *Essentials of Management*, Prentice Hall of India, New Delhi.

Mescon, M.H., Albert, M. and Khedouri, F. (1986), *Management*, Harper and Row Publishers, New York.

Nair, Suja R. (2004), *Organisational Behaviour*, Himalaya Publishing House, New Delhi.

Newman, W.H. and Warren, E.K. (1979), *The Process of Management*, Prentice Hall of India, New Delhi.

Newstorm, J.W. and Devis, K. (1995), *Organisational Behaviour*, Tata McGraw Hill Publishing Co. Pvt. Ltd., Delhi.

Pareek, V., Rao, T.V. and Pestonjee, D.M. (1989), *Behavioural Processes in Organisations*, Oxford and IBH Publishing Co. Pvt. Ltd., New Delhi.

Prasad, L.M. (1989), *Principles and Practice of Management*, Sultan Chand and Sons, New Delhi.

Rao, M.G., Rao, V.S.P. and Narayana, P.S. (1994), *Organisational Behaviour*, Konark Publishers Pvt. Ltd.

Rao, P. Subba (2004), *Management and Organisational Behaviour*, Himalaya Publishing House, New Delhi.

Robbins, S.P. (1993), *Organisational Behaviour*, Prentice Hall of India Pvt. Ltd., New Delhi.

Sekaran, U. (1994), *Organisational Behaviour*, Tata McGraw Hill Publishing Company Ltd., New Delhi.

Sharma, R.A. (1994), *Organisational Theory and Behaviour*, Tata McGraw Hill Publishing Company Ltd., New Delhi.

Sherlekar, S.A. (1982), *Principles of Management*, Himalaya Publishing House, New Delhi.

Shukla, M. (1996), *Understanding Organisations*, Prentice Hall of India, New Delhi.

Stanford, M.J. (1986), *Management Policy*, Prentice Hall of India Ltd., New Delhi.

Starr, M.K. (1981), *Management: A Modern Approach*, Freeman Book Company, Delhi.

Stoner, A.R., Freeman, R.E. and Gilbert, D.R. (1996), *Management*, Prentice Hall of India Ltd., New Delhi.

Stuart, R. (1980), *Introduction to Organisational Behaviour: A Situational Approach*, Reston Publishing Company Inc., Virginia.

Tandon, J.K., Gar, S. and Handa, S. (1996), *Indian Management*, Arihant Publishing House, Jaipur, India.

Terry, G.R. and Franklin, S.G. (1994), *Principles of Management*, All India Travellers Booksellers, New Delhi.

Tripathi, P.C. and Reddy, R.N. (1993), *Principles of Management*, Tata McGraw Publishing Company, New Delhi.